ST. LOUIS CRIME CHRONICLES
THE FIRST 200 YEARS
1764–1964

To Tom and Jill Long

Best of wishes

Bill Lhotka

BILL LHOTKA

REEDY PRESS
St. Louis, Missouri

Copyright © 2009, Reedy Press, LLC.
All rights reserved.

Reedy Press
PO Box 5131
St. Louis, MO 63139, USA

No part of this publication may be reproduced or transmitted in any form or by any means, electronic or mechanical, including photocopy, recording, or any information storage and retrieval system, without permission in writing from the publisher.

Permissions may be sought directly from Reedy Press at the above mailing address or via our website at www.reedypress.com.

Library of Congress Control Number: 2009936329

ISBN: 978-1-933370-44-6

Please visit our website at www.reedypress.com.

cover design by Eric Hirsch

Printed in the United States of America
09 10 11 12 13   5 4 3 2 1

TO SUE, MIKE, KIM, PAUL,
NANCY, AND ROB

CONTENTS

Acknowledgments ix

Introduction, by Bill McClellan xi

Duels
 James Shields vs. Abraham Lincoln, 1842 1
 Shadrach Bond vs. Rice Jones, 1808 4
 James A. Graham vs. Bernard Farrar, 1810 5
 Thomas Hart Benton vs. Charles Lucas, 1817 6
 Timothy Bennett vs. Alphonso Stewart, 1819 7
 John Smith T vs. Lionel Browne, 1819 9
 Joshua Barton vs. Thomas Rector, 1823 10
 Spencer Pettis vs. Thomas Biddle, 1831 11

Chief Pontiac, 1769 13

Slaves Executed for Murder, Cahokia, 1779 18

Daniel Boone Makes an Arrest, 1804 22

Manuel Lisa's Expedition and Frontier Justice, 1807 25

The Ioways Went That Away, 1808 27

St. Louis's First Convicted Murderer, 1809 30

A Rarified Murder, the Stephenson House, 1825 34

Francis McIntosh, Elijah Lovejoy, 1836–37 37

Beaumont and Geyer: A Case of Malpractice, 1840 46

Giving the French a Bad Name, 1849	50
Joseph Charless, Jr., 1859	53
James Utz, Confederate Spy, 1864	57
The Whiskey Ring, 1875	59
The *Post-Dispatch* Newsroom Shooting, 1882	65
Southern Hotel Trunk Murder, 1885	70
Marion the Outlaw, 1891	78
A Clayton Courthouse Confrontation, 1892	82
Ballad of Frankie and Johnny, 1899	85
The Boodlers, 1901–02	89
Belleville Lynching, 1903	98
Downtown St. Louis Shootout, 1904	101
Desperate Lord Barrington, 1903–04	106
Edward Garner Lewis, 1905–12	113
They Stole the Locomotive, 1910	118
Arson Trust, 1915	122
East St. Louis Riots, 1917	126

Robert Prager Lynched as German Spy, 1918	130
The Mob, 1920s and 1930s	135
Jack Daniel Heir Acquitted of Murder, 1924	149
Pretty Boy Floyd, 1925	154
Bertha Gifford, Poisoner, 1928	157
Kidnapped: Busch Family Heir, 1930–31	160
Homer G. Phillips, 1931	164
Nellie Tipton Muench, 1930s	169
August Luer Kidnapping, Alton, 1933	177
Kellar's Last Supper, 1933	181
The Strange Case of Mary Catherine Reardon, 1947	184
The Kefauver Committee, 1951	190
Popular Pol, Corruption, 1951–52	205
The Ammonia Bomb Holdup, 1952	210
The Great St. Louis Bank Robbery, 1953	212
Greenlease Kidnapping, 1953	215
Stalking the Stalker: The North County Rapist, 1957	222

Not Guilty: An Insanity Plea, 1959	225
Pulitzer Prize–Winning Reporter Shoots Handyman, 1960	229
Frank "Buster" Wortman, Crime Boss, 1960s	236
Bibliography	239
About the Author	249

ACKNOWLEDGMENTS

On a sunny May morning in 1992, I was working my beat at the courthouse in Clayton when an aerospace technician fatally shot his estranged wife, wounded his attorney, her attorney, a bailiff and a security guard, and terrorized hundreds before he, in turn, was shot nine times by police but managed to survived. In the aftermath of the tragic events involving Kenneth M. Baumruk, I happened to engage in a conversation about the shooting with Judge Arthur Litz, who told me that the Baumruk rampage wasn't the first shooting to take place in a courthouse in Clayton.

Nearly a hundred years earlier and less than one hundred yards from where we were sitting, the St. Louis County sheriff shot and killed the county assessor, explained Litz, who is also a local historian of note. That conversation was probably the genesis for this book as I researched the Dosenbach-Smith affair of 1892. I then began to look into some other cases and went back over the crimes I had covered since 1962 when I began my career in journalism. The emphasis was on more current and recent crimes and trials, many of which I covered for the *Post-Dispatch* where I have worked since 1973 and some of which I had covered for the *Alton Telegraph* before then.

Over the next three years, I collected information and set aside data for a book on crime, then I decided to put off the project until my retirement. Last year, as retirement neared, a friend and author, Marianna Riley, put me in touch with Josh Stevens of Reedy Press. Josh expressed interest in the concept of a book on historic crimes. By then, I had decided to limit my research to cases over the first two hundred years since the founding of St. Louis by Pierre Laclede and Auguste Chouteau. My reasons were multiple. Many of the stories I had considered important in the more recent past have faded quickly from public consciousness. And, having covered many of the death penalty and other major cases over the past twenty-five years in the St. Louis area, I didn't want the emotional strain that would come with revisiting the crimes and my memories of the anguish of both victims' families and the relatives of the criminals. Another factor has been the in-depth coverage of many of the high-profile crimes of the last thirty years in book form by other authors such as Charles Bosworth, Ellen Harris, Bill McClellan, and Tim O'Neil.

Several people have been very helpful in bringing this book to print. I would like to thank my wife, Sue, for her forbearance as I often prattled on about events of 150 years ago; and my son, Mike, for his constant encouragement and his help with an interview. A special word of thanks is due my stepdaughter, Kim Good, for taking so much of her time from her frame shop, the Artery, to tend to personal family matters so I would, in turn, have the time to write and edit.

Her husband, Rob Good, provided the initial information that led to the unusual story of a poisoning in Cahokia in 1779. Likewise, friend and colleague, Roy Malone, told me about the sad case of a lynching in Belleville just after the turn of the last century.

Post-Dispatch colleagues the late John McGuire, Pat Gauen, and Tim O'Neil provided helpful information. Assistant St. Louis County prosecutor Doug Sidel, with assistance from law librarians Mary Dahm and Bernard Lewandowski, researched the statute of limitations in the early nineteenth century for me; while Alton Cemetery and Hazelwood Park employees dug up—not literally—information I needed. Sharon Smith and Donn Johnson of the Missouri History Museum helped with the Southern Hotel story, and the staff at the archives building helped me find several documents for my research.

To the fourth floor staff at the St. Louis County Library headquarters, a thanks for keeping the microfilm machines churning for the three months I used them, despite my fumbling mechanical abilities. And a thanks to Matt Heidenry and Josh Stevens of Reedy Press for their editing and design work, as well as the trust in my ability to get the book done by deadline—or close to it. Lastly, a thanks to friend and colleague Bill McClellan for his kind introduction.

—Bill Lhotka

INTRODUCTION

If I were looking to construct a giant novel about the history of a city, I would say, "Let me first see the police blotters." That's because one can get a true sense of place and character in the underbelly of a city. Besides, what's more fun than reading about old crimes and meeting the villains and heroes of the past?

Longtime *St. Louis Post-Dispatch* reporter Bill Lhotka has gone through all the old police blotters. Actually, he has gone back into the days long before police blotters to recount the first two hundred years of St. Louis crimes. He starts with the 1769 murder of Pontiac in Cahokia and ends with the demise of gangster Frank "Buster" Wortman, who died in 1968.

In between is a collection of scalawags and nobility, people who show us the best and worst of human nature. Consider the 1859 murder of Joseph Charless, Jr., who was gunned down on a downtown street. The shooter, Joseph Thornton, was immediately arrested and taken to jail. A lynch mob quickly formed. The Reverend William Greenleaf Eliot, a founder of Washington University (did I not say the history of a city can be found in its police blotters?) realized that things were getting out of control and summoned a relative of the victim, who spoke to the crowd. "No course could be pursued more terrible to the family of Mr. Charless, more in violence to their feelings, than for you to visit upon this unfortunate criminal the merit of his crime." Ah, the eloquence of the antebellum days! A man faces a mob and appeals to its better nature with language that could have come from Shakespeare. But St. Louis was a rough place and eloquence went only so far. When words could not disperse the mob, the sheriff had to call in the army. For the rest of that story, you'll have to read the book.

There are whodunits and what-ifs. In the latter category, Lhotka recounts a number of duels that were fought between 1808 and 1842. In those days, honor was a sacred thing, worth one's life.

Perhaps the most interesting of these duels is one that did not take place. James Shields, who went on to be a U.S. senator in three states, was going to fight a political rival, a young lawyer from Springfield. It is interesting to think that had the duel taken place, and had Shields come through as the survivor, the duel hardly would be worth noting. The world would scarcely have noted the passing of Abraham Lincoln.

Skipping through the years to a whodunit, I'd recommend the murder of J. Vincent Reardon. He was murdered in 1947. He was a prominent businessman and a loving father. The city was shocked when his fourteen-year-old daughter Mary was arrested for his murder. She had spent the night with her thirteen-year-old boyfriend at a motel in Wentzville when Reardon found them. He was driving them home when he was shot in the back of the head. The car plunged down an embankment. Reardon and the boyfriend died. Police found Mary sitting calmly in the back seat. The murder weapon was in the car. Mary confessed—to police, to reporters, to the coroner. An open and shut case? So it would seem, but then this unusual case got even stranger.

By the way, Lhotka gives us a sense of history and place as he tells these stories. For instance, as he recounts Mary's trial, he mentions that the defense began its presentation on the day that more than one hundred workers died in a coal mine disaster in Centralia, Illinois.

If you think of a book like this as sort of a newsreel, it is not surprising that some characters appear more than once before fading from view. For instance, one of Mary Reardon's lawyers, Henry Morris, appears in a trial in 1961. That was when *Post-Dispatch* reporter Ted Link, a Pulitzer Prize winner and the grandson of the architect who designed Union Station, went to trial for the murder of Clarence Calvin. That was not a whodunit. Link readily admitted that he shot Calvin after the two argued at Link's farm in Franklin County. He shot him first with a shotgun and then with a .38-caliber revolver.

Perhaps because I'm a newspaperman, or perhaps because Lhotka is a newspaperman, I especially enjoyed the story inside the story about the case. Jake Wolf, the *Post-Dispatch* reporter who had to report the story about the shooting of Calvin, was interviewed about his recollections. After rushing to the scene and talking to police and then Link, his older and much decorated colleague, Wolf raced into nearby St. Albans to phone the story into the newspaper. This was in the days of rewrite men. He found an old-fashioned crank phone in a general store. As he dictated the story, he heard clinking sounds. People were picking up to listen in as he told the rewrite man what he'd learned. Then one of the listeners spoke. It was Calvin's mother. She announced that she was heading to the scene. Wolf hung up and hurried back to the farm to alert police and Link that she was on her way.

Link was charged with first-degree murder and was facing the death penalty when he went to trial. What happened? I'll let Lhotka tell you. I'll just tell you this: This is real life. This is history. Straight from the police blotters.

—Bill McClellan

DUELS
SHIELDS VS. LINCOLN
1842

Late in the afternoon of a fall day in 1842, Illinois State Auditor James Shields met his opponent near St. Louis on the Missouri bank of the Mississippi River in what was to be a duel to the death with cavalry broadswords.

Had Shields succumbed to a fatal blow, the nation would have lost a man who was destined to be a general in the Mexican War, where he would be wounded at Cerro Gordo Pass, and a general in the Civil War, where he would be the only Union officer to defeat Stonewall Jackson on the battlefield. The country also would have lost the only man who ever served as a United States senator of three states: Illinois, Missouri, and Minnesota.

Had Shields won that duel, however, the country would have suffered an even greater loss: the man who later would be elected as the sixteenth president of the United States.

The other duelist?

Abraham Lincoln.

Shields instigated the challenge. Lincoln was a Whig who would be elected to Congress under the party's label in 1846. Shields was a Democrat in the camp of Stephen Douglas. Both men lived in Springfield, where Lincoln was involved in the middle of an on-again, off-again engagement to Mary Todd, a woman who had flirted with Shields and had been courted by Douglas.

In a letter to Lincoln five days before the meeting on the Missouri shore, Shields wrote: "Articles of the most personal nature and calculated to degrade me have made their appearance" in the *Sangamon Journal*. The articles critical of Shields had been written under the pen name of "Rebecca." Some writers suggest that they were the work not only of Lincoln, but also of Todd and her friend Julia Jayne, later the wife of Senator Lyman Trumbull. Shields said he had learned that Lincoln was the author and demanded an immediate retraction.

Lincoln was coy in his initial hand-delivered response saying, "Without stopping to inquire whether I really am the author, or to point out what is offensive in them, you demand an unqualified retraction of all that is offensive, and then proceed to hint at consequences."

Shields replied immediately that his source of information was the newspaper's editor, who told Shields that Lincoln had written the article of September 2 that was signed "Rebecca." Are you "Rebecca?" Shields asked, and if so, Shields reiterated his demand for a retraction. Two days later, in a letter delivered by a friend who would be Lincoln's second at the upcoming duel, Lincoln admitted to writing the article of September 2, but added he "had no participation in any other article alluding to you"—an indication that Todd and Jayne may indeed have been the authors of prior critiques of the auditor under the pen name of Rebecca.

Lincoln told Shields he had written the article "for political effect" with no intention of attacking Shields's character. Along with that comment, Lincoln wrote he was choosing broadswords, and the duel should take place three miles from Alton on the opposite bank of the Mississippi at "a spot to be approved by you."

Lincoln's choice of Missouri for the duel of 1842—and Shields's agreement—was no surprise. Illinois had a long history of frowning on duels as a means of settling disputes, while Missouri found them a way of resolving issues involving the so-called honor of gentlemen and generally ignored their illegality. Both Lincoln and Shields were self-taught lawyers who had worked their way up from poverty. Shields, an Irish immigrant, had been a teacher in Kaskaskia before embarking on a career in politics. Lincoln had built a reputation as one of Illinois's most talented lawyers as he traveled the state. Both men had probably heard about all or most of the duels that took place on both sides of the Mississippi over a thirty-year period.

Whether Lincoln's planned duel had been scheduled for Bloody Island—the scene of several fatal encounters and now part of the Illinois shore—has been the subject of some speculation. In his reply letter to Shields that he also enclosed in a letter to a friend in Kentucky two weeks after the aborted duel, Lincoln gave the site as three miles from Alton on the opposite side of the river. This scenario would have put the location closer to Fort Bellefontaine and the meeting of the Missouri and Mississippi rivers or farther downriver at the Chain of Rocks. Three miles upriver from Alton would have placed the duel near what is now Portage des Sioux. Lincoln was not a native St. Louisan, and he may have gotten the distance from Alton wrong. He may have meant Bloody Island.

Fortunately for the youthful contestants, cooler heads prevailed on the afternoon of September 22, 1842, and managed to talk Shields, thirty-six, and Lincoln, thirty-three, out of their plan to fight to the death. Some historians believe Shields realized that Lincoln, at six feet four inches, and a former rail-splitter with long, strong arms, could have easily overpowered the shorter swordsman.

Lincoln and Todd married six weeks after the would-be duel, and Lincoln and Shields remained political rivals for years. In 1856, Shields and Douglas were the two incumbent senators from Illinois, and Lincoln tried to capture Shields's seat. Senators were then chosen by the state general assembly, not by direct vote. Whigs backed Lincoln, who got as high as forty-seven votes in a series of ballots, with fifty-one needed to win. Shields received the vote of forty-one Democrats, but five others backed Trumbull. In subsequent balloting, the majority of Democrats dumped Shields and switched their support to Governor Joel Matteson. Aware he couldn't win, Lincoln then directed his supporters to back Trumbull, who was elected. Mary Lincoln never forgave Julia Trumbull, and never talked to her again.

Between 1808 and 1831, at least five infamous duels had taken place on Bloody Island, another on an island near Ste. Genevieve, another on an island near Herculaneum, and another in the town square of Belleville.

BOND VS. JONES
1808

Shadrach Bond, who would later become Illinois's first governor, quarreled with Rice Jones of Kaskaskia. Bond was living in St. Clair County when Illinois was then part of Indiana Territory. Jones was an elected representative of the territorial government. Dr. James Dunlap, an enemy of Jones, served as Bond's second in a duel on an island between Kaskaskia and Ste. Genevieve.

Jones fired his weapon before the order to fire was given and said it was an accident. Bond accepted the explanation, and no duel occurred. However, Dunlap was irate, claiming Jones deliberately discharged the gun. The feud between Jones and Dunlap escalated until December 7 of that year, when Dunlap shot down Jones on the streets of Kaskaskia and fled to Texas. In 1810, the territorial government declared the death of someone resulting from a duel the crime of murder for everyone involved, seconds as well as the shooter.

GRAHAM VS. FARRAR
1810

James A. Graham, a lawyer, and Bernard Farrar, a doctor in frontier St. Louis, were close friends. However, they ended up at Bloody Island firing pistols at each other, resulting in dire consequences.

Graham claimed he saw an army officer cheating at cards in a downtown hotel and publicly denounced him as being a card cheat. The officer sent Dr. Farrar, a relative, to challenge Graham to a retraction or a duel. Because the officer was a cheater, he couldn't possibly be a gentleman and was therefore unworthy of a duel, Graham responded. The strange code of early nineteenth-century chivalry required Farrar to take up the cause of his relative, and with no personal grudge against Graham, Farrar was compelled to demand the duel on behalf of the officer.

The doctor and lawyer ended up on Bloody Island, where both fired three shots and both were wounded—Graham severely. After being bedridden for four months, Graham then attempted to ride a horse on a visit back East and died en route.

BENTON VS. LUCAS
1817

A pair of Bloody Island duels drew crowds to the riverfront the summer of 1817 to await the outcome of the shootouts between two St. Louis leaders.

Thomas Hart Benton had arrived in St. Louis from Tennessee in 1815 after a public brawl with war hero and future president Andrew Jackson. Benton would serve nearly thirty years in the U.S. Senate. A lawyer, he quickly aligned himself with a group of wealthy landowners and businessmen, headed by city founder Auguste Chouteau and explorer William Clark. Charles Lucas played a major role in a rival landowning faction headed by his father, James B. C. Lucas. Charles owned substantial acreage of his own in the area that he called Normandy.

The feud between the two men led to a duel on Bloody Island on August 12, 1812. Benton shot Lucas in the neck; Lucas's shot grazed Benton's leg. Lucas survived the shooting, and Benton, at first, seemed satisfied that his honor had been restored. But six weeks later, the pair was back on the island after Benton alleged Lucas had made derogatory remarks about Benton's sudden arrival in Missouri from Tennessee. Once again, Benton didn't miss; Lucas did. Lucas died of a chest wound at the age of twenty-five.

THOMAS HART BENTON

6 BILL LHOTKA

BENNETT VS. STEWART
1819

The Illinois law banning duels was put to the test after a so-called duel—whether it was an actual duel, a murder, or an accident was at issue—between Timothy Bennett and Alphonso C. Stewart on February 8, 1819, outside the courthouse in Belleville at the southwest corner of Main and Illinois streets. (*Stewart* is spelled *Stuart* in some versions, with a first name of Alonzo, and Bennett's first name is at times listed as William.)

Bennett's horse, Stewart's cornfield, and plenty of drinks at Tannehill's tavern led to the confrontation. Witnesses later described Stewart as a lawyer who spent most of his practice at the tavern. Bennett owned a horse that frequented Stewart's cornfield. Stewart warned Bennett he would shoot the horse if the nag trespassed on Stewart's field again. The warning went unheeded, and Stewart hired a farmhand to shoot the horse with salt, sending the animal fleeing in pain. Bennett became angry, and he was drinking with friends who goaded him into challenging Stewart to a duel.

Other revelers told Stewart the duel would be a sham and that the guns would be loaded with powder but no cap. Stewart agreed to meet Bennett. The contestants marched twenty-five steps, turned, and on the word to fire, Bennett shot Stewart, who pitched forward and died instantly. The second to Bennett grabbed Stewart's gun and fired it into the air. No one knew if Stewart had put a ball in his weapon.

Bennett later escaped from the Belleville jail by boring holes in its log wall and took off for Arkansas Territory. He stayed a fugitive for almost two years until he met his wife in Ste. Genevieve. A posse from Belleville had followed her and caught the duelist.

The seconds in the shooting of Stewart had gone on trial in June 1819 for their role in his death. Both were acquitted. A new grand jury indictment in 1821 accused, "Timothy Bennett, laborer . . . not having the fear of God before his eyes, but being moved and seduced by the instigation of the Devil, on 8 February 1819, shot Alphonso C. Stewart in Belleville."

Bennett got an expert in duels to defend him: Benton, the successful and uncharged duelist in Charles Lucas's death. Benton had already defended in court the seconds in the Bennett-Stewart duel and got them off.

A key prosecution witness was the tavern owner's daughter, Rachael Tannehill, nine, who said she saw Bennett putting a bullet in his gun without the seconds knowing it. The jury of twelve men convicted Bennett of murder, despite Benton's best efforts. Pleas to the governor for a pardon failed. Before a large crowd that included women and children, Bennett was hanged on September 3, 1821.

SMITH T VS. BROWNE
1819

The same year that Bennett killed Stewart, Colonel John Smith T and Lionel Browne picked either an island near Herculaneum or the Illinois shore in what is now Monroe County to settle their dispute with pistols. Smith T was a gun-toting, buckskin-wearing entrepreneur who gave himself a title and added "T" to his name to distinguish himself from all the other Smiths in Tennessee, where he owned land. In Missouri, where he settled, Smith T owned substantial acreage in Ste. Genevieve, a lead mine in Washington County, and a salt mine on land in west-central Missouri. He often bragged that he had killed fifteen men in his lifetime.

One of those victims was Browne, the sheriff of Washington County. Ironically, Browne was the nephew of former Vice President Aaron Burr, infamous for fatally shooting founding father Alexander Hamilton in a duel in July 1804.

BARTON VS. RECTOR
1823

On June 23, 1823, Bloody Island was the site of yet another fatal duel. With crowds again lining the riverbank, it pitted Joshua Barton against Thomas Rector. Joshua Barton, a lawyer, was the brother of David Barton, who had been picked as a U.S. senator along with Benton after Missouri gained statehood two years earlier. Rector also had a famous brother: General William Rector, surveyor-general of the United States. Thomas Rector took umbrage at a critical article written by Joshua Barton about the general and challenged Barton to a duel. Rector achieved his revenge for Barton's writings that day on Bloody Island. He fatally shot Barton, who should have known the dangers of dueling. He had been Charles Lucas's second at both of the Benton-Lucas duels.

PETTIS VS. BIDDLE
1831

Perhaps the most infamous and possibly last duel on Bloody Island took place in August 1831. Called "the nearsighted duel," the gun-toters fired from five feet apart and their weapons overlapped as they shot each other simultaneously. One would think that a congressman and an army major would have known better. However, tempers seemed to have outdistanced any rational thought.

Spencer Pettis was the local congressman, having defeated Edward Bates—later attorney general in Lincoln's cabinet—in the hard-fought election contest of 1828. A lawyer from Virginia, Pettis had served as Missouri's secretary of state. He was a Democrat and supporter of President Andrew Jackson, who had declared war on the National Bank of the United States and its chief executive, Nicholas Biddle.

Residing in St. Louis as an army major and paymaster, Thomas Biddle was the bank president's brother. A branch of the National Bank had opened in 1829 in St. Louis with Biddle, William Clark, and wealthy businessman John Mullanphy among its directors. Biddle was also married to Mullanphy's daughter.

As the election of 1830 approached, Pettis sought reelection as a U.S. representative. Biddle wrote a series of critical articles and made derogatory comments about Pettis, who responded similarly to the character attacks. Shortly before the election, and after Pettis had refused to see the major, Biddle found Pettis in the hallway of the City Hotel. Biddle began whipping Pettis, who pulled out a sword-cane to attack Biddle and stop the assault. Biddle was charged with assault. His father-in-law posted bond.

After Pettis won reelection, he challenged Biddle to a duel. Biddle agreed to pistols, and both combatants received training in their use before their confrontation on Bloody Island. Biddle was nearsighted and demanded a distance of five feet; Pettis agreed, and both crossed the river to Bloody Island.

"The whole town was assembled to see them depart. There were several thousand people on the levee, at the windows, and on the tops of the houses facing the river," wrote John F. Darby, a future mayor of St. Louis, in his memoirs. "Old Mr. Mullanphy, the father-in-law of Major Biddle, sat on his old roan mare in the midst of the great crowd on the levee. At last there was a report of a pistol shot—both pistols fired so simultaneously that it seemed as if there was one shot."

Pettis died the next day, August 27, 1831, from the gunshot wound; Biddle, two days later.

Nicholas Biddle went on to spar famously with Old Hickory Andrew Jackson in 1834.

CHIEF PONTIAC
1769

The town of Cahokia, downtown St. Louis, and Starved Rock State Park on the Illinois River all have something in common: they are connected to the 1769 death of Ottawa Indian Chief Pontiac. He was murdered in Cahokia and buried in St. Louis. Legend has it that a band of Indians were either starved to death in retaliation on the 125-foot promontory near LaSalle, Illinois, or were massacred when they attempted to escape the siege.

In April 1769, Pontiac was visiting his friend Captain Louis St. Ange de Bellerive in St. Louis. Pontiac was in full military regalia, wearing the dress uniform of a French army officer that Marquis Louis Joseph Montcalm had presented him during the French and Indian War. St. Ange and Pontiac had been colleagues since fighting the British and colonials together. St. Ange was then the commander in St. Louis. Pontiac told St. Ange he was going to attend a Creole ball in Cahokia, but St. Ange, worried his friend's life would be in danger, warned him against it.

Ignoring the warning, Pontiac went anyway to Cahokia, founded by French missionaries in 1699 and boasting a population by 1769 in excess of three thousand. However, the village had changed hands at the end of the French and Indian War, and the British were in control. On April 20, a Peoria Indian pretended friendship with the former Indian leader, then fractured Pontiac's skull with a blow from behind. Some accounts of the murder allege that Pontiac was lured into nearby woods, where he was attacked. John Allen's *Legend and Lore* suggests a British trader hired the Peoria Indian to kill Pontiac for a barrel of whiskey.

Carl Baldwin, in his *Echoes of Their Voices*, places the murder at Second and Elm streets in the village outside the English trading post of Boynton, Wharton, and Morgan. Baldwin writes that in

1768, Pontiac had fatally stabbed Black Dog, a Peoria chief, during an argument. The man who accosted Pontiac in Cahokia was Black Dog's nephew.

St. Ange retrieved Pontiac's body and had him buried in downtown St. Louis. When word spread that Pontiac had been killed by a Peoria Indian, Ottawa, Potawatomi, and other tribes near the Great Lakes took revenge on the Illini Confederation, a loosely knit group of a dozen tribes including the Peoria, Cahokia, and Kaskaskia Indians. The Illinois Indians were no match for their northern and eastern neighbors. They were decimated in attacks on their villages that bordered on genocide. Many of the survivors were forced to move west of the Mississippi River. Some mounted a fight and ended up under siege at Starved Rock. Rather than surrender to the Potawatomi or Ottawa, who surrounded them atop the bluff overlooking the river, one legend has the warriors starving to death. Another version suggests they made a break for freedom from the rocky top but were massacred.

At the time of his death, Pontiac was in his mid-forties, a drifter and an alcoholic. Just six years earlier, he had been at the height of his powers, leading as many as forty-seven tribes into war against the British, which became known as Pontiac's War. Not many individuals have wars named after them.

Pontiac was born between 1713 and 1720 in northeast Indiana of an Ottawa father and a Chippewa or Ojibwa mother. By the time the French and Indian War began in 1754, Pontiac was an Ottawa chief aligned with the French and taking part in the battle of Fort Duchesne (modern-day Pittsburgh) on July 9, 1755. Imagine Pontiac on one side and a young George Washington on the other. The English marched in formation into a French and Indian ambush with more than 450 British soldiers dying on the battlefield along with their commander, General Edward Braddock. Pontiac's side suffered only a handful of casualties. That battle was one of the high points for the French in a war that spread to other continents.

Montreal fell to the British in 1760, and two months later,

the French garrison at Fort Detroit turned it over to the British. Instead of trading goods with the French, Indian tribes had to deal with the less generous British. While the French were merchants and traders, the British were colonizers and settlers, moving into land belonging to the Indians, clearing the forests, and reducing the wild game the Indians needed for sustenance. This was the picture Pontiac faced, and his trading experience at Fort Detroit exacerbated it.

On April 27, 1763, Pontiac addressed an assembly of warriors estimated at nine thousand. He was of average height. He wore white porcelain beads dangling from his ears, silver bands on his arms, and a silver disk on his head with three feathers. He was painted for war. Like a mystic, Pontiac told the warriors he had spent ten days in the forest and prophesied that the Great Spirit was upset with them. Only by ridding the earth of the English, a war of extermination, could He be appeased.

In the harangue, the chief told the warriors that the English were destroying the forests, and when the Indians complained, they were subjected to reprisals. He urged a simultaneous uprising throughout the country. Several tribes agreed to the undertaking. The main target would be Fort Detroit, ten days later.

On May 7, Pontiac entered the fort with three hundred men carrying blankets concealing sawed-off muskets, but Major Henry Gladwin was ready for them. He had been forewarned by an Indian woman who may have been his lover and a French trader with the unusual name of Jacques Baby. Suspecting the British were ready, Pontiac took his men out of the fort. Soon, ten English soldiers were killed in an ambush, and Pontiac's War had begun.

The Indian chief laid siege to the fort and its 120 soldiers, who had boats with cannons on the river alongside the fort. The British repelled an attack by six hundred warriors after Pontiac's offer of safe conduct to Fort Niagara in New York was rejected. In late May, Fort Sandusky, in what is now northern Ohio, fell with twenty-seven British casualties and captives who were later taken to the area outside Detroit, tortured, and mutilated, their bodies left to float downriver in view of the fort.

Indians captured Fort Miami in what is now Fort Wayne, Fort St. Joseph on the Michigan peninsula, and a fort along the Wabash River in southern Indiana.

A supply convoy led by Lieutenant Abraham Cuyler heading for Detroit was ambushed by two hundred Indians the same day that Fort Sandusky fell, and sixty-one of ninety-six were either killed or captured. In July, the British, then considered to have the best soldiers in the world, sent a relief column. It attacked Pontiac at a place called Parent's Creek. Pontiac won what is called the Battle of Bloody Run, for the English blood flowing down the creek.

Indians under Pontiac's confederation attacked but failed to capture Fort Pitt in what is now western Pennsylvania and Fort Niagara in New York. Pontiac was a ruthless leader, and British settlers and colonials were often the targets of his attacks. The British, too, had their brutal moments and even resorted to biological warfare at Fort Pitt, giving blankets and a handkerchief that had been taken from the beds of smallpox victims to three tribes. An epidemic ensued that failed to distinguish between warriors, women, and children. In a British counterattack on July 4, an Indian was scalped, and in response Pontiac gave the Chippewas permission to kill an English captain.

French settlers and traders, however, were immune from any Indian reprisals. Their military men had suggested that French troops would take the field on Pontiac's behalf. The promises proved hollow. Unbeknown to Pontiac, the French and English had signed a peace treaty in February, three months before Pontiac's War began. The treaty officially ended the French and Indian War. Pontiac met St. Ange at Fort Chartres and asked for French help. He was refused any military aid. The Indian chief sent emissaries to New Orleans and was again rebuffed. Also reneging on their promises of military aid were chiefs of the Illini Confederation. As the number of warriors surrounding Detroit dwindled, on October

31, nearly six months after it began, Pontiac decided to end the siege of the garrison. By April of 1765, Pontiac signed a treaty ending the war.

Historians disagree over Pontiac's place in the history of Indian leadership. His star has diminished as the years have progressed, and chiefs such as Tecumseh, Sitting Bull, and Chief Joseph of the Nez Pearce have achieved greater fame.

However, Baldwin argues vigorously for Pontiac's place, writing, "Pontiac had united tribes from the Hudson to the Mississippi and Minnesota to Kentucky, including tribes that had been enemies for centuries." In a year's time, Pontiac had overrun ten forts, failing only at Detroit, Niagara, and Pitt and had caused the deaths of two thousand soldiers and settlers, his enemies, Baldwin noted.

At the Southern Hotel in downtown St. Louis in 1901, where a plaque was established in Pontiac's honor, the *American Monthly Magazine* of the Daughters of the American Revolution reported the mostly backhand comments of principal speaker, Bishop Daniel S. Tuttle, who told the assembly, "We come not to bury Pontiac, nor to praise him. He was a savage and the son of a savage."

Tuttle conceded that Pontiac was an astute military leader and organizer who "gave his efforts, his life, for the protection of his country." His major fault, it seemed, was that he was on the wrong side of history. Tuttle called him "a leader of the opposition to the white man's march of progress." The magazine reported that Pontiac had been buried near the hotel where the plaque was erected.

In his book, *Here's Where,* author Charlie Brennan places the site where St. Ange had the Indian chief buried at the southeast corner of Broadway and Walnut Street.

SLAVES EXECUTED FOR MURDER, CAHOKIA
1779

The trial took place in a house in Cahokia, and the execution just six days later in Kaskaskia. The defendants were a pair of slaves accused of multiple crimes. Jurisdiction over the whole affair—in a quirk of history—rested with the state of Virginia.

Leading citizens of the frontier village gathered on June 10, 1779, at the Cahokia home of a man named Saucier whose first name was not listed in the Cahokia transcripts. Pierre Godin served as president of the group, and the records show that six other men heard some or all of the testimony along with Godin and Saucier.

The panel heard from witnesses Catherine, Paul, Sasa, Francois, and Cupidon. The story they heard was chilling: four murders by poison in 1778, another attempted poisoning, and an aborted plot to kill two more. All five witnesses were slaves, and they were exposing two other slaves, Moreau and Manuel, as the criminals.

Francois provided perhaps the most damaging evidence. He testified that Moreau had sex with Janette, another slave, who had also bestowed sexual favors on another man. Out of jealousy, Moreau poisoned his rival. Suspecting what was happening to him, the slave went to Moreau and, according to Francois, said, "My countryman, take away the sickness you have given me." Francois added that the victim offered to pay Moreau for a cure. He gave Moreau a wash basin and a handkerchief and promised more if he didn't die. It was too late. "It is not in my power to take it from you," Moreau told his dying victim, who later moved to St. Louis and eventually died.

Cupidon and Francois provided additional evidence that Moreau had murdered Mr. and Mrs. Nicolle after he was asked by two of their slaves to make the masters more gentle. Cupidon described the following confrontation after the Nicolles were poisoned. Moreau told Mrs. Nicolle's female slave, "You ought to be content now. There are your master and mistress dead, and you can walk and go where you wish."

Her husband replied, "We did not ask you to make them die, only [be] a little gentler."

Moreau then asked the woman for the sex he claimed she had promised him, but she told him he was too old. The cutting remark angered the killer and prompted him to reply, "You find me too old, and well you shall repent it."

Francois described what happened next: "For this reason, the said Moreau poisoned her, and she died." Francois said several friends of the victim approached Moreau and pleaded with him to cure her. He told them, Francois testified, "It was no longer in his power to take from her that which he had given her."

Next, Sasa told the panel he had been in the cottage of M. Martin—one of the panelists who voted guilty was listed as Martin—and asked Martin's slave, Janette, for some tobacco. He found a horn filled with what he called boiling blood. Janette told Sasa not to touch it, that Manuel had given it to her "to put her master and mistress to death." Sasa quoted Janette as saying that she was told by Moreau that Manuel had prepared the liquid in the horn that was "used to poison Monsieur and Madame Nicolle."

Catherine also testified that she was told by Moreau that Manuel wanted to kill the Martins. Only an intervention by a slave named Guanga, who threatened to expose Manuel and Moreau, prevented another double murder, Catherine said. Guanga made them dig up poison they had secreted under the threshold to the Martin house.

Catherine's own husband had been poisoned by Moreau and Manuel, and the tone of her testimony suggested that she had no doubt he would die too. She said her husband had gotten permission from his master, Saucier, to visit Kaskaskia. Manuel and Moreau gave him a pint of tafia (a West Indian rum-based drink) to take along. No sooner had he drunk the tafia than he felt sick "and is still sick," Catherine testified. She confronted Manuel and Moreau after their arrests. Manuel said he had wanted Catherine's husband to die quickly but was overruled by Moreau. Moreau said it "was better to make him die slowly." Catherine said her husband "has been pining," an indication that his condition had not improved.

After hearing the testimony, the panel voted. Godin signed a document saying, "Manuel and Moreau had done that of which they are accused." He listed the time as 8 p.m. and the date as June 10.

During the trial, the Revolutionary War was in full bloom. A year earlier, Lieutenant Colonel George Rogers Clark had defeated the English at Vincennes and Kaskaskia and had driven the British from Cahokia. The British had taken over the town in 1763 as part of the spoils of winning the French and Indian War. Founded by French missionaries in 1699, Cahokia had grown from a spot on the map with twelve people in 1729 to a town of three thousand by 1763. However, many of its occupants moved to fledgling St. Louis or prosperous New Orleans over the next decade. In both predominantly French cities, the new settlers preferred the Spanish rule over the British.

When Americans took control after the victories by Clark, a native Virginian, there was a Continental Congress and thirteen colonies at war with England. Virginia took jurisdiction over Cahokia, and Patrick "Give me liberty or give me death" Henry, Virginia's governor, became Cahokia's governor as well.

State's Attorney Jean Girault got the trial report from Godin. A master of six languages, Girault had purchased land in Cahokia and had served as Clark's interpreter for interactions with the supportive French at Kaskaskia. Girault would later be a commissioned lieutenant in the American army. After the war, he moved from Cahokia to New Orleans and finally to Natchez, Mississippi, where he died in 1813.

Girault held the official title of state's attorney of Virginia, District of Kaskaskia. In forwarding his findings for a final decision,

Girault said Moreau and Manuel appeared to be "really guilty of the horrible crime of which they are accused . . . from which poisons several of the good subjects of this republic and soldiers of the garrison have died."

Girault's declaration of June 12, 1779, leaves open the possibility that the two accused men committed more murders than the testimony at the hearing in Cahokia revealed. However, there had been no mention in the transcripts from the official Cahokia records of poisoned troops. This also raises the issue of Moreau and Manuel working for the British.

From Girault, the murder case went to John Todd. In December 1778, Patrick Henry appointed Todd, twenty-eight, as lieutenant-commander of the county of Illinois with the seat of government in Kaskaskia. Todd arrived at his post in May 1779 with a long list of instructions from Henry on what to do, including cultivating the affection of the French and Indians.

Two days after the case came to him, on June 14, Todd issued the order to Sheriff Richard Winston to hang the defendants two days later. Both Virginia rule and Todd's life turned out to be short-lived. Virginia and several other states gave up their claims to western land in 1781 to the United States. Todd died in a battle with Indians in Kentucky a year later.

DANIEL BOONE MAKES AN ARREST
1804

As the chief law enforcement officer in the Femme Osage Valley in what is now southern St. Charles County, legendary frontiersman and pioneer Daniel Boone had no choice in December of 1804 when he was told about a shooting: he had to do his duty. However, it must have been gut-wrenching for Boone, then seventy, to arrest James Davis, take him to jail in St. Charles, and convene a grand jury to determine if there was probable cause to charge the defendant.

What must have been going through the woodsman's mind that day? Davis was the husband of Boone's granddaughter, Jemima. The man Davis killed was Will Hays, Boone's son-in-law and the father-in-law of Davis. Davis, Hays, and their families had migrated to Femme Osage with Boone from Kentucky after Boone received a Spanish land grant to settle the area in 1799. Hays's wife—Boone's daughter—had died from a fever a year later, in 1800.

That same year, St. Louis–based Lieutenant Governor Charles de Hault de Lassus, the Spanish leader of Upper Louisiana, made Boone the syndic—in effect, the official administrator—for the settlement Boone had founded northwest of the Missouri River. Included in his duties were hearing disputes and resolving minor crimes. Boone dispensed his homespun version of justice beneath a big elm tree, but a shooting required more than Boone's sole determination; a grand jury had to be convened. Of the twelve that met to consider the case in St. Charles in December 1804, only one could write. He became the foreman while the other eleven signed the indictment with an "X." Earlier that year in ceremonies in St. Louis, the Louisiana Territory, covering what would later become all or parts of thirteen states, had been transferred from Spain to France and then to the United States—courtesy of the best land buy in U.S. history by President Thomas Jefferson from Napoleon.

The indictment returned by the grand jury against Davis then was probably the first ever in the United States west of the Mississippi River. In the colorful language of the times and a typically lengthy legalistic sentence, it read:

> That one James Davis, late of the District of St. Charles, in the Territory of Louisiana, not having the fear of God before his eyes, but being moved and seduced by the instigation of the Devil, on the 13th Day of December, in the year of our Lord one thousand eight hundred and four, at a place called Femme Osage, in the said District of St. Charles, with force or arms, in and upon William Hays, in the peace of God and the United States, there and then Feloniously, willfully, and with malice aforethought, did make an assault and that the said James Davis, with a certain rifle gun, four feet long, and of the value of five dollars, then and there loaded and charged with gun powder and one leaden bullet, with said rifle gun the said James Davis, then and there in his hands had and held, fired and killed William Hays.

The grand jurors concluded there was probable cause to bind Davis over for trial on a charge of murder. Boone posted a three thousand–dollar bond for Davis. Boone also testified at the trial in favor of his granddaughter's husband. Hays had been a heavy drinker and a wife-beater during his fifteen-year marriage to Susannah Boone. Daniel Boone and Susannah's siblings had punished Hays for his actions by beating him in turn.

DANIEL BOONE

While Hays was drinking, he and Davis had argued, and Hays told Davis to stay away from the Hays farm. On the day of the shooting, Davis went to the Hays land to look for a horse he thought had run onto the property. Hays went for a rifle in his cabin. Father-in-law then chased son-in-law around the farm. Davis cocked his own rifle and fired one shot, hitting Hays in the chest and killing him.

Daniel Hays, the son of the victim, told the jury he had witnessed the shooting and said his brother-in-law had killed his father in self-defense. Davis was acquitted.

Daniel Boone lived another sixteen years. He died at the house he had helped his son, Nathan Boone, build. The four-story limestone structure is located near Defiance, Missouri, and is owned by Lindenwood University, which has added over a dozen buildings to form Boonesfield Village. It is open to the public. Near the house is the remains of an old elm, believed to be the Judgment Tree where Daniel Boone handed down frontier justice.

MANUEL LISA'S EXPEDITION AND FRONTIER JUSTICE
1807

At the mouth of the Osage River about ten miles from present-day Jefferson City, the expedition of Manuel Lisa and his band of forty-two awoke on the morning of May 14, 1807, to find that one of their number was gone, along with blankets and some other articles.

Antoine Bissonet was missing. He had disappeared during the night and had hidden expedition supplies in a tree, apparently intending to use them on his way back to St. Louis or wherever he planned to go. He didn't get far.

The angry expedition leader sent George Drouillard to hunt down Bissonet. Drouillard, an expert rifleman, tracked Bissonet, caught up with him, and shot him. Bissonet was brought back to camp wounded but still alive. He was sent downriver by canoe to St. Charles but died of his gunshot wound on the way. Lisa and his men moved on.

Nearly one year after Bissonet's murder, Lisa and his men returned to St. Louis, and one of the expedition members, Antoine Dubriel, swore out a complaint against Drouillard and Lisa. Drouillard went on trial on September 19, 1808, accused of the murder of Bissonet and faced a hanging if convicted by the jury of twelve men. Dubriel was to be the key prosecution witness.

In a frontier town like St. Louis, everybody knew everyone. There was, of course, the defendant, Drouillard. Of French and Shawnee descent, Drouillard had been a charter member of the expedition of Meriwether Lewis and William Clark to the Pacific Ocean and back. In their journals, the explorers described Drouillard as an outstanding hunter and woodsman. He was also singled out for his ability to interpret Indian sign language.

Then there was his boss, Manuel Lisa, who had arrived from New Orleans during Spanish occupation. An astute businessman, he soon became a leader in the fur trade, and he wasted no time raising sixteen thousand dollars to finance the first trading trip after Lewis and Clark returned. The plan was to follow the explorers' route to the Great Falls of the Missouri River, about fifteen hundred snaking, upriver miles. Lisa and his men succeeded where two subsequent expeditions were forced to turn back by hostile Indians.

The judges of the trial were city founder and fur trader, Auguste Chouteau and John C. B. Lucas, a rival of Chouteau over land ownership. The prosecutor was John Scott, who would later become the area's first congressman. The defense team consisted of Edward Hempstead, considered the best trial lawyer in the city; Rufus Easton, a future founder of Alton; and William C. Carr, a future judge.

Dubriel testified that he heard Lisa tell Drouillard, "George, go and find this Bazine. Go after him and bring him dead or alive." Bissonet was also known by the name of "Bazine." Dubriel and other witnesses said they heard gunfire, and Drouillard returned, saying he had shot Bissonet. Dubriel quoted Lisa, "It is well done. He is a rascal who got what he deserved." Scott argued that Bissonet was shot in the back, near his shoulder, and therefore, it was murder "in the fullest and most strict sense of the term."

Hempstead argued that Drouillard held no malice toward Bissonet, so murder was an improper charge, and the defendant was guilty of manslaughter, if guilty of anything. Carr contended that the hunter was fulfilling "the commands of his superior" when he fired the shot that eventually killed Bissonet. Easton argued that Bissonet was a deserter who had signed on for a term of three years and had left his post. He was also a thief, Easton said, and he quoted the Bible that no blood should be shed for a thief who is caught and dies. By contrast, Drouillard had "braved the unparalleled hardships of a desert and howling wilderness" and never left Clark, Easton told the jury.

The twelve men agreed, acquitting Drouillard. Lisa was never tried for the dead-or-alive order he gave Drouillard, who was soon back in the wilderness. The adventurer was killed two years later by Blackfeet Indians at the three forks of the Missouri River. Lisa made thirteen more trips up the Missouri, covering more than 26,000 miles.

THE IOWAYS WENT THAT AWAY
1808

On July 26, 1808, Joseph Charless's fledgling *Missouri Gazette* reported in its third issue that "two Ioway Indians who were committed to prison some time ago for murder, were tried and found guilty. Sentence of death will be pronounced on them this day." In the same issue, Charless reported that the U.S. government had allowed Shawnees and Kickapoos to make war on the Osage Indians because of many "outrages on the frontier" by the Osage.

Picture St. Louis in 1808—a true frontier town with a polyglot of French merchants at the top of the local hierarchy, followed by frontiersmen, adventurers, tradesmen, visiting Indians, and a handful of African American slaves.

The first trial of the two Indians from the Iowa tribe, who roamed through what is now Iowa and southern Minnesota, must have caused a stir. In perhaps its first correction of clarification—no death penalty had been levied—the *Gazette* reported on August 2 that a second trial was ordered after the attorney for the Indians claimed the verdict was against both the law and the evidence. The article identified the murder victims as Joseph Tibbeau and Joseph Marshall.

When the second trial began on August 2, sixty-seven jurors were excused because they had already formed opinions, the *Gazette* reported. It is not hard to imagine what their opinions were, given the natural bias of the day toward Indians. The trial began at 2 p.m. that day and concluded at 1 a.m. that night. The jury deliberated until 5 p.m.—sixteen hours—before again convicting the unnamed Indians.

What was the evidence against them? Had they ambushed Tibbeau and Marshall? Or were the Frenchmen killed in battle? And whose territory was it? The *Gazette* does not say. The

Ma-Has_Kah (White Cloud), an Ioway chief, 1837.

newspaper does say the deaths took place at the mouth of the Grand River in what is now northwest Missouri.

The second trial drew a crowd, and it wasn't just the locals. The trial of the Iowas may have been St. Louis's first major tourist attraction. According to a letter signed "A Bystander," the streets of St. Louis "teemed with Indian warriors." They were there, the letter writer said, to demand the freedom of the two men, a request denied by Governor Meriwether Lewis and General William Clark. Lewis and Clark, however, promised the chiefs a fair trial.

When the jury brought back its murder verdict, Rufus Easton, one of the Iowas' attorneys, approached the two judges presiding over the trial with a novel argument: because the killings took place at the mouth of the Grand River, the judges lacked jurisdiction to mete out the death penalty. The judges decided to sleep on it.

The next day, Easton's argument prevailed. But what to do with the Indians just convicted of murder? The solution: pass the dilemma on to someone else. The judges promptly turned the men over to the jurisdiction of Governor Lewis, who also took the same no-decision route after jailing the Indians. Lewis said he would ask President Thomas Jefferson to settle the matter.

The "Bystander" had nothing but praise for the whole procedure and trial. He wrote, "The Universal outcry was 'bang them, bang them,' but the judges and lawyers were above reproach. . . . They have done themselves much honor in their conduct in this trial, and some of their decisions would grace even Westminster Hall."

So the two Iowas were back where they had started—in jail—and were now awaiting a decision on their fate from a man a thousand miles away. The Iowas waited almost a year and then made a decision of their own. In its July 19, 1809, edition, the *Gazette* had a one-sentence entry: "The two Ioways escaped from jail."

Lewis demanded their return from Iowa chiefs, who refused, and Lewis initiated a boycott against the tribe. However, Lewis died soon thereafter, and his successor, Frederick Bates, did not press the matter.

As eastern tribes were pushed westward across the Mississippi by white settlers over the next thirty years, they fought the Iowas, and the tribe eventually signed a treaty with the government in 1836, ceding its land and moving to a reservation on the Kansas-Missouri border.

ST. LOUIS'S FIRST CONVICTED MURDERER
——————— 1809 ———————

A blended family that didn't meld, adultery, divorce, threats, dueling lawsuits, stealing, and finally a murder, a trial, a plea for mercy, and an execution. The plot for a twenty-first-century true-crime television show or an episode of *Law & Order*? Instead, two hundred years ago this scenario describes the first recorded murder conviction in the history of the fledgling frontier town of St. Louis.

It began in the 1790s, courtesy of extensive genealogical research that John A. McCullough, a descendant of the murder victim in this case, reported in the Missouri Historical Society's *Gateway*. The family of George Gordon moved from Pennsylvania to 680 acres of land near the mouth of Bonhomme Creek at the Missouri River in what is now Chesterfield. Locally, the area was known as St. Andrews, and Lewis and Clark noted it on their outbound trip to the Pacific Ocean in 1804 as an area with several farms and a large creek. The family of Lawrence and Priscilla Long from Virginia, the parents of nine, including John Long, moved onto nearby land.

Lawrence Long died; so did Mary Gordon. The surviving spouses decided to marry on November 30, 1806, and George Gordon moved into the Long homestead.

In March of 1809, Gordon was staying with a friend, Joseph Conway, who heard a commotion coming from the barn and found Gordon in the hay with Molly, a slave. Conway ordered Gordon off his farm. He suggested Gordon had been drunk.

The Longs reacted quickly. On March 28, Priscilla filed for divorce and moved out of the Long home. Then three of Priscilla's sons and her son-in-law broke into what was once their parents' home and carted off scores of items.

Gordon countered the divorce petition with a pair of lawsuits filed by St. Louis attorney Rufus Easton. One suit for three thousand dollars specifically accused John Long of taking Gordon's slaves; the second asked for damages of five thousand dollars for the break-in and theft. Among the items Gordon alleged missing were one thousand pounds of bacon, seven slaves, two dozen chairs, fifty pounds of sugar, and thirty yards of calico.

On June 5, according to a court deposition, Gordon told Justice of the Peace Andrew Kinkaid, "John Long is going to kill me." Three weeks to the day, Gordon was fatally shot in the chest outside the former Long home, in which he was still living.

A grand jury indicted Long on August 12, and he went on trial on August 21 in the court of Judge John B. C. Lucas. The jury heard more than two dozen witnesses. None could place Long at the scene of the shooting, and the victim, Gordon, told two people before he died that he did not see who shot him.

One witness, Moses Kinney, told the jury he heard Long complain about Gordon living at the former Long homestead. Kinney quoted Long as saying, "Before Gordon should have the property, one or the other of them would be carried off dead." Other witnesses also reported they had heard death threats by the defendant, who didn't testify. Lucas instructed the jury that the evidence against Long was only circumstantial, but circumstantial evidence did not bar a murder conviction. The jury wasted little time in finding Long guilty of murder.

Lucas imposed the death penalty, saying, "You have deprived your fellow creature, your stepfather, of a right which he had from God and which society had pledged to protect. Your situation is dreadful may serve as an awful example to evil doers." The judge later denied a defense request for a new trial.

The *Missouri Gazette*'s issue of August 30, 1809, carried lengthy stories on the state of European affairs and a smattering of ads selling slaves and goods. John Long's pending demise garnered only one paragraph: "John Long, the Younger, who was found guilty of murder, has received sentence to be hanged on the 16th of September next."

Gordon's descendant, McCullough, discovered in his research that the law at the time allowed the oldest son of a murder victim to intercede in a death sentence. "George Gordon Jr., undoubtedly present for the trial, had no intention of relieving his father's murderer from his prescribed outcome, and surely was standing in the crowd when the sentence was carried out," wrote McCullough in *Gateway*.

Before the hanging, Long appealed to the St. Louis populace in a letter in the *Gazette* that was signed: "I am your most unhappy and unfortunate. John Long, Gael, St. Louis, September 6, 1809." Long implored St. Louisans "to view with mercy my wretched condition." His reasoning was twofold: mercy for him and a living father for his kids. Long argued that he had not run away when he was charged with his stepfather's murder. He considered that a major plus. Instead, he said, "I surrendered myself a willing victim to popular suspicion, viewing with anxiety the kind acquittal of a friendly jury."

Sadly for Long, the jury had been neither kind nor friendly, and the townsfolk, Long noted, were well aware of the verdict. What people didn't know, Long insisted, was that he was married to "an amiable wife" and was the father "of two helpless infants, whose cries are insufficient to save their all, the author of their existence. You that are fathers," the letter continues, "can best appreciate my forlorn state and view my orphaned children tottering in the rugged path of life without a friend to guide their erring steps. . . . The grave opens to receive me. I sink into its bosum, unless rescued by your pity . . . I live or die by your mandate . . . and trust you will suffer me to remain a living monument of heaven born mercy."

No such luck. Once again, Long's trust in St. Louis kindness and mercy was misplaced—or the people concluded that Long's children were better off without a living murderer for a father.

Long was executed on September 16, 1809. The *Gazette* reported in its September 20 edition that Long assisted the executioner in adjusting the rope as he stood on a chair on a cart, and "without waiting for the cart being drawn off, he kicked the chair from him and launched into eternity."

Long was listed as a resident of Bonhomme Township, St. Louis District, Louisiana Territory. He was the first recorded individual in St. Louis to be hanged.

There had been no reports of murders in St. Louis during the forty years of colonial rule under the French and Spanish and only one disputed case in the five years of American rule before the Long-Gordon affair. In 1806, a man had killed an Indian, but a jury acquitted him on the grounds that he had come to the defense of two others.

A RARIFIED MURDER, THE STEPHENSON HOUSE
1825

On January 29, 1825, Daniel D. Smith stopped in Edwardsville on his way home to Pike County, where Governor Shadrach Bond had appointed him the county's recorder four years earlier. Smith, a prior Edwardsville resident, was visiting friends. He never left Edwardsville that night. Someone stabbed him and he died.

Smith went by the nickname of "Rarified Smith" and was described by former St. Louis Mayor John Darby in his *Personal Recollections* as "a man of much humor and wit, and a great caricaturist." Charged immediately with his murder was Palemon Winchester, son-in-law of Lucy and the late Benjamin Stephenson, a colonel in the War of 1812, a founder of the town, and a builder of Edwardsville's finest—and still-standing—mansion where Winchester was arrested. Also charged were Lucy's son, James W. Stephenson; and local resident James D. Henry, later a general in the Black Hawk War. Only Winchester went to trial.

Winchester, a young lawyer, had moved to Illinois from Tennessee and married Julia Stephenson. He convinced one of that state's leading criminal defense lawyers to make the trip from Nashville to Edwardsville to represent him. The lawyer, Felix Grundy, served in a career that spanned forty years as an attorney general of the United States, a U.S. senator and congressman, and as a state chief justice. Illinois Attorney General Alfred Coles and Greenville lawyer Ben Mills were the prosecutors.

According to Darby, in jury selection, Grundy limited his picks to persons who were born, raised, or had lived in Tennessee like Winchester and himself, and excluded anyone with a hint of Yankee blood. Both the prosecutors and Smith were Northerners.

Grundy also strategically arranged the courtroom so that former Territorial Governor Ninian Edwards, a major force in Illinois and local politics, was sitting in the front row, with Winchester's wife and family around him.

The prosecution provided two witnesses who said they had seen Winchester approach Smith with a knife. Grundy pressed the men about their alcohol consumption and implied they were too drunk to know what was going on.

Like the Skidmore, Missouri, bully case of the 1990s, no one admitted to seeing the stabbing that night, and the jury verdict in March 1825 was not guilty. Neither of the co-defendants was ever tried. According to research by Karen Campe Mateyka, who wrote columns about the case for the *Edwardsville Intelligencer* in November 2002 under the pseudonym of "Henry the Stephenson House Mouse" as well as a book about the historic Stephenson dwelling and the families who lived there, the local paper, the *Edwardsville Spectator*, said only that Smith had been "killed in an affray." So what was the motive?

That year, John Quincy Adams became president courtesy of the U.S. House of Representatives after neither Adams nor Andrew Jackson was able to get a majority in the Electoral College. Could a quarrel have erupted between Smith and the Yankee supporters of Adams of Massachusetts for president on one hand and the Southern backers of Tennessee's Old Hickory on the other?

Or was the antagonism more personal in nature? Darby suggests that drawings by Smith led to a quarrel, without hinting at what the caricatures were about. In an article in the *Intelligencer*, Mateyka cites a local historian, Louise Travous, who speculated that a Smith cartoon lampooned Lucy Stephenson and Ninian Edwards and suggested intimacy between the widow and the politician. The Edwards and Stephenson families, as the first families of Edwardsville, were close. Mateyka notes that a fire damaged the Edwards home the year before, and the Stephensons took in the Edwards family. A caricature of the matriarch of one family in some sort of intimacy with the patriarch of the other—whether true or not—would certainly have enraged Lucy's son and son-in-law. Fueled by alcohol at a party in the mansion, a quarrel over a cartoon could have prompted Winchester and Stephenson to lash out at Smith, perhaps demand an apology, and upon getting none, stab him.

THE RESTORED STEPHENSON HOUSE

FRANCIS MCINTOSH, ELIJAH LOVEJOY
1836-37

Whatever George Hammond or William Mull told Francis L. McIntosh on April 24, 1836, on the St. Louis riverfront, their words—in jest or reality—triggered an unforeseen series of tragic events that tarnished the reputations of two frontier cities, St. Louis and Alton. McIntosh fatally stabbed Hammond and severely wounded Mull. A mob then tied McIntosh to a tree and burned him to death. Abolitionist Elijah P. Lovejoy wrote about it. Nineteen months later, Lovejoy, too, was dead—killed in a shootout in Alton by another angry mob and proclaimed as a martyr in defense of a free press.

Hammond was a deputy sheriff, and Mull a city constable. That fateful day, they had arrested two men for some minor infraction, possibly drunkenness, peace disturbance, or fighting. The men were part of the crew of the steamship *Flora*, a Pittsburgh vessel docked at the waterfront. McIntosh, a free black, was either a crew member, a cook, or steward. He joined the fracas and his friends fled, but he was arrested for his interference with police and was being escorted to jail between the two officers when he asked what his punishment would be.

Various accounts say McIntosh was told that he would get either thirty lashes, six years in prison, or a hanging. Whether the men were kidding or suggesting that a slave-owning state like Missouri would show no mercy to a free black from Pennsylvania has never been determined. Whatever the context, McIntosh took it the wrong way. He grabbed a knife from his pants; slashed Hammond's jugular, killing him; stabbed Mull in the side; and fled, hurtling a fence and hiding in an outhouse. Mull yelled, "Catch him," as he fell, and passersby gave chase, catching the attacker and taking him to jail.

A crowd soon gathered, stormed the jail, grabbed the defendant, and took him to a locust tree at what is now Market and Tenth streets. After gathering wood and tying McIntosh to the tree, they set him afire. An alderman allegedly threatened anyone who would consider helping the dying McIntosh. McIntosh prayed and sang hymns. At one point, he pleaded with the crowd to put a bullet in his head to end his agony. McIntosh burned to death in eighteen minutes. His remains were left in the street as the mob dispersed.

Mayor John Darby was home ill and unavailable to call out the militia. In his personal recollections several years later, Darby downplayed the whole event. He insisted Easterners had kept the sorry episode alive.

"From Hammond's death to the capture and burning of the negro was not more than one hour's time. In fact, three fourths of the citizens did not know anything about it till the tragic affair was over," Darby wrote. "For two or three years afterwards, strangers and visitors from the East—particularly from Pittsburgh—would go to that locust tree, cut off pieces of it, and take them away, so that the tree was greatly cut to pieces, and large portions of it carried away."

Darby did not discuss the failure of St. Louisans to cut down the tree immediately to wipe out a shameful episode. So the tree stood as a daily reminder of the atrocity.

The *Missouri Republican*, the leading newspaper of the day, called the burning at the stake "a revolting spectacle" but philosophized that it could have happened anywhere and that a "veil of oblivion" should be drawn over it, lest St. Louis's reputation be damaged. The *Missouri Argus* emphasized the stabbings of the officers, and one of its writers said flippantly, "The punishment was, as once said an old preacher, awfully emphatic, and we trust another occasion for its administration will never present itself. It is certainly as well, however, for impudent free negroes to be cautious."

A German newspaper wanted to know why concerned citizens failed to stop the lynching and why the civil guard was not called out. The *Alton Telegraph* weighed in with an editorial critical of mob justice.

The Reverend Elijah P. Lovejoy, a Presbyterian minister and publisher of the abolitionist *St. Louis Observer*, had no firsthand knowledge of McIntosh's death, but he went to the Market Street scene the next day. He found McIntosh's decapitated body and witnessed boys throwing stones at the corpse. He reported the sight in the *Observer*'s May 5 edition under the heading "Awful Murder and Savage Barbarity." "We must stand by the Constitution and laws or all is gone," he wrote.

Lovejoy was thirty-three years old and one of seven children of the Reverend Daniel and Elizabeth Lovejoy of Albion, Maine. A graduate of Waterville College in Maine, Lovejoy arrived in St. Louis a year later, 1827, as a teacher and later a newspaper editor. In this role, Lovejoy showed a vituperative streak in his writing, partly the fashion of the day. Of President Andrew Jackson, Lovejoy wrote he was "an adulterer and murderer," and his staff consisted of "fools and knaves."

In 1832, Lovejoy converted to Presbyterianism—his father had been a Congregationalist preacher—and he studied at the Princeton Theological Seminary in New Jersey. He then preached in New York before being called to St. Louis to edit the *St. Louis Observer*, a Presbyterian newspaper. He was also assigned by the American Home Missionary Society to serve as pastor of the Des Peres Presbyterian Church. He preached in a one-room limestone church, still standing at what is now 1834 Geyer Road. The minister and editor married Celia Ann French of St. Charles in March 1835, and a son, Edward, was born in March 1836.

In May of that year, while Lovejoy was attending a church function in Pittsburgh, Judge Luke E. Lawless announced a grand jury investigation into the burning of McIntosh. A law partner of U.S. Senator Thomas Hart Benton, Lawless was a Democrat who backed the city's elite. They, in turn, generally held slaves or supported slavery.

In instructions to the jurors, Lawless made it all but impossible for them to hand up a true bill. He declared the grand jury could not return an indictment if it found McIntosh's death was "not the act of numerable and ascertainable malefactors, but of congregated thousands, seized upon and impelled by that mysterious, metaphysical, and almost electric frenzy, which in all ages and nations, has hurried on the infurcated multitude to deeds of death and destruction."

All those "thousands" acting together were "beyond the reach of human law," he said. In a shot across Lovejoy's bow, he added that religious zealots were convinced that they alone knew God's will. Lawless went even further: Abolitionists stirring up hatreds had caused McIntosh's death.

It is no surprise that the grand jury found no one to blame for burning a man at the stake. Not a soul in the self-perceived civilized St. Louis was charged.

Similarly, it was no surprise that Lovejoy's offices became the target of reprisals. Vandals damaged the offices on May 23, 24, and 31. Lawless claimed he had intervened to keep mobs from doing further damage. Lovejoy retaliated in an editorial in the *Observer* on July 21. In it, he denounced mob rule, as well as the judge's instructions that allowed the grand jury to determine the burning was "an act of the populace" for which no individual could be charged.

In keeping with his style, Lovejoy went over the line, way over the line: "Judge Lawless is a Papist, and in his charge we see the cloven foot of Jesuitism peeping out from under the veil of almost every paragraph." In one sentence, the abolitionist editor succeeded in offending every Irish Catholic in St. Louis, as well as the Benton-Lawless political faction.

He went on to write, "The real origin of the cry 'Down with the *Observer*' is to be looked for in its opposition to Popery. The fire that is now crackling through this city, was kindled on Popish altars and has been assiduously blowed up by Jesuit breath."

On the same day the *Observer* published Lovejoy's words, about two hundred people broke down the door of his offices and destroyed print material.

Lovejoy crated his press and shipped it to Alton. He also crated his furniture, but it too was destroyed by a mob before he could get it out of town. The press arrived at the Alton dock on Sunday, July 24, and Lovejoy left it there. At about 2 a.m. the next morning, the press was gone—damaged and toppled into the Mississippi. In a mass meeting that night, Alton residents denied any involvement in the destruction and declared such acts would not be tolerated in their city. They suggested St. Louisans had followed the boat upriver and destroyed the press after it was unloaded. They even contributed money for a new press.

In response, Lovejoy made comments placating his audience and suggesting he would be more tolerant in his writing. But he warned that he was "an uncompromising enemy of slavery, and so expected to live and so to die." He added, "I shall hold myself at liberty to speak, to write, and to publish whatever I please on any subject."

Lovejoy founded the *Alton Observer* in September and moved his family to Alton that fall. He was printing on borrowed presses and raising capital to replace the press he had lost in July 1836. He became pastor at the Second Presbyterian Church.

On July 4, 1837, Lovejoy used the anniversary of the founding of the country as an opportunity to call for a meeting of those opposed to slavery to form a state auxiliary to the American Anti-Slavery Society. The editorial brought resentment from Altonians divided over the slavery issue and unhappy with being dragged into the controversy. Missouri was a slave state; Illinois, a free state. However, many of its residents along the border had property in Missouri and slaves on that property.

The *Missouri Republican* denounced Lovejoy, the *Alton Observer*, and its call for a renewed war on slavery. It carried a flaming editorial against the Presbyterian minister in August, and from that point forward, Lovejoy seemed a marked man.

Lovejoy's second printing press arrived by boat from Cincinnati via St. Louis on August 21. Lovejoy was home with Celia, who was sick. A mob gathered, threw rocks through office windows, threatened workers who fled, and destroyed the press. Lovejoy was forced to take out an ad in the *Alton Telegraph* and appealed for funding.

On September 21, a third press following the same water route—Cincinnati through St. Louis to Alton—arrived at the Alton wharf. Mayor John M. Krum told an angry group who had gathered to disperse. They ignored him. Press No. 3 lasted six hours before it was destroyed and joined the first two in the river bottom mud.

Lovejoy was in ever-increasing danger. On October 3, Lovejoy was preaching in St. Charles, his wife's hometown, when a mob attacked him, and he narrowly managed to escape by foot and on horseback. One of the Illinois leaders verbally attacking Lovejoy was Attorney General Usher F. Linder. He denounced the *Observer*, saying it was brought to Alton "to teach rebellion; to preach murder in the name of religion; to strike dismay into the hearts of the people, and spread desolation over the face of the land."

At a mass meeting on November 3, Krum introduced a resolution that passed easily. "Resolved, that as citizens of Alton, and friends of order, peace, and constitutional law, we regret that persons and editors from abroad have seen proper to interest themselves so conspicuously in the discussion and agitation of a question, in which our city is made the principal theatre."

Lovejoy addressed the hostile crowd about his view and their view of slavery, as well as about his rights and their rights. His ringing speech eventually served as his figurative epitaph:

> Mr. Chairman, it is not true, as has been charged upon me, that I hold in contempt the feelings of this community, in reference to the question

which is now agitating it. I respect and appreciate the feelings and opinions of my fellow citizens, and it is one of the most painful and unpleasant duties of my life that I am called upon to act in opposition to them.

If you suppose, sir, that I have published sentiments contrary to those generally held in this community, because I delighted in differing from them, or in occasioning a disturbance, you have entirely misapprehended me.

But, sir, while I value the good opinion of my fellow citizens as highly as anyone, I may be permitted to say that I am governed by higher considerations than either the favor or fear of man. I am impelled to the course I have taken, because I fear God. As I shall answer it to my God in the great day, I dare not abandon my sentiments or cease in all proper ways to propagate them.

Lovejoy went on to state that he had asked only that his rights as a citizen be protected, that he broke no laws, that he never published anything injurious of Alton or its individuals, and that if he had committed any crimes he could easily be convicted:

I know, sir, that you can tar and feather me, hang me up, or put me in the Mississippi, without the least difficulty. But where shall I go? I have been made to feel that if I am not safe in Alton, I shall not be safe anywhere . . .

If the civil authorities refuse to protect me, I must look to God; and if I die, I have determined to make my grave in Alton. I have sworn eternal opposition to slavery, and by the blessing of God, I will never turn back. With God I cheerfully rest my cause. I can die at my post, but I cannot desert it.

Four days later, he was dead.

The fourth press arrived on November 7, following the same route through St. Louis; Lovejoy supporters rushed to the warehouse of Wynthrop Gilman, where about twenty defenders had gathered. The defenders had tried to enlist Mayor Krum to lead them, but he had refused to take sides between the anti- and proslavery factions. The Lovejoy group then called itself a militia. A mob gathered outside the brick building. Its members had been alerted when the boat carrying the press left St. Louis. One of its self-styled leaders was local doctor Horace Beal.

Mayor Krum tried to get the mob to disperse. They ignored him, and when he tried to get Lovejoy and his advocates to give up the press to avoid bloodshed, they refused.

Shots were fired into the building and from the warehouse into the crowd. First to fall fatally wounded was Lyman Bishop, one of the rioters. The mob tried to lift a makeshift ladder to set fire to the roof, but Lovejoy and two of his aides toppled it. During a second attempt to get a ladder to the roof, Lovejoy and two others made another charge to dismantle it. Lovejoy was shot three times in the chest and once in the stomach and arm. He managed to stagger back into the warehouse before he died. His colleague, Royal Weller, was shot in the leg.

The mob then allowed Lovejoy's defenders to leave. They fled. The wounded Weller watched the crowd tear the press into pieces, cart the ruins out of the building, and dump them in the river. Lovejoy's body was left where it was. His brothers, fearing more violence, waited until the morning of November 9, his thirty-fifth birthday, before recovering it.

In January, Gilman went on trial in Alton, accused of causing a riot. Some members of the mob were tried for rioting. The case was unsuccessful. Neither side was convicted of anything.

Some historians, such as James Neal Primm, author of *Lion of the Valley*, have speculated that St. Louisans were part of the mob the night Lovejoy died. After all, individually, they had the most to lose. Lovejoy may have been able to identify many of those who had played a role in the death of McIntosh. A judge less lenient than Lawless could reopen the case at any time. In 1837, Missouri had no statute of limitations for murder, according to research for this book by assistant St. Louis County prosecutor Doug Sidell.

The news of Lovejoy's death spread throughout the country, and—deservedly or not—he became a martyr for both the abolition movement and the defenders of freedom of the press.

One hundred years after the death of Lovejoy, the *St. Louis Star-Times* reviewed the events and noted that the *New York Post* had sensed the importance of the tragedy a century earlier. In an editorial from 1837, the *Post* emphasized:

> For our part, we approve, we applaud, we would consecrate, if we could, to universal honor, the conduct of those who bled in this gallant defense of the freedom of the press. Whether they erred or not in their opinion, they did not err in their conviction of their rights, as citizens of a democratic government, to express them.

BEAUMONT AND GEYER: A CASE OF MALPRACTICE
1840

The world-renowned army surgeon Dr. William Beaumont had been in private practice for less than a year in St. Louis when a colleague called him to the National Hotel to treat a man who had been beaten. On June 1, 1840, Beaumont recommended and then performed a trephine operation, sawing into the patient's skull to relieve pressure and to remove skull fragments. The patient, Andrew Jackson Davis, died seven days later. His attacker, William P. Darnes, went on trial in November of that year, with the most prominent lawyer of the day, Henry S. Geyer, as one of his defense attorneys.

Geyer's defense was twofold: He blamed the press for the initial attack, and he blamed the doctor for the victim's death. The jury even had a portion of the dead man's skull to view during the lengthy trial that was moved to a larger courtroom because the smaller one had been filled to capacity. Prosecutors Peter Engle and Thomas Gantt and defenders Geyer and Joseph B. Crockett put on more than twenty witnesses and told the jury the following story:

Davis had taken over the *St. Louis Argus*, a Democrat newspaper, in 1839 and had selected William Gilpin as its editor with complete control over its contents. The Democrats were divided over support or opposition to a national bank, and the *Argus* was firmly opposed, like Davis's namesake, Andrew Jackson.

Darnes was a self-taught carpenter and active in politics. He was secretary of a Democrat political club that favored the bank. His group was the target of criticism by Gilpin in the *Argus*, prompting Darnes to write Davis to complain about Gilpin. Davis, however, defended Gilpin. Gilpin claimed sole responsibility for what the *Argus* printed. Gilpin called Darnes a common street loafer and vagabond. Gilpin wrote that Darnes was a "half-witted drone who stands at corners or roams about the streets . . ." and challenged Darnes to come to the offices of the *Argus* on Olive Street.

Instead, prosecutors said, an angry Darnes went out and bought a special cane, in effect, a small iron rod, and began a search for Davis. He found the publisher, described as a small, mild-mannered individual, on Market Street. Davis had been walking down Chestnut, carrying an umbrella, and cut over to Market at Third Street. In the center of the intersection, Darnes punched Davis in the jaw, knocking him down, and then beat him about the head and face with the iron cane before walking up Third Street, leaving the bleeding publisher in the middle of Market.

Davis was taken into the lobby of the National Hotel, where Dr. Thomas McMartin and Dr. James Sykes attempted to treat the wounds. Sykes brought Beaumont to the hotel, and the trephining was performed. Doctors described to the jury how Beaumont cut into Davis's head to relieve pressure on the skull.

Sykes and other doctors testified that Beaumont had done his best to save the patient. Drs. Franklin Knox and Thomas White, however, disagreed and said the operation had been dangerous. "It is difficult to say whether Mr. Davis would have lived if no medical treatment had been afforded him," added White, who, like Knox, was a rival of Beaumont. Dr. William Carr Lane, a former St. Louis mayor, also testified that trephining should only be a last resort and suggested that Davis had not reached that stage. The implication? Death by surgery.

In his closing arguments, Geyer pounced on Beaumont's very celebrity as a surgeon and scholar whose book on gastric fluids had been read by a worldwide audience. Geyer suggested that Beaumont was prone to experiment rather than cure. "It was upon the same principle of curiosity that he bored a hole in Davis's head, to see what was going on in there," Geyer alleged.

The prosecutors painted Darnes as angry and vindictive, attacking the wrong man because physically he had nothing to fear from Davis. They also argued the assault was a deliberate murder because Darnes had been searching downtown for his victim. However, Geyer blamed the newspapers, not Darnes, for the attack itself, saying the public was without a remedy "for over all these [people] a licentious press asserts its usurped jurisdiction and all are equally exposed to its blighting and withering influence, all equally unprotected."

Geyer was convincing, and the jury rejected a murder conviction and found Darnes guilty of fourth-degree manslaughter. Jurors said the defendant should be fined five hundred dollars.

Interestingly, Beaumont and Geyer had much in common. They were born five years apart, and both served the country in the War of 1812. By the time they clashed in court, both had become famous in their chosen professions. Beaumont has since had a high school and a scout reservation named after him; Geyer, a road in Kirkwood and an avenue in Soulard.

After the War of 1812, Beaumont had served off and on as a surgeon in the army. In 1822, Alexis St. Martin, a trapper, near Fort Mackinack on Lake Michigan, where Beaumont was stationed, had been shot accidentally in the stomach. Beaumont treated him, even though he expected St. Martin to die in twenty minutes. But St. Martin lived—with an open hole, or fistula, in his stomach. Beaumont later hired St. Martin as a handyman, and the doctor performed experiments on the man's stomach. Beaumont would put food on a string and place it in the hole in the stomach wall, retrieving it every few hours to see what was happening. Beaumont performed more experiments in 1831 and 1832 on the stomach of St. Martin, who lived until 1880 despite the open sore.

In 1833, Beaumont produced a textbook from his experimental work and showed for the first time in medical history that digestion was a chemical process. He has been called the father of physiology. His book *Experiments and Observations on the Gastric Juice and the*

Physiology of Digestion was reprinted in several languages.

A year later, Beaumont came to St. Louis as a surgeon at Jefferson Barracks. He later served the same position at the St. Louis arsenal, resigning from the military to go into private practice in 1839. He became the first head of the surgery department at Saint Louis University. He died in 1853 and is buried at Bellefontaine Cemetery.

DR. WILLIAM BEAUMONT

His nemesis, Geyer, is also buried at Bellefontaine. He died in 1859. In the 1830s, Geyer was active in promoting a public school system in Missouri. One of his biographers claimed he had tried more cases before the U.S. Supreme Court than Daniel Webster. One of the early cases involved Spanish land grants, and Geyer won praise for his erudition and scholarship from Chief Justice John Marshall.

He also defended the owner of slave Dred Scott before the high court, and some of the language Chief

HENRY S. GEYER

Justice Roger Taney used to defend slavery came from Geyer's brief. Geyer served in the territorial legislature in 1818, was later Missouri's Speaker of the House, and succeeded Thomas Hart Benton as a U.S. senator in 1851 as a proslavery Whig.

GIVING THE FRENCH A BAD NAME
1849

The year 1849 proved to be bad for St. Louis—possibly the worst year ever in the annals of the Mound City. From January to July of 1849, a cholera epidemic took the lives of 4,574 people in a city with a population of 70,000. Then, on May 19, a good portion of St. Louis—as many as four hundred buildings—burned down from a fire that began on the levee aboard the steamship *White Cloud*. It spread to twenty-three other vessels before jumping ashore and wreaking havoc throughout downtown. Finally, two popular young men were fatally shot for no apparent reason at about 11:50 p.m. on October 29 in a downtown hotel the fire had missed. The shooter and his brother narrowly escaped a lynching.

Gonsalve and Raymond de Montesquieu arrived in St. Louis on Sunday morning, October 28. They were wealthy French noblemen who had sailed to America, arriving at New York in June, and had traveled leisurely westward. They showed up with large wardrobes and an assortment of weapons for hunting. At Barnum's City Hotel, the brothers were assigned a room off a hallway that led to a piazza behind the hotel. Opposite them, in a room with a door to the garden, were Albert Jones, H. M. Henderson, and Captain William Hubbell. In another room with a window providing a view of the piazza were T. Kirby Barnum and a man identified as Mr. Macumber. Barnum was the nephew of the hotel owner, Theron Barnum, a relative of impresario P. T. Barnum.

That fatal night, Barnum heard a tapping on the window from the piazza. When he pulled back the curtain, he was shot immediately and died. Macumber was hit in the wrist. Hearing the gunshot from the piazza, Jones opened his door and was immediately gunned down. Henderson and Hubbell suffered minor wounds. They saw their assailants, the two Frenchmen, in the garden. No arguments had taken place. In fact, not a word had been spoken by either the killer or the victims.

Officers went immediately to the room of the Frenchmen and arrested the brothers. Raymond said his brother had been acting strangely recently so he tried to follow him wherever he went. Gonsalve admitted his guilt. He claimed he had an uncontrollable urge to shoot two men and couldn't stop himself. He absolved his brother, saying Raymond had followed him to prevent a tragedy, but everything had happened too quickly for Raymond to stop him. Both men were taken to jail.

After the funerals for Jones, a carriage maker, and Barnum, a large crowd started to gather at the jail. Its intention? Hang the Frenchmen. Isaac Sturgeon, a businessman who had sold lumber to Jones for the latter's carriages, had attended Jones's funeral and heard the plot to lynch the assailants.

Years later, Sturgeon would explain his actions: "I satisfied myself the next day after the murder that it was an act of an insane man, and my deepest sympathy was aroused for the poor unfortunate Raymond, who had so suddenly thrust upon him the insanity of his brother and in danger of losing his life for the act of his insane brother."

Sturgeon said the fact the men were French counts or some kind of nobility enflamed public sentiment against them even more, and he determined to try to "save my city the disgrace of murdering one innocent and one crazy man."

After discovering the plot, Sturgeon was able to find Sheriff Louis Le Beume, and they, in turn, recruited Judge J. B. Colt. When the trio got to the jail, they found the mob out front but were able to secrete the defendants out a back door into an alley and then to the nearby home of a bishop. From there, they took the brothers to the federal arsenal, only to be told there were insufficient numbers of soldiers to stand up to a large crowd. Their cab-drawn horses were unable to make the trip to the next post of safety, Jefferson Barracks. Sturgeon said the group spent several tense hours finding horse-drawn carriages to make a thirty-mile night run, but they finally accomplished their mission, turning the brothers de Montesquieu over to the post's commander for safekeeping shortly before midnight.

With Gonsalve's lawyers pleading insanity and Raymond's lawyer protesting his innocence, the brothers were tried twice, both with the same results. Jurors could not agree if Gonsalve should be found guilty of two murders and executed or not guilty by reason of insanity. Witnesses were imported from France to testify that the brothers came from a family with a history of mental illness.

After the two trials and diplomatic exchanges between France and the United States, Governor Austin A. King stepped in and pardoned both, Gonsalve because he was insane, Raymond because he didn't participate in the homicide. King said a third trial would bring "renewed trouble and increased expenses to the state." The brothers left almost immediately for New York and sailed to France. Gonsalve died insane. Before they left St. Louis, however, Raymond made at least one visit: the offices of Isaac Sturgeon, to thank him.

JOSEPH CHARLESS, JR.
1859

After Joseph W. Thornton had gunned down prominent businessman Joseph Charless, Jr., on a downtown street, only the moving speech of a relative of the murder victim and the U.S. Army saved a revenge-minded Thornton from a lynching by an angry mob on June 3, 1859.

Charless was walking from his home at Fifth and Walnut streets to his wholesale drug business on Main Street when he encountered Thornton on the south side of Main between Third and Fourth streets. Thornton abruptly greeted him: "You are the son of a bitch that swore against my character." Without another word and before Charless could reply, Thornton drew a pistol and shot Charless in the stomach. Charless went down. As he got up, Thornton fired a second round into his left side. Charless fell again, managed to rise again, and staggered into a lace shop, where workers made a bed for him in a back room. They summoned a doctor and his relatives.

"Having thus consummated his murderous purpose, the assassin coolly replaced the revolver in his pocket, and began deliberately to resume his morning stroll," the *St. Louis Democrat* later reported. The stroll did not last long. Several men raced to the scene, including the bartender from the Leviathan Saloon, and seized Thornton, who fought with them. The head of a Market Street horse and buggy line intervened and took the shooter to the calaboose.

It did not take long for a mob to form downtown, and they marched in two columns to the jail. Court officials had already locked the building, though, and policemen were guarding the door. A committee from the crowd headed by a Dr. Spaulding entered the jail and checked on the prisoner. Spaulding then reported to the crowd that Thornton was safe in a cell and could not escape. Spaulding added, "If ever a time when the Lynch law was justifiable, this is the time. But I am satisfied upon reflection to let the law take its course." The newspaper reported that Spaulding's comments were met with cries of "No, no, hang the foul assassin. Let us make a sure thing of it. There is no security in the law. He will escape. They will say he is insane and on that ground acquit him. Lynch him. Lynch him."

Spaulding tried yet again to reason with the crowd: "Let the law deal with the bloody scoundrel; let the hangman punish the assassin."

Meanwhile, the mayor called out all of the city's deputy marshals and sheriffs to prevent a breach of the jail-yard wall. The Reverend William Greenleaf Eliot of the Unitarian Church, a founder of Washington University, realized the seriousness of the situation and summoned C. D. Drake from Charless's deathbed at the lace store. Drake was the brother-in-law of the victim.

Drake stood in front of the mob and told them he had a relationship with the victim by marriage for a quarter of a century. A lynching was something the family wanted no part of. Drake said, "I felt it is my duty to come to you and say to you as friends, as neighbors, that no course could be pursued more terrible to the family of Mr. Charless, more in violence to their feelings, than for you to visit upon this unfortunate criminal the merit of his crime."

Drake managed to quiet the crowd but it would not disperse, and Sheriff Michael Cerre decided he needed substantial reinforcements. He called upon the army for help. Companies of soldiers were mustered and in place by late afternoon. The mob finally broke up. Charless died the next day, forgiving his attacker before he passed away.

Thornton had the trial the mob would have denied him in September, and as one wag in the mob had predicted, his lawyers pleaded insanity. It didn't work. The jury convicted Thornton, and he was sentenced to death. He expected executive clemency or a pardon or a commutation from the governor. It never came.

From a large crowd that had gathered, about seventy-five

people got to see the hanging on November 11. People climbed to nearby rooftops to get a glimpse of Thornton in the jail yard. He was thirty-eight when he died.

The trial in 1859 had been Thornton's second, but the first one—in May 1858—had set in motion Thornton's hatred for Charless. Thornton had been on trial for his alleged role in the disappearance of some eighteen to nineteen thousand dollars on April 5, 1855, from the safe of Boatmen's Savings Association, where Thornton had worked for fifteen hundred dollars a year as a bookkeeper. The initial suspicion was robbery. But locks to the safe required keys, and Thornton had one. Thornton was terminated or resigned. He was later accused, arrested, held on bail, and indicted for theft.

One of the business and civic hats that Charless wore was president of the State Bank of Missouri. In that role, he surfaced at Thornton's trial as the main witness against the former bookkeeper. After Thornton left Boatmen's, he had begun making deposits of $120 to $340 at the State Bank, Charless testified, and in each deposit was a stained or dirty fifty- or hundred-dollar bill. The bills appeared as if they had been buried.

The accumulation of the small deposits by Thornton amounted to several thousands of dollars, testimony disclosed. In one instance, Thornton had brought in a ream of bills amounting to $1,070, so dirty and stained they could not be pried apart. When questioned about the bills, Thornton claimed he got them from a boatman who found them under an uprooted tree. Instead of depositing the roll in Thornton's account, the bank advertised that anyone who lost the money could claim it.

Despite the dirty money evidence and the testimony of Charless, Thornton was acquitted, but he was so angry at Charless that he even considered a defamation lawsuit. A year later, Thornton sought his revenge. Charless was fifty-five when he died.

Charless was the son of Joseph Charless, who in 1808 founded the *Missouri Gazette*, the first newspaper west of the Mississippi

River. He worked for his father for a time in the printing business but returned to Kentucky, where he got a college education. Back in St. Louis, he eventually prospered in wholesale drugs and finance. He married Charlotte Blow in 1831 and had one daughter.

Among the contributions of Joseph Charless to St. Louis and Missouri were his service as director of public schools, his founding of Westminster College, and his membership on the Board of Aldermen. Charless also was a director of a railroad company and president of the Mechanics Bank, as well as the State Bank of Missouri.

Charless and his wife supported Dred Scott both morally and financially in the slave's legal efforts to obtain his freedom. At one time, Charlotte's father, Peter Blow, had owned Scott. After Scott lost his case before the U.S. Supreme Court, he was transferred from his owner to Taylor Blow, Charlotte's brother. Blow immediately granted Scott his freedom.

Charlotte Charless wrote a book about her husband extolling his virtues. In 1853, she founded the Home of the Friendless to care for older women no longer able to take care of themselves. The Charless House celebrated its 150th anniversary in 2003. Charlotte had outlived her husband by forty-six years when she died in 1905.

JAMES UTZ, CONFEDERATE SPY
1864

Just before midnight on September 24, 1864, a union cavalry unit stopped a wagon near the corner of Clayton and Ballas roads in what was then rural western St. Louis County. Seven men were in the wagon, along with guns, ammunition, and medicine. The leader of the group was James Morgan Utz. In his possession were a cipher book and letters for rebel officers. Utz was a major in the Confederate Army and a spy. He would pay with his life for his activities. He was found guilty of spying, recruiting soldiers for the Confederacy, and transporting weapons and medicine by a Union tribunal headed by Colonel W. A. Barstrow, of Wisconsin.

Utz was a native of Missouri—a state and region torn by the Civil War. He was the son of Franklin and Amelia Utz. He joined the rebel forces at the age of twenty in 1861. He was captured in September 1862 and involved in an exchange for federal prisoners. According to the Missouri Division of the Sons of Confederate Veterans, Utz took part in several battles in the West. He fought with Confederate troops at Prairie Grove in northwest Arkansas on December 7, 1862; at Pleasant Hill in northwestern Louisiana on April 9, 1864; and at Jenkin's Ferry in south-central Arkansas twenty-one days later.

Promoted to major from captain in the summer of 1864, Utz was sent behind enemy lines in advance of General Sterling Price's foray into Missouri that would end with a victory at Pilot Knob in southeast Missouri and subsequent defeats in Independence and Westport. In St. Louis, Utz got a wagon from a partisan and acquired federal uniforms from Paul Fusz and medical supplies from a druggist sympathizer. Four recruits were hidden in the wagon along with the druggist, Fusz, wearing a federal uniform, and Utz when the cavalry patrol stopped them.

Utz was confined at Gratiot Street Prison in downtown St. Louis where his father had been housed as a rebel sympathizer since July. Fusz, eighteen, an ancestor of the car dealership's family, was transferred to Jefferson City where he was later paroled by President Abraham Lincoln.

Major Utz's uncle was St. Louis County Judge Frederick Hyatt, who petitioned Lincoln on his nephew's behalf. The petition was successful—almost. Lincoln granted the pardon. But it arrived in St. Louis too late; Utz had already been executed. He was hanged at 2:20 p.m. on December 26, 1864, and buried at Fee Fee Cemetery, not far from the home where he was born on March 9, 1841. The war ended four months later.

The historic, three-dormered Utz family home at 615 Utz Lane has been saved from demolition and moved to Greene Park in Hazelwood, where it shares green space with the refurbished Knobbe House and an old single-room school.

THE WHISKEY RING
1875

In a hushed, crowded courtroom in downtown St. Louis on February 17, 1876, Defense Attorney J. K. Porter got formal permission from U.S. District Judge John F. Dillon to address the jurors and to read to them a document in the case of the *United States vs. Orville Babcock*. The document was the deposition of the president of the United States taken at the White House five days earlier—and Ulysses S. Grant was praising the character of Babcock, his private secretary and unofficial chief of staff. Never before or since has a president testified on behalf of a defendant in a criminal case.

Consider also the fact that Grant was, in effect, the country's law enforcement chief—the prosecutors were under the umbrella of the Justice Department, and the special prosecutor in the case was Grant's appointee. That put the president in the position of testifying against his own administration. But loyalty to Babcock, Grant's top aide during the closing years of the Civil War, won out.

Grant had wanted to travel to St. Louis to testify in person for Babcock, but Hamilton Fish, his secretary of state, had talked him out of it. So the unusual deposition took place in the White House, with Lucien Eaton, an assistant prosecutor, given the unenviable task of cross-examining his antagonistic boss. Babcock's lawyer had already drawn volumes of praise from the president about Babcock's loyalty, honesty, efficiency, and overall good character. Morrison Remick Waite, chief justice of the U.S. Supreme Court, was also present at the deposition. He signed off as Grant's official witness. Attorney General Edward Pierrepont was also in the room.

So, too, was Benjamin Bristow, the secretary of the treasury, whose investigation of a whiskey ring had led from distilleries in St. Louis to minor Treasury agents who took bribes and then up the ladder to regional politicians and officeholders until it came knocking at the White House door and included Babcock as one of the alleged ringleaders. Babcock was accused of participating in and covering up a criminal conspiracy that had been ongoing for five years and had cost the U.S. Treasury more than $4 million in unpaid liquor taxes.

In his Pulitzer Prize–winning biography *Grant*, author William S. McFeely wrote that the Treasury secretary "possessed that sticky double commodity, principle and ambition, and he was in an uncommon position of being able to rise to the first while advancing to the second." Bristow and the Treasury Department's solicitor, Bluford Wilson, had worked behind the scenes; had employed a secret investigator in St. Louis, newspaperman Myron Colony; and had stunned the country with raids in May 1875 on sixteen distilleries that resulted in more than 350 arrests. Those arrests yielded more than 200 indictments and eventually 100-plus convictions. More than half of the lost tax revenue was traced to the whiskey ring in St. Louis, but raids also took place in Chicago, Milwaukee, Indianapolis, Kansas City, and New Orleans.

Babcock was one of the five men U.S. Attorney David Dyer had targeted as the ringleaders of the St. Louis operations. Appointed by Grant as special prosecutor to assist Dyer had been General John Brooks Henderson, a former Missouri senator. But Henderson had made disparaging remarks about the president, and he was dismissed. Grant chose as his replacement St. Louis lawyer James O. Broadhead, who would one day become the first president of the American Bar Association. Dyer would eventually reach the federal bench and served as a judge in St. Louis for decades.

Dyer and Broadhead did what prosecutors often do: they cut deals, they granted minimal sentences to lesser lights, and they let distillers off easy in order to go after the five top guys. They were:

1. WILLIAM MCKEE

McKee was a businessman, newspaper publisher, and Grant's patronage boss in Missouri. He had owned the *St. Louis Democrat* with John Fishback, but they had a falling out over what Fishback considered McKee's lack of morals, and Fishback bought out McKee. McKee then bought the *St. Louis Globe*, pushed its circulation to outstrip the *Democrat*, and then bought out Fishback, forming the *Globe-Democrat*. It became the official Republican voice in St. Louis.

Getting a measure of revenge, Fishback wrote Bristow secretly in February 1875 about the corruption in St. Louis and suggested Bristow hire Colony, who was the commercial writer for the *Globe-Democrat*. Based on revenue receipts—or the lack thereof—Bristow was aware there was something amiss and took up Fishback on his offer. Colony set up surveillance at suspected distilleries; watched the amount of grain going in and the amount of liquor coming out; and then compared the results to tax receipts. A lot more liquor was going out than federal tax dollars were rolling in.

McKee went on trial in Judge Dillon's court in January 1876. Testimony disclosed that the ring spent $35,030 in buying off revenue agents and investigators to keep secret their payoffs from distillers. A jury deliberated eleven hours on January 31 and found the publisher guilty of criminal conspiracy.

McKee faced Dillon for sentencing on May 1. The *New York Times* noted that the whiskey ring had garnered national attention, but none of Bristow's allegations about the fraud had found its way into print in first the *Globe* and then the *Globe-Democrat*.

McKee's case was "a peculiar one. He was not an official, nor was he directly concerned in any way of the distillers," the *Times* reporter wrote. "He was a superserviceable friend of the Administration, which with him came the power that controlled the offices."

"The *Globe-Democrat* gave aid and comfort to the indicted enemies of the Government," said the *Times*, no friend of the Grant administration. "The political engineer, who conducted the extraordinary campaign, is sentenced to two years in the common jail."

2. JOHN MCDONALD

A Civil War general, McDonald got the appointment as internal revenue supervisor for Missouri and eight other states, with headquarters in St. Louis. McDonald had the support of McKee and Babcock for the position. McDonald also had the support of friends of the Dent family, wealthy St. Louisans. Grant had married Julia Dent on August 22, 1848. They had three sons and a daughter. Grant had built their cabin, "Hardscrabble," on land his father-in-law had given Julia, and he had farmed the land from 1854 to 1858 before moving to Galena, Illinois, to help run his brother's store. The Civil War had revived Grant's career as a military man and leader. He had been elected the eighteenth president of the United States in 1868 and was reelected to a second term in 1872. When he took office in 1869, at the age of forty-seven, Grant became the youngest person to ever serve as president.

McDonald's appointment was political. It was aimed at keeping Missouri in the Republican column in 1872. The former general was in the thick of the ring's activities. A jury convicted him in the fall of 1875, and he got a three-year prison sentence.

After his release from prison, McDonald released a book and gave a series of interviews to the fledgling *St. Louis Post-Dispatch* in which he complained that Babcock had escaped a prison sentence. He also alleged that Grant was in on the ring's operations and got payoffs, but no evidence of that has ever surfaced, and Grant's biographers consider the attack the result of McDonald's bitterness.

3. JOHN A. JOYCE

Joyce was the politically attuned collector of revenue in St. Louis, who didn't collect—except money for payoffs—the excise taxes due from favored distillers. He, too, was convicted. He served twenty-one months of a three-year sentence at the Missouri State Penitentiary in Jefferson City.

Joyce was interviewed by the *New York Times* in Chicago after he got out of prison and told the reporter he was moving to Colorado to devote his life to literature. He showed the bitterness he felt toward Babcock and other ring members, believing that he got a raw deal in the prosecution. "When I was taken up as a first-class goat, trotted into the synagogue, and loaded down with the sins of the whole jubilee, I think common sense as well as equal justice will say that I have been punished more than I deserve," said Joyce, who added he intended to earn henceforth an honest living and was leaving politics forever.

4. WILLIAM AVERY

Avery was chief clerk of the Internal Revenue Department of the U.S. Treasury. His role in the ring was to protect its members from investigations run from Washington, where he was based. The evidence against him consisted of the testimony of a bagman who said part of the payoffs were sent to Washington and Avery got a share. He was also accused of alerting McDonald and Joyce of movements of revenue officers and tipping them off about special agents to be sent to St. Louis by Bristow to look into the distilleries. Avery was convicted and got a three-year sentence. He was pardoned in 1877.

5. ORVILLE BABCOCK

Born in 1835 in Vermont, Babcock graduated from West Point in 1861 as the Civil War was getting under way. He served with distinction throughout the conflict and rose steadily in rank until he made brigadier general as the aide-de-camp to General Grant in the waning months of the conflict. Babcock delivered Grant's final surrender terms to Confederate General Robert E. Lee and escorted Lee to the meeting with Grant at Appomattox Courthouse in Virginia where the war, in effect, ended.

When Grant became president, he chose Babcock as his private secretary. In that capacity, Babcock often controlled who got to see Grant and who didn't. He had the president's total confidence. Babcock also married a woman from Grant's hometown of Galena.

As the whiskey ring investigation developed, it became clear to authorities that Babcock was the ring's top man in Washington, that he was running a coverup of the matter, and that investigators had found a series of telegrams involving McDonald, Joyce, Avery, and Babcock that pointed to Babcock's guilt.

Newspaper reporters from around the country packed the courtroom in St. Louis for Babcock's trial in February 1876. The consensus was that Dyer and Eaton, the prosecutors, appeared to be scoring points and the trial was going badly for Babcock until the deposition from Grant attesting to Babcock's good moral character. In *Lion of the Valley,* St. Louis historian James Neal Primm suggested that Grant's testimony put the jury in the almost impossible situation of either repudiating their president or finding Babcock not guilty.

The president, however, wasn't the only character witness for the defendant. The jury also heard witness testimony of five Civil War generals including William Tecumseh Sherman, who had decided to make St. Louis his home after the war. Sherman said Babcock always had a good reputation.

Babcock was acquitted. He returned to the White House, but cabinet members insisted that Grant fire him. Babcock resigned. He eventually got an appointment by the president as a lighthouse inspector.

Babcock drowned on June 2, 1884, when a boat capsized in Mosquito Inlet on the east coast of Florida, where Babcock, forty-nine, was planning to build a lighthouse. He is buried in Arlington National Cemetery.

THE *POST-DISPATCH* NEWSROOM SHOOTING
1882

> "He left home at 9 a.m. yesterday in good health and was brought home dead at 8 p.m."
> —*Alice Slayback in a written statement to a coroner's inquest jury in St. Louis on October 14, 1882*

Actually, Colonel Alonzo W. Slayback, former Confederate cavalry officer and, in the words of the *Globe-Democrat*, "a prominent attorney of St. Louis, as well known as any citizen within her limits," had been dead since 5:30 p.m. on October 13. He was killed in the newsroom of the *St. Louis Post-Dispatch*. Its managing editor, John A. Cockerill, shot him.

The fallout from the shooting was both short-term and long-lasting—not to mention the immediate effect it had on Slayback's widow and their six children.

With vitriolic attacks by the *St. Louis Republican*, which flatly declared before any sort of hearing that Slayback, forty-four, had been murdered, a drunken crowd descended on the newspaper and threatened to burn down the building at 515 Market Street. Before it was dispersed, the mob had also talked about lynching Cockerill and *Post-Dispatch* founder Joseph Pulitzer.

At a higher social level, the St. Louis Bar Association decried the *Post-Dispatch*'s sensationalism and what lawyers considered personal attacks on individuals in it columns.

Going one more step up the social ladder, St. Louis's high society, which had never accepted Pulitzer to its inner circle, had another reason to shun him. Even before the shooting, wrote Harry

Wilensky ninety-nine years later in the *Story of the Post-Dispatch*, "Many of the 'big people' in town remained hostile because of his continual exposure of misdeeds of the wealthy."

From a financial standpoint, the shooting was also a disaster for the newspaper. It lost thirteen hundred subscribers that year and another thousand the next year. Advertising went down, revenue went down, and Cockerill was forced to resign, replaced as managing editor by the more conservative John Dillon, a former partner of Pulitzer's in the newspaper and a member of the St. Louis aristocracy.

On May 10, 1883, after several weeks of negotiations with railroad czar Jay Gould, Pulitzer bought the nearly defunct *New York World*, leased an apartment, and began life anew as a full-fledged New Yorker.

There was little doubt that Slayback had been "big people" in St. Louis. He had been a founder of the Veiled Prophet organization, and his daughter, Susie, had been its first queen of love and beauty. He was a partner of James O. Broadhead, a founder and first president of the American Bar Association.

It was Slayback's connections to Broadhead that led to the confrontation in Cockerill's office in the *Post-Dispatch* newsroom. The *Post* opposed Broadhead in his bid for the congressional seat vacated by Thomas Allen and backed another Democrat, John Glover. In a series of editorials, the *Post* vilified Broadhead. He had once represented St. Louis in a franchise agreement with a gas company, then he switched sides and defended the gas company in court when the city sued and alleged the company had to pay exorbitant fees.

As his law partner and political supporter, Slayback took to the stump on behalf of Broadhead. In a speech at a meeting of the Eighteenth Ward Democrats, Slayback called the *Post-Dispatch* "a blackmailing sheet."

When Cockerill found out about Slayback's speech, he dug out a letter that Glover had written the *Post-Dispatch* the year before in which Glover wrote that Slayback "notwithstanding his military title, is a coward."

Pulitzer had refused to run the original letter, but Cockerill put it on page four and made reference to it in an editorial.

Slayback read the article in the afternoon paper, grabbed fellow lawyer John Clopton, charged the two blocks from his offices to the *Post*, climbed the stairs to the second floor, and barged into Cockerill's office. In a matter of seconds, Cockerill had fired a revolver, and Slayback was dead.

In interviews with the *Globe-Democrat* immediately after the shooting and at the coroner's inquest the next day, two versions of the shooting emerged.

The first to enter the office after the fatal shot was city editor Henry Moore. He said he heard a pistol shot as he approached the office, Clopton emerged and walked away rapidly, and Moore ran in. "Cockerill, on his knees, was holding Slayback in his arms," Moore told the *Globe*. "Blood was welling from the mouth of Slayback. [*Post* business manager John] McGuffin had an uncocked pistol in his hand, held loosely, almost dangling. [Composing room foreman Victor] Cole was bending anxiously over the heavy breathing burden in Cockerill's arms."

"My God, what is the matter?" Moore said he asked.

"He pulled a pistol on me and I shot him," Moore quoted Cockerill as replying. "And then with a blanched face, he looked upon the countenance of the man who was dying in his arms. In a few minutes, very few, the genial soul of Slayback had gone forth."

McGuffin gave the following account, also to a *Globe* reporter: "He was near the window to Cockerill's left, and Cole was on Cockerill's right when Slayback and Clopton walked in. As Slayback advanced toward Cockerill, he said, 'Well, sir, I am here.' Slayback drew a revolver. He saw Cockerill's revolver on the desk. He asked, 'Is that for me?'"

"It is not except to defend myself," Cockerill answered. They were face to face, guns drawn, no more than three feet apart. Clopton was moving forward. "Don't you do it, don't you do it, step away," Cockerill said.

"I made a lunge for the gun," McGuffin told the *Globe*. "As I caught hold of the weapon, the hammer fell on my hand. Cockerill said, 'Oh, Mac, don't let him do it.' Slayback was pressing the trigger, and I heard the report of a revolver. I felt him wilt and then fall over on Mr. Cockerill."

In few words, Cole supported the story, saying Slayback was armed and the aggressor.

In a written statement to the *Globe* and testimony at the coroner's inquest, Clopton said, "Mr. Slayback had no pistol or other weapon in his hand when he was killed." Slayback had gone to the editor's office with the intention of slapping Cockerill's face, in that a retraction would be insufficient, Clopton said.

Slayback was taking off his coat when Cockerill said, "Don't you draw that pistol on me." "Simultaneously, with that remark, Cockerill fired," Clopton said, adding that Slayback closed with Cockerill after he was shot.

"I caught hold of Cockerill at once, forcing his right arm against the window to prevent him from shooting again," Clopton said. Clopton said he held Slayback in his arms as Cockerill stepped past him and out the door. An excited man (presumably McGuffin) held a revolver over him, Clopton said.

In his testimony at the inquest, Cockerill gave the same basic version as McGuffin, saying, "Slayback was pointing his pistol at me, and I fired."

Cockerill said he told McGuffin, "Don't let these men kill me." Cockerill said McGuffin took Slayback's gun and pointed it at Clopton's head.

In conclusion, Cockerill told the jurors, "Of course, it is unnecessary for me to express the sorrow that I feel for the deplorable event. Every man who knows me can realize the poignancy of my regrets. I believed in the horror of the moment that my life was being taken and there was but one dread alternative."

Slayback had a gun, Cockerill, McGuffin, and Cole testified.

Clopton said his friend was unarmed. A person believing his life is in danger can use self-defense even if it turns out later that his belief was erroneous. The coroner's jury took just forty-five minutes to decide it was a clear case of self-defense. A grand jury failed to return a true bill after two weeks of hearings.

Cockerill also had nothing to worry about from Pulitzer. The publisher had been on vacation back East, returned immediately to St. Louis, and wrote a defense of his managing editor. Pulitzer said, "The charge of blackmail is the worst that can be preferred against any honest paper or editor."

Had Cockerill taken no action after Slayback's derogatory remarks about the *Post-Dispatch*, Pulitzer suggested, he would soon have lost his job. Cockerill did resign as managing editor when the public uproar persisted, but after taking over the *New York World* the following May, Pulitzer wasted little time in bringing Cockerill aboard with the same title he had in St. Louis.

McGuffin, the business manager and key witness who had testified on Cockerill's behalf, also moved to New York. Broadhead, the initial target of the *Post-Dispatch*'s political attacks, moved to Washington, where he filled the congressional seat that he won.

SOUTHERN HOTEL TRUNK MURDER
1885

On the day in 1888 when St. Louis hanged Walter H. Lennox Maxwell—a murderer the newspapers had dubbed "The Little Chloroformer"—a writer for the *St. Louis Post-Dispatch* waxed poetic and wrote, "Another will soon occupy his place in the city prison, and in a few years the public will have almost entirely forgotten that Maxwell ever lived. He and his crime will be numbered among the relics of the unrecalled past."

Wrong.

Charles Arthur Preller's death at the hands of Maxwell would actually be known to several generations of St. Louisans as the "Southern Hotel trunk murder" because relics of the crime, like a shrine, would be displayed by police in the Palace of Education at the St. Louis World's Fair of 1904, then in the Jefferson Memorial in Forest Park for several decades after it opened in 1913.

Visitors to the history museum could read about the murder and see the trunk into which Maxwell had stuffed Preller; they could read the cable police sent to catch the fleeing killer; and they could see the handcuffs used on Maxwell and the miniature noose sent to him while he awaited execution. The display came down from its second-floor location in the early to mid-1990s, according to curator Sharon Smith, and the museum has most of the artifacts in storage.

Victorian inhibitions kept any direct reference out of the newspapers of the day that Maxwell and Preller were probably lovers. The closest writers came to outing the English couple were occasional innuendos, descriptions of their relationship as companions who had lived together, or descriptions of their personalities. In a reference to his flamboyant dress, a prosecutor, for example, went so far as to call Preller "a perfect gentleman though with peculiarities of action and appearance that caused him to be noticed."

The companions had met in Liverpool in January 1885 while waiting to sail to America aboard the steamship *Cephalonia*. Preller was thirty-two and an international clothing and tapestry salesman for a prestigious London company; Maxwell said he was thirty. He was a doctor on his way to start a practice in Massachusetts. A fellow traveler aboard the steamship said the relationship developed around the piano bar on the Atlantic crossing. According to the traveling companion, who later visited the pair in Boston, Maxwell's extravagant conversations—he insisted, for example, that he was of noble birth, and he claimed he was an Oxford man—got Preller's attention.

However, Maxwell complained he couldn't find work and that Boston was overstocked with doctors. Maxwell said he was considering a small town, and Preller recommended Auckland, New Zealand. The two decided to meet in St. Louis after Preller completed a business trip to Canada. Maxwell later claimed that Preller was going to finance Maxwell's trip to New Zealand along with his own.

Maxwell got to St. Louis first, arriving on March 31, 1885. He took Room 144 at the Southern Hotel for a week. The second-floor room of the posh hotel faced Fourth Street. Preller arrived on April 3 and took Room 385 on the fourth floor but spent most of his time in 144. The pair dined together on the night of April 4 in the hotel restaurant, but Maxwell dined alone the next night and showed the head waiter a big roll of paper money. He was often in a bragging mood when he dined, and he had told the waiter in the past that he had been a surgeon in Manchester, England, and had served in the Turkish medical service.

The next day, April 6, Maxwell bought new trunks in downtown St. Louis and a German flute for eight dollars at a pawnshop after flashing a one hundred–dollar bill. The previous week, Maxwell had pawned items for cash in the same shop. Maxwell left St.

Louis that day by train for San Francisco using the name of Hugh Brooks.

On April 12, hotel management got complaints about a smell emanating from Room 144 but found nothing amiss inside the room. Two days later, the odor became unbearable, and employees hauled three trunks out of the room. The one from which the smell originated was taken outside and opened. Inside was the decaying body of Preller, clad only in white knit shorts. A cross was carved into his chest above his heart. A note on the side of the trunk said, "So perish all traitors to the great cause."

Dr. James C. Nidolet, the city coroner, performed the postmortem and established the date of death about a week earlier. He decided that poison was the cause. The victim's stomach was taken to Washington University, where Dr. Charles Luedeking, a chemistry professor, examined it and later told a coroner's jury that an overdose of chloroform had proven fatal. Among Maxwell's personal effects that he left behind, police found a half-full vial of chloroform and a diploma from the Royal College of Surgeons in England.

Maxwell arrived in San Francisco and stayed at the Palace Hotel posing as a French general with poor English by the name of T. C. D'Auguier. He argued with a prostitute and said, "I have just killed a man, and I will kill you." A step ahead of police, he caught the steamship *City of Sydney* for New Zealand with stops in Hawaii and Samoa.

In their search for Maxwell after a cable from St. Louis, San Francisco police found that Maxwell had swapped watches at a pawn shop, and the one he gave up said "H. M. Brooks" on it. The investigation soon led police to the conclusion that Maxwell was really an English bloke named Hugh Mottram Brooks, whose medical background was nil. His surgical diploma was a forgery. And he was six years younger than the thirty he pretended to be—a very young doctor indeed.

Having missed Maxwell in San Francisco and aware that he had sailed on the *City of Sydney*, St. Louis Police Chief Laurence Harrigan cabled the U.S. consul in New Zealand. The telegram read, "Arrest Walter E. Lennox-Maxwell, alias T. C. D'Auguier, who left San Francisco on Steamer *City of Sydney* April 12th for Auckland. He is wanted for the horrible murder of Charles A. Preller, a British subject, on the 5th instant. Age 30, 5 feet, 5 or 6 inches high, 140 pounds, light hair worn short, light mustache and imperial, fair complexion, large blue eyes, nose full at the nostrils, had a large gray covered trunk and grip sack marked A. S. Aloe, St. Louis. Smoked cigarettes constantly. Is an Englishman but assumes to be a French or Turkish military officer. His profession is doctor. Will you arrest and hold him for extradition. Answer."

When the ship arrived, Maxwell was arrested onboard without a struggle and taken into custody, but New Zealand officials expressed concern about Maxwell's rights and how long they could hold him. Their worries prompted another cable from Harrigan to the U.S. consul: "Hold Maxwell by all means; evidence conclusive; State Department cables you today. I will send officer for him as soon as possible."

After brief disputes involving the governor's office over who would foot the bill, how many men to send for Maxwell's return, and who should pick him up, St. Louis detective James Tracy and special officer George W. Badger left St. Louis on May 30 and caught the steamship *Zealandia*, arriving in Auckland on June 30. At the end of the return trip with a handcuffed Maxwell, the officers got back to St. Louis on August 16 and faced a crowd of more than two thousand who wanted to see "the little chloroformer."

Maxwell's trial began on May 10 of the following year, with three hundred prospective jurors from which to choose. Most were stricken for two reasons: by the defense because they had already made up their mind about the case or by the prosecution because they said they would not convict based on circumstantial evidence.

The *Globe-Democrat* reported about every juror who was questioned. For example, Gustavus Edward Fluhr, senior partner in a downtown firm bearing his name (but not listing what the firm did), said he had formed his opinion of the case when it was first publicized. John Overton, a book-news dealer at the Southern Hotel, said he was acquainted with all of the state's witnesses and had seen the defendant at the hotel. John Bassett, a carpenter living downtown, said he was not in favor of hanging people for murder "except when guilty" and opposed the use of circumstantial evidence to convict. All three were excused.

The *Globe* printed the names and artist portraits of all twelve men—women did not serve on juries in the nineteenth century—before the opening statements. Among the jurors: a book publisher, a fire insurance agent, and a builder.

Meanwhile, Maxwell was busy giving interviews. Before the opening statements, he had given an interview to John J. Jennings of the *Post-Dispatch*. The *Globe* was forced to report snatches of Jennings's story when Assistant Circuit Attorney C. Orrick Bishop quoted from it in his opening remarks to the jury.

Before the trial, during it, and even two years later, Maxwell stuck to the same story. Preller was stricken with an illness, presumably a venereal disease, though the purported affliction was never disclosed by the media. The defendant claimed Preller had a stricture that Maxwell agreed to unblock using his medical knowledge. First he had prescribed medicine that he mixed from the vials he carried with him. The drugs didn't work, and Preller agreed to let Maxwell insert a catheter, Maxwell told Jennings in the interview. Maxwell claimed he had used the device and chloroform for anesthesia successfully on a man named Harrison in Liverpool.

At about 5 p.m. on April 5, Easter Sunday, Maxwell said he had held a saturated cloth to the victim's nose. "I discovered too late that he was dying. Imagine my horror when the fact dawned on me. I had the presence of mind to cut the shirt and undershirt from the body and getting a wet towel to beat him around the neck and shoulders for an hour or more."

Maxwell continued, "What did I do when I saw my friend

dead? I didn't know what to do, except drink, and I drank freely. I drank everything I could get: wine, whiskey, everything. What were my thoughts? I hadn't any."

Maxwell said he put a pair of drawers on the victim and put Preller in the trunk about an hour after he died. He said he had no other recollection. Jennings asked Maxwell about Preller's money. "I know nothing of Preller's money. I had plenty of money of my own, or I couldn't have made the long trip which I did make."

Maxwell's statements to Jennings gave Circuit Attorney Ashley Clover the ammunition he needed to obtain a search warrant for the exhumation of Preller's body at Bellefontaine Cemetery. Dr. T. F. Prewitt, dean of the Missouri Medical Society, Dr. Nidolet, the coroner, and Dr. T. V. Brokaw examined the remains.

In his opening statement, Bishop, the trial prosecutor, argued that Maxwell deliberately killed Preller for money, and he cited all of the purchases Maxwell made on April 6, the day he caught the train for the West Coast.

Prosecutors put on scores of witnesses for seven days, including the three doctors who had examined the victim's body when the trial began. The trio said they found no evidence of any disease, any damaged organs, or any strictures.

Then came witness Frank Delfinger, only his real name was John P. McCullough, a railroad detective who had pretended for forty-seven days to be a jail inmate and had befriended Maxwell. Clover, the circuit attorney, was paying McCullough out of his own pocket. Despite often contemptuous cross-examination for his role-playing by Defense Attorney P. W. Fauntleroy, McCullough stuck to a story that Maxwell had confided in him and told him he killed Preller for money and as payback because Preller was reneging on financing Maxwell's travels to New Zealand.

The prosecution rested on May 25, and Maxwell took the stand, admitting he wasn't a doctor, admitting he had never been to Oxford, admitting he had forged documents in the past, and following the same storyline he had told previously—Preller's death was an accident, and everything after that was the result of panic. Cross-examined by Clover, however, Maxwell could explain neither the note he wrote in the trunk about traitors nor the cross he had carved on the corpse nor the reason he had shaved Preller's mustache. Maxwell claimed he was drunk, and he couldn't remember.

For the finale, onlookers gathered for hours and stormed the courthouse on June 1. "The crowd defied deputy sheriffs and police and poured into the courtroom, despite the announcement the building was unsafe," the *Globe* reported. "Once they were in, there was no getting out, and the deputies got even during the proceedings by taking various measures against anyone caught whispering."

Judge G. S. Van Wagoner virtually sealed Maxwell's fate in the jury instructions. The twelve were told they had to declare Maxwell guilty of murder if they found that he chloroformed and strangled Preller, he chloroformed and suffocated Preller by putting him in a trunk, or he killed Preller in the perpetration of a robbery by means unknown.

To acquit the defendant, the judge said, the jury would have to find that Maxwell was treating Preller for some disease, that he had administered chloroform "in a careful and prudent manner," and that the defendant had died despite Maxwell's best efforts.

In his closing arguments, Bishop cited the forged medical diploma, the horror caused by the discovery of the murder, and the chase around the world. On the Easter Sunday that Preller died, Maxwell could have summoned immediate help if his story was true because Room 144 of the Southern Hotel was equipped with the latest fashion, an electric bell. To Maxwell's claims that he was continuously drunk after Preller's death, Bishop noted Maxwell's ability to buy trunks and tickets and check his baggage for the train trip.

Fauntleroy argued accidental death, that it was the result of Maxwell's "foolish, vain, naked boyish nature. . . . He came to St. Louis filled with vanity but with no design to harm anyone."

The *Globe* reported that as the courtroom cleared with the jury on its way to deliberate on the afternoon of June 4, several hundred dollars changed hands in betting on the outcome. One man offered ten dollars to five dollars that Maxwell would be cleared. The bet was taken immediately.

The jury returned its verdict at 12:15 p.m. on June 5, 1886. Maxwell was guilty and should die for the murder. The appeals began. Finally, in January 1888, the U.S. Supreme Court refused to hear the case, and the Missouri Supreme Court set the execution for July 13. Governor Albert Morehouse granted the defense a stay until August 10.

On August 2, U.S. Secretary of State Thomas Bayard cabled Morehouse that the British government had asked for a delay for further investigation. One of the allegations by Maxwell's lawyers was juror prejudice. They alleged one of the jurors had been heard to say Maxwell "ought to hang without a judge or jury."

A week later, Morehouse said he had reviewed the matter, saw no likelihood that new evidence would be forthcoming, and decreed that the execution would go forward as scheduled at 6:30 a.m. the next day in the jail yard of the Four Courts Building. The *Post* reported that no one told Maxwell. "There was a fear he would commit suicide if he knew his doom was sealed and thus cheat the hungry gallows which had waited so long and impatiently for its prey."

A crowd of two hundred gathered for the hanging, but only fifteen witnesses, a coroner's jury, and court officials were allowed to attend. Sheriff Joseph Harrington read the death warrant at 8:45 a.m., and the trapdoor dropped at 8:56 a.m.

"The fight which Maxwell has waged for over three years against the laws of the land has ended," the *Globe* concluded. "Charles Arthur Preller has been avenged; and Hugh Mottram Brooks, alias Walter H. Lennox-Maxwell, whose name has constantly been on every lip, is no more. He died this morning, and the old scaffold in the jail yard was his deathbed."

MARION THE OUTLAW
1891

Wyoming had Butch Cassidy, the Sundance Kid, and the Wild Bunch; Kansas City and St. Joseph had Jesse and Frank James, as well as Cole Younger and his brothers; the Dalton gang hit trains in Oklahoma territory; and the Doolin gang roamed in Kansas. The best St. Louis could do in the pantheon of outlaws of the West in the second half of the nineteenth century—a good thing perhaps—was a man named Marion, and he actually lived here only a few weeks. Women swooned over tall, lanky, horse-faced, jug-eared Marion Hedgepeth, whom Richard Patterson declared in his book *Train Robbery* was more of a media creation than a successful long rider, while top detective Robert Pinkerton had called Hedgepeth "one of the really bad men of the West." So popular was Hedgepeth with the women of St. Louis that they filled his jail cell with bouquets of flowers and later formed committees to petition the governor for his release from prison.

Born in Prairie Home in western Missouri, Hedgepeth was a runaway at fifteen, a cowboy out West, and an outlaw by twenty. He purportedly killed a man both in Colorado and Wyoming and taught himself the quick draw. He was so fast, legend has it, that he could outdraw and kill a man whose pistol had already left the holster. Hedgepeth dressed in black and wore a large wing collar and a cravat with a diamond stickpin in it.

Hedgepeth had been a robber and a safecracker in Kansas City. He was finally convicted of larceny and escaping from the Cooper County jail. For those offensives, he was sentenced in November 1883 to five years and three months in prison. Upon his release, Hedgepeth began forming his gang. It consisted of his brother-in-law, Adelbert "Bertie" Slye; James "Illinois Jimmie" Francis, a St. Louis burglar; and Charles "Dink" Wilson of Omaha.

A series of daring robberies throughout the Midwest—the office of a Kansas City streetcar company, a car barn headquarters in Omaha, a Missouri Pacific train in Nebraska near Omaha, and a Chicago, Milwaukee, and St. Paul train at Western Union Junction in Wisconsin—brought the gang plenty of Midwestern notoriety, if not national attention. The robberies, the newspapers said, were reminiscent of some of the heists the James gang had pulled off a decade earlier.

At about 9:45 p.m. on November 30, 1891, the gang held up the St. Louis and San Francisco Night Express at Glendale after it had made a stop in Old Orchard, in today's Webster Groves. Hedgepeth, tall and thin, and Slye, short and heavyset, climbed down from the cab into the locomotive and ordered the engineer and fireman to stop the train on a bridge. The robbers argued with the engineer and fireman about the amount of coal needed to get to the bridge. They relented, and fireman H. S. Daly shoveled more coal into the boiler furnace, and the train made it to the bridge before it was stopped by the engineer on the span. The outlaws then blew up the door to the express car and ordered a guard to open the safe. When he refused, they blew it up.

In the passenger car and smoker, robbers fired as many as twelve to twenty shots. This got the attention of the riders, who huddled between seats as they were methodically robbed of their money and jewelry. One passenger went out on the platform of the smoker and found a pistol against his head with orders to return.

Conductor James Douthitt and passenger John Chandler estimated the time of the entire robbery from the train stopping to the disappearance of the bandits as fifteen minutes. A guard from whom they had stolen a gold watch said the outlaws "took to the bluffs in the neighborhood of the Glendale station."

The quartet made its way to St. Louis. The estimated haul from the Glendale holdup was as much as fifty thousand dollars. All four moved temporarily into a rented house along with Hedgepeth's wife, Maggie, in the 4200 block of Swan Avenue.

Slye, Maggie's brother, was caught in Los Angeles just fifteen days after the robbery. He had purchased a saloon with his share of the holdup. For his role in the robbery, Slye got a twenty-year sentence. Francis didn't live long. He orchestrated a train robbery in Lamar, Missouri, and died in a gun battle with a posse in neighboring Kansas. Before his demise, Francis bought a farm in Kansas with the proceeds of the Glendale heist. Wilson died in the electric chair in New York for the murder of a police officer.

At the house in St. Louis, Marion and Maggie buried guns and other items in the dirt floor of a shed behind the residence. The couple left for San Francisco. A little neighborhood girl playing in the shed found the guns and told her parents, and they called the police. The house had been rented in the Hedgepeth name, and police learned the Hedgepeths had made arrangements to ship a trunk to Oakland. When Maggie showed up to get the trunk at a Wells Fargo office, police were waiting, but she would not reveal her husband's location.

On February 10, 1892, police arrested Hedgepeth in San Francisco. He became an instant celebrity upon his return to St. Louis, and the bouquets from women began to flow into and overcrowd his jail cell. Because of the publicity, the trial was held in St. Charles. The outpouring of support for the popular bandit was of little help. He was convicted on November 28, 1893, and received a twenty-five–year prison sentence.

While he had been in jail awaiting trial, Hedgepeth roomed with a man calling himself H. H. Holmes, who had been incarcerated in an insurance scam. Holmes agreed to pay Hedgepeth five hundred dollars for a good lawyer to get him a light sentence. Hedgepeth found him a lawyer, and Holmes got a good deal. However, Holmes never paid the bandit the five hundred dollars he owed him. From prison, Hedgepeth got even. He wrote insurance officials in Pennsylvania with particulars about Holmes's scam, which led to a multi-state investigation. Holmes was actually Herman Webster Mudgett. When the police focused on the castle Mudgett had built in suburban Chicago, they found a house of horrors and evidence that Mudgett was a serial killer who may have been responsible for the deaths of two hundred women.

Hedgepeth was paroled by Governor Joseph Folk in July 1906 after serving about half of his sentence. The parole was reward for Hedgepeth's revealing an escape plot to prison authorities. A year later, Hedgepeth was back in prison for a burglary in Iowa, a conviction that was set aside in 1909.

On December 30, 1909, Hedgepeth died in a gun battle with police in a Chicago saloon he was trying to rob. Six weeks earlier, Hedgepeth had been in St. Louis and had told the city's chief of detectives that he was going straight. He wrote letters to the detective from St. Paul, Milwaukee, and Louisville saying the same thing.

A CLAYTON COURTHOUSE CONFRONTATION
──────── 1892 ────────

Emil J. Dosenbach and Major Winfield Scott Smith had a lot in common during the Gilded Age. Families of both had been early settlers of St. Louis County, they were prominent in the social circles of the county and Clayton, and both men were public officials: Dosenbach the county sheriff, Smith the county assessor. Dosenbach and Smith were also Republicans in a county that was as heavily Republican as the city of St. Louis was Democrat. Both men took their politics seriously—too seriously, as a matter of life and death, it turned out.

On the night of July 12, 1892, Chapter Seventy-seven of the Sons of Veterans—that's Civil War veterans—met at the Saegerbund Hall in Clayton, and Emil Dosenbach, the sheriff's son, tried to steer the group to endorse Dr. Richard Barthold as the GOP candidate for congress. A faction led by Smith backed a different candidate for the eleventh congressional seat and blocked Dosenbach's attempt to get an endorsement from the club.

The next morning, the argument between the two groups spilled over into the court of Probate Judge A. J. Shores. Smith was seated when the senior Dosenbach walked into the courtroom. Smith yelled at the sheriff about his son's attempt to grab the nomination for Barthold the night before. Dosenbach replied, "You are a damned liar." Smith was out of his seat, charging Dosenbach and grabbing him by the neck. In the struggle, Smith was thrown to the floor and tried to crawl behind a desk as Dosenbach drew his pistol. Witnesses said three shots were fired. One struck Smith over his right eye; a second pierced his heart.

So who's in charge when the sheriff has been charged? Prosecuting Attorney R. Lee Mudd accused Dosenbach of first-degree murder. The prosecutor put the county coroner, Dr. M. W. Caster, in control of the county jail. Because Smith's friends were angry over his death and fearing possible reprisals, Caster moved Dosenbach to the jail in the city.

The case was moved out of Clayton ten months later because of pretrial publicity, although the matter had largely faded from the newspapers of the day. Dosenbach went on trial in May 1893 in St. Charles on a reduced charge of second-degree murder. Dosenbach claimed self-defense; the prosecution said Smith's death was murder. The jury found Dosenbach had acted recklessly and convicted him of fourth-degree manslaughter, assessing his punishment at six months in jail and a fine of five hundred dollars. Dosenbach thought the punishment too severe; he asked for a new trial and later appealed unsuccessfully. Smith's widow, Apolonia, filed a wrongful death suit six months later and won the maximum then allowed by law: five thousand dollars.

After the verdict in the criminal case, the *Globe-Democrat*, the Republican newspaper, gave the story one paragraph at the bottom of an inside page of its May 6 edition. The *Post-Dispatch*, generally the Democrat paper, gave it three paragraphs on page three of its May 5 edition. In summarizing the shooting, the *Post* said, "They quarreled. Epithets were exchanged. Smith rose from his chair and moved toward Dosenbach. The latter used his pistol with fatal affect."

Ninety-nine years to the day of that verdict—May 5, 1992—aerospace technician Kenneth Baumruk fatally shot his wife, wounded four others, and terrorized hundreds at the courthouse in Clayton, less than a hundred yards from the site of Smith's death. One of Baumruk's trials, like Dosenbach's, took place in St. Charles. The outcome was a wee bit different: Baumruk got the death penalty.

Dosenbach later went into the land title business and was elected president of the Clayton School Board. Smith's son, W.

Scott Smith, became city clerk of Clayton, a position he held for several years.

In his history of Clayton, author Dickson Terry summed up the sheriff-assessor shooting: "Politics was never taken lightly in St. Louis County."

BALLAD OF FRANKIE AND JOHNNY
1899

> Frankie and Johnny were lovers.
> Oh, Lawdy, how they could love.
> They swore to be true to each other,
> Just as true as the stars above.
> He was her man, but he done her wrong.

"If America has a classical gutter song," wrote Carl Sandburg, historian, poet, and folk-song collector, "it is the one that tells of Frankie and her man." Sandburg thought the melody and perhaps some of the trashy lyrics could be traced back to the Civil War days of the 1860s. Some musicologists say the ballad originated in Memphis in the 1840s; others place it in New Orleans ten years later.

"No song in all of musical Americana has been subject to so much conjecture or has appeared in so many guises and disguises, with so many variations in form and so many aliases in name," says Jack Burton in his *Tin Pan Alley Blue Book*. Burton and a majority of musicologists lean toward St. Louis as the origin of the song: specifically a flat on Targee Street—where Scottrade Center stands today—and a fatal shooting in 1899.

> Frankie went down to the corner,
> Stopped to buy some beer.
> She said to the fat bartender,
> "Has my Johnny man been here?"
> He was her man, but he done her wrong.
> "Ain't goin' to tell no story.
> Ain't goin' to tell no lie.
> But your Johnny went by about an hour ago
> With a girl named Nellie Blye."

In various versions of the song, Johnny is spelled Johnnie, or Johnny is Albert or Allen; Frankie is also Billie or Josie or Rosie or Sadie, and the other woman has been called Nelly Blye or Alice Bley or Nellie Fly and even Alkali.

Over the years, different versions of the legend put the shooting in different locations—tavern, hotel, bordello. Artist Thomas Hart Benton chose a bar for the shooting in his famous murals in the House Lounge on the second floor of the Missouri State Capitol in Jefferson City. In a panel all to themselves, Frankie is shooting Johnny in the back. The bartender and Nellie Blye are astonished. Johnny is toppling over a table, a chair, and Nellie's beer as he falls to the floor.

Another version has Frankie spotting Johnny with Nellie through a transom of a hotel on Clark Street. In that version:

> Johnny saw Frankie a comin'.
> Out the back door he did scoot.
> But Frankie aimed the pistol,
> And the gun went root-toot-toot.

In still another version, Johnny has no chance to run because:

> Frankie threw back her kimono.
> She took out the little .44.
> Root-toot-toot, three times she shot
> Right through the hardwood door.

Then there is the Western version, which sounds more like Dodge City than St. Louis, Memphis, or New Orleans:

> Johnny he grabbed off his Stetson.
> "Oh, Good Lawd, Frankie, don't shoot."
> But Frankie she fingered the trigger.
> And the gun went root-toot-toot.

The song went through several transmutations and adaptations. Irving Berlin used it in a musical in the 1920s, and Mae West sang it in *She Done Him Wrong*, a 1933 movie. Sammy Davis, Jr., sang it in *Meet Me in Las Vegas* in 1956, Sam Cooke had a hit with the number in 1963, and Elvis Presley, the King himself, played Johnny in 1966. The most controversial adaptation was a movie in 1938 starring singer Helen Morgan as Frankie and actor Chester Morris as Johnny. It was a box-office dud in a year that moviegoers were treated to such hits as *Boys Town* with Spencer Tracy and Frank Capra's *You Can't Take It With You*.

Frankie Baker, of Portland, Oregon, came forward in a suit that year, alleging libel and privacy violations and seeking two hundred thousand dollars from Republic Pictures. She had also sued Mae West and the 1933 movie production, but that case was thrown out of court.

Baker claimed to be the Frankie of the song, and Johnny was actually Allen Britt, her teenage lover, whom she shot in 1899 after catching him with another woman. She said she met Allen when she was twenty-one and Allen was fifteen. Both lived on Targee Street. She was a prostitute; he played piano. Baker complained about an affair between Britt and a woman named Alice Pryor. When the case got to trial in 1942 in St. Louis Circuit Court, she testified that Britt, on one occasion, had beaten her badly after she confronted him about Pryor. Baker testified she provided Britt with fancy clothes from her earnings on the street. Baker said Britt came to her room in October 1899. He was drunk. She told him to leave. He refused. He threw a lamp at her and then pulled out a knife. She grabbed a .32-caliber revolver. "I shot him, intending to scare him, and the bullet hit him," she told a coroner's jury in 1899 and a jury in her civil case forty-three years later.

The brief reports that appeared in the newspapers in 1899 in what seemed to be a humdrum shooting say the coroner's jury found Baker had acted in self-defense. The *Post-Dispatch* had reported that Allen Britt was fatally wounded on October 15, 1899, by a woman at a rooming house at 212 Targee Street. The *Globe-Democrat* said the woman had accused Britt of paying attention to a rival.

Britt's age was listed at seventeen. Subsequent articles identified the killer as Frankie Baker. At her trial nearly a half-century later, an old friend, Richard Clay, recalled that he and Britt had double-dated, taking their dates to such night spots as the Bachelor's Club and the Lonestar.

According to Nathan Young, an attorney, a judge, and an authority on African American folklore, after Britt's death and Baker's release from custody on the self-defense argument, a local musician, Bill Dooley, put words of the ballad to paper and sold the lyrics throughout downtown. Britt became Johnny, a street slang for a man. Young was a witness for Baker.

Sigmund Spaeth, a nationally known expert on music, wrote in 1926 that the ballad originated in St. Louis, but he testified at the trial in 1942 and put the date before the Civil War, saying he had changed his mind. A Duke University professor sided with Frankie Baker, but a Washington University expert contended that the Frankie of the song was obsessive and a stalker, while Frankie Baker shot a drunken, violent lover in self-defense. Baker had been cleared. The ballad's Frankie had been hanged.

The real-life Frankie Baker lost her case. The jury found in favor of the movie studio.

> Bring out your long black coffin.
> Bring out your funeral clothes.
> My Johnny's gone and cashed his bad checks.
> To the graveyard Johnny goes.
> He was her man, but he done her wrong

THE BOODLERS
1901-02

In November 1902, two groups of people rode the Wabash Railroad from St. Louis to Columbia. One side was loud and boisterous, treating the one-hundred–mile trip to Boone County as a lark, a week's vacation in the countryside. The other group was serious, self-contained, almost morose.

It was showdown time in Missouri politics: Colonel Ed Butler, the boss of bosses, versus Joe Folk, the upstart circuit attorney. All bets were on Butler. His railroad coach was party time. He was joined by his wife and sons, Edward and James, and the usual gaggle of hangers-on. James Butler had just been elected to congress from St. Louis. Dad had delivered the vote once again. The Butlers thought they had little to fear from Folk, a former corporation lawyer. After all, the trial was going to be in a rural county, and what did country farmers care about big-city corruption?

Besides, Boone County was a Democrat Party stronghold, and Butler was Mr. Democrat in Missouri. A week earlier, for example, the Democrats had once again won control of the legislature. Half in admiration and half in consternation, the *Globe-Democrat* alluded to the fact that Butler controlled thirty-eight votes in the legislature-elect. If "the Old Man at the head of the Democracy of Missouri" wanted to be a U.S. senator, all he had to do was say so, ran the sarcastic editorial.

Butler's barrage of attorneys and ex-judges had gotten the trial moved to Columbia in the nick of time. Just a month earlier, the corruption of Butler and the Boodlers, as they were nicknamed—and Folk's underdog efforts to stop it—had gone national. Sentiment in St. Louis was turning toward the dour lawyer and away from the flamboyant, self-proclaimed colonel. A World's Fair was coming to St. Louis in just two years, and how would the city's lurid underbelly look to thousands of visitors?

Lincoln Steffens, one of the leading muckrakers of the early twentieth century, had just published an exposé in *McClure's Magazine*. The title to the article minced no words: "Tweed Days in St. Louis." Butler, of course, was Tweed, the corrupt boss of New York's Tammany Hall in the late nineteenth century. And Steffens was hard at work on an encore: "The Shamelessness of St. Louis," an article that would run in March of 1903 in *McClure's* and would propel Folk into the national limelight.

With jury selection on November 10, Butler had even more reason to be optimistic. Thirty-three of the forty potential jurors were farmers. Eleven of the twelve chosen to serve were farmers, or as the *Post-Dispatch* reported, "agriculturists." That was good for Butler, his advisers said. Farmers would be uninterested in city corruption. Farmers would be hard put to follow all the Machiavellian political maneuvers or to understand the motives behind them.

The *Post* concentrated on Butler's attire: a light gray suit and vest, but the trousers were too loose at the ankles to qualify the colonel as a faultless fashion plate. Butler wore a broad-brimmed black hat that hid his face. Missing, however, was the twelve hundred–dollar diamond stickpin Butler usually wore. Don't patronize the locals, the *Post* suggested.

In its overnight story, the *Globe* analyzed the jury pool and found that thirty-nine of forty potential jurors were Democrats. The lone Republican was disqualified after he told the judge that he had already formed an opinion about the case.

Of the twelve chosen for duty, four were actually members of the Democrat Party Central Committee in Boone County, an ominous sign for Folk. When jury picking ended the first day's work, everyone left the courtroom except the twelve men who would decide Butler's fate. They had to spend the night on cots guarded by sheriff's deputies.

Who were these two men who had forced jurors to be locked in a courtroom and had brought the attention of a country to a small town in mid-Missouri?

EDWARD BUTLER

Born in Ireland in 1838 or 1839—he was never sure—Butler migrated to the United States and ended up in St. Louis in 1857 as a blacksmith when the city had a population of about 160,000. By the time of his trial forty-five years later, St. Louis had 600,000 people and was the nation's fourth largest city.

On the Fourth of July in 1859, businessman Erastus Wells unveiled his new enterprise and gave anyone who wanted one a free ride in it. The horsecar had come to St. Louis, the city's first commuter line. The business was an overnight success and eventually grew to 119 miles of horsecar tracks, on which 2,280 horses pulled 496 cars.

All of those horses needed shoes, special shoes. Butler provided them. With a strong-armed band of smithies and farriers, Butler made sure he held the monopoly. Butler was on his way to becoming a very wealthy man.

As the Democrat Party began to return to power in post–Civil War St. Louis, Butler turned his horseshoe gang into ballot stuffers and strong-arm intimidators at the polls. He became the boss of Kerry Patch, an Irish enclave near downtown. By 1870, he had moved on to boss the city's Democratic machine. Seven years later, Butler delivered the mayoral election to Henry Overstolz. Massive fraud was alleged. One of the accusations had Butler literally eating the ballots of opponents.

In 1883, Butler showed his political might with the police department, forcing the removal by the police board of Chief John W. Campbell. A grand jury indicted Butler, crony Joe McEntire, and two police commissioners, alleging a criminal conspiracy. The indictment was Butler's ninth in seven years. This time, he was accused of threatening Campbell. The defendants went on trial on October 27, 1883. It was short-lived. A judge ordered the jury to return a verdict in favor of the quartet.

In 1885, Butler's boys got David R. Francis elected as mayor by 1,526 votes. Francis went on to careers as Missouri governor, president of the 1904 World's Fair, and ambassador to Russia. Butler had become a kingmaker, a man to be reckoned with. His tactics weren't subtle.

John K. Murrell was the Republican candidate from the Nineteenth Ward in that 1885 mayoral election. He watched Butler's men vote and vote and vote again. One man, Murrell counted, had gone through the polls seven times. Murrell complained to a police sergeant, who promptly threw Murrell out of the polling place. Murrell watched strong-arm squads that day beat other complainers at other polls. What he couldn't beat, he later joined. Murrell became a member of "The Big Cinch" or "The Combine"—Butler had nineteen members of the Municipal Assembly. They controlled everything that had to do with City Hall. To do business in St. Louis, to get a contract from the city, the steps were twofold: see Colonel Butler and ante up to the Combine. By 1899, even the city itself was for sale.

The Boodlers tried to sell the waterworks for $1 million but discovered to their dismay that the city charter prevented it. They tried to sell Union Market and backed down only after a twenty thousand–dollar bribe was paid to Butler to stop it. They even tried to sell the courthouse, with each Boodler promised one hundred thousand dollars while the city got to use two floors of its own building. But the title to the courthouse required that the building had to be used for city purposes only, and the Boodlers couldn't find a way around that.

The new City Hall was unfinished. The Boodlers had diverted to private use money donated to finish its interior walls. In the election of 1900, Butler backed for Mayor Rolla Wells, the wealthy grandson of the horsecar executive and a man Butler considered a political dilettante. For circuit attorney on the Wells ticket, Butler found it politically expedient to support Joseph Folk, a young political unknown, who had been campaigning quietly against political corruption.

JOSEPH WINGATE FOLK

Born the seventh of ten children in Tennessee, Folk graduated from Vanderbilt University in 1888. He had joined his uncle's law firm in St. Louis in 1893 and had advanced quickly to become a top corporation lawyer. Like his friend Rolla Wells, Folk had dabbled in politics through a Democrat political club. At the age of thirty, he ran for circuit attorney on a reform platform. With backing from Butler, Folk won.

Folk had a slight physique and eschewed the demagogic speeches then in favor by most politicians. He was described as cool, reserved, and dignified. Some perceived him as an opportunist. Steffens, who became a confidante of Folk, described him as "a thin-lipped, firm-mouthed dark little man who never raises his voice . . . he goes ahead doing, with a smiling eye and set jaw, the simple thing he said he would do."

When he ran for election, Folk promised voters he would prosecute corruption. Butler, his gang, and most politicians took Folk's words as the sentiments of an office seeker, words that would soon be forgotten.

Throughout 1901, rumors swept the city about an attempt by the Boodlers to force Charles Turner to pay $145,000 in bribes to extend the franchises of the St. Louis and Suburban Railway. Turner was its president. He had also been part of Butler's inner circle. But he wouldn't pay. Folk heard the rumors.

In January 1902, St. Louisans turned to their half-dozen newspapers to read—some with glee, some with shock, nearly all with surprise—that Folk had given to the sheriff the names of one hundred people to be summoned before a grand jury investigating corruption. It was Folk's first move against the Boodlers, and it was a failure. Every witness denied knowledge of a corruption fund.

Folk then resorted to what turned out to be one of the most successful bluffs ever undertaken by a prosecutor. He called into his office two of the witnesses he felt were the most vulnerable. Folk stared at the pair and, in his quiet voice, told them, "Unless you appear before the grand jury within forty-eight hours and tell everything you know about the placing of money in escrow for the purpose of bribing members of the Municipal Assembly, I shall send you both to the penitentiary. That is all. Good morning, gentlemen."

Within the allotted forty-eight hours, both men caved in. They told what they knew about the Suburban Railroad bribery case. Folk was on his way. In 1902, the grand jury returned sixty-one indictments against twenty-four people for bribery or perjury.

Some of the accused skipped the city and even the country. One of them was brewer and businessman Ellis Wainwright. In 1890, Wainwright had commissioned renowned architect Louis Sullivan to design the downtown skyscraper that still bears Wainwright's name. In 1892, he hired Sullivan again to design the classic tomb at Bellefontaine Cemetery for his wife. In 1902, Wainwright was in Egypt when he heard about the Suburban Railway indictments. His signature happened to be on a $135,000 note that found its way into the escrow bribery fund. Paris seemed a better option than St. Louis. That's where Wainwright took up residence—for the next ten years.

Folk became the target of threats, both political and lethal. He began taking Boodlers to trial one after another, and the public saw another side of the public figure—a skillful lawyer who was a master with a jury. He could also attack defense lawyers with finely honed rhetoric. Consider this portion of an opening statement:

When you find paint upon the lily or artificial perfume on the rose, there is suspicion, in the one instance, of the original whiteness of the lily, and, in the other, of the original sweetness of the rose. So when you find so-called innocence defended with such eloquence, there is a suspicion of the innocence so much eloquence defends.

But all of the rhetoric, the indictments, and the convictions of other players meant nothing to Folk's political future if Butler walked free.

THE TRIAL

On November 11, 1902, in Columbia, the farmer jury was sworn, opening statements were made, and a half-dozen minor witnesses testified. The case was about garbage: who got the contracts to haul city refuse and how were they awarded.

In the fall of 1901, the St. Louis Sanitary Company bid on a new city contract that would pay the hauler $134,000. Butler owned 185 shares of St. Louis Sanitary and also got a salary of $2,500 a year for "good will and services." The previous contract had been for $65,000 a year. A witness testified that the amount of garbage was the same. There was no obvious benefit to the city that justified the higher amount.

To make matters more confusing, St. Louis Sanitary paid Excelsior Hauling Company $62,000 a year as a subcontractor to haul away the garbage. Guess who is the largest stockholder in Excelsior? Folk asked. His name is Butler.

To the stand strode Dr. Henry A. Chapman, a member of the St. Louis Board of Health. On September 16, 1901, Chapman said Butler came to his home and offered him "a present of twenty-five hundred dollars" if St. Louis Sanitary got the contract.

"I couldn't take it. It would be a bribe," Chapman replied.

"Oh, no, it would be a present," Chapman quoted Butler as saying.

Between September and November, the Board of Health

approved the bid of St. Louis Sanitary. That prompted another visit to Chapman's house by Butler. The following exchange took place, according to Chapman:

Butler: "I am a man of my word, and I have come to make that present."

Chapman refused.

Butler: "You're not a millionaire. You may need this."

Chapman: "I would never have another peaceful moment if I took it."

Butler: "Well, you are a man in a million. If I can do anything for you, let me know."

Following Chapman to the stand was Dr. Albert N. Merrell, another board member. He testified that Butler had offered him twenty-four hundred dollars for his vote on one occasion and "gold and greenbacks" at a second meeting. Merrell refused.

Defense lawyers called company officials to testify that Butler had no logical reason to bribe anyone because St. Louis Sanitary was the only bidder. Butler's sons, James and Edward, provided an alibi for their dad, saying he was sick at home when he was supposed to be bribing Chapman.

Probably against the advice of his battery of lawyers, Butler decided to take the stand and put down the uppity young attorney he had helped elect. That was a disaster. Butler denied bribing anyone or even meeting the two doctors. Then he described his occupation as master blacksmith. Folk asked him if he had any other occupation.

Butler: "I have some other business. I speculate. I buy bonds. I buy stocks."

Folk: "Have you ever been a legislative agent?"

Butler: "I think not. I have never been directly engaged in legislation except so far as my personal business is concerned."

Folk went for the jugular. He asked about Suburban Railway and then about getting bills passed in the Municipal Assembly. Butler's lawyers were on their feet objecting, and the judge was sustaining the objections, but Butler was already yelling at Folk: "I have been engaged in no legislation. I have not been in the general bribery business. I was only engaged in matters that I owned stock in and was looking out for my own interest." And Butler's own interest was just about every bill that went through City Hall.

"Behold the Siamese Twins, Mr. Butler of the sanitary company and Mr. Butler of the hauling company," said a sarcastic C. O. Bishop, an assistant prosecutor, in closing arguments.

Jurors found Butler guilty of attempted bribery and recommended three years in prison. Three Columbia residents posted an appeals bond, and a silent Butler took the Wabash home. Only son James, the congressman, spoke out, and his comments carried a delicious irony for St. Louisans. James Butler said his father was innocent. "It was an outrage. That jury was fixed."

In a day-after editorial, the *Globe* described Butler as a millionaire and the most powerful politician in Missouri. "Butler has not cared to hold office. He prefers to distribute offices by the hundred." The editorial predicted that Butler would never spend a day in jail. It also declared that if there were more Democrats like Folk, the Democrat Party would be vigorous instead "of a divided and decaying remnant."

Folk took the words to heart. Buoyed by the Butler conviction and dozens of others, Folk rode a good-government platform into the governorship in 1904. He also threw his hat into the ring for the presidency in 1912, only to lose the nomination to Woodrow Wilson. Wilson then brought the Missourian into his cabinet in Washington.

Butler never did serve a day in jail. The Missouri Supreme Court threw out the conviction on a technicality.

In an unusual burst of candor in 1904, Butler told a *Post-Dispatch* reporter that he was through fixing elections. The colonel acknowledged that he had been stealing elections from the Republicans in St. Louis for thirty years, "and I have decided to quit. Yes, sir, quit is the word."

Butler died at his home in the 3500 block of Pine Street in 1911. He left an estate of $5 million.

BELLEVILLE LYNCHING
1903

David Wyatt must have wondered if anyone would come to his rescue on the night of June 6, 1903, as a mob outside the Belleville jail banged on its doors. Then Wyatt may have given up hope, as hour after hour ticked by and he could hear the continual pounding. He was locked in what officials called "the murderer's cell," with no place to go and no place to hide.

Wyatt was an African American schoolteacher from nearby Brooklyn, Illinois. Charles Hertel was the county superintendent of schools. Hertel was a popular Freeburg farmer who had been elected three times to the St. Clair County post. The county offices were in Belleville.

Wyatt had gone to Hertel's office that afternoon. Some parents in Brooklyn had complained about Wyatt in a school system where Wyatt had taught for a decade. They wanted Hertel to oust him by not renewing his teacher's certificate for the 1903–04 school year. Wyatt went to see Hertel to find out what the superintendent planned to do. In front of Hertel's son, Garfield, Wyatt asked directly if his teaching certificate would be renewed. Hertel said it would not.

According to Garfield Hertel and a friend who was in the senior Hertel's office, Wyatt then drew a handgun and fired one shot, hitting Charles Hertel in the right breast. Garfield and the friend then wrestled the gun from Wyatt, grabbed him, and dragged him to the jail nearby.

So Wyatt was in jail as a crowd—estimated at as many as fifteen hundred men, women, and children—gathered outside. Mayor Fred J. Kern told the crowd to go home and to let the law take its course. He was ignored. Firefighters tried to rush the crowd with fire hoses, but the water wasn't turned on, and the bluff didn't work. The crowd sliced the hoses into pieces, tied them into bows, and resumed their assault on the front door, using a plank as a battering ram. Eventually, the first door gave way, but the mob failed to get through a steel second door. The crowd leaders turned their attention to the jail's back door and hammered away at it with sledgehammers until it broke, about six hours after Wyatt's arrest.

What followed was gruesome. Wyatt was dragged from the cell about 11:30 p.m. and taken to Belleville's public square, where he was hanged from a telephone pole. But the mob wasn't done. People approached the hanged man and prodded his ribs with canes and umbrellas while women and children watched. Then the body was doused with kerosene and set afire.

"No effort whatever was made by police to prevent the lynching," the *St. Louis Post-Dispatch* reported the next day. "Some of the officers witnessed it." Members of the crowd, the newspaper said, "appeared to regard it as a matter of course that Wyatt should be hanged, and they hanged him."

Belleville area churches denounced the lynching, but no one came forward as a potential witness, leading the coroner's jury to declare, "We, the jury, find that the deceased came to his death at the hands of parties unknown to the jury." Moreover, prosecutors said no one would identify the lynchers—despite the six hours it took to get to Wyatt and to kill him.

There had been no effort by police or city officials to defend Wyatt, the *Post-Dispatch* noted. Not a single shot was fired on his behalf. Moreover, the newspaper said, the mayor himself had ordered police to stand down and had refused to allow firefighters to hook up their water hoses. After three days of criticism, Kern came firing back. Besides serving as mayor, Kern was a former congressman and the publisher of the *Belleville News-Democrat.* Had the community not acted over the shooting of Hertel, said Kern with some sort of twisted logic, "it would not be made of desirable or right stuff."

Kern glibly described the lynching of Wyatt as "a somewhat

irregular execution," and he acknowledged that he ordered police not to use force to defend the suspect. His reason? He didn't want "to see innocent blood flow on account of the guilty wretch in the jail."

Just as St. Louis leaders somehow managed to blame Elijah Lovejoy and other abolitionists for the death by burning of Francis McIntosh in 1836 because they stirred up people's passions, so, too, did Kern find a scapegoat. An African American minister had sued a barber in St. Clair County Circuit Court because the barber had refused to give the minister a shoeshine. That lawsuit by a black against a white was so brazen, Kern theorized, that it led to widespread antagonism in Belleville against blacks in general. Kern's remarks led to threats against the minister, who eventually moved to Chicago, where he was active in civil rights.

Perhaps the only person who didn't take part in the lynching of Wyatt either as a participant or as a spectator was the man Wyatt shot—Charles Hertel.

Hertel lived.

DOWNTOWN ST. LOUIS SHOOTOUT
1904

Friends, family, and fellow police officers gathered on November 21, 1904, for a funeral Mass at St. Alphonsus "Rock" Church on North Grand Boulevard. They came to mourn officer Daniel P. Shea, a rookie patrolman, who had died of what was described as heart failure. He had lived with his mother and sister on Thomas Street. Daniel had joined the police department, following in his older brother's footsteps, earlier that year, when the police force had expanded by five hundred for the World's Fair. He had been assigned to the Sixth District. Only a handful of mourners made the trip to Calvary Cemetery, where Daniel was buried near his brother John, who had been a year older.

Daniel Shea had been one of more than ten thousand mourners—the biggest funeral since General William T. Sherman in 1891—to attend the Mass and line the route to the cemetery a month earlier for the burial of his brother and Thomas Dwyer. The Shea family attributed Daniel's subsequent depression and death at the age of thirty-two to the tragedy that had stunned St. Louis.

John Shea, Dwyer, and James McCluskey had perished in a gun battle with train robbers in a run-down apartment at 1324 Pine Street. Two of the robbers also died in the shootout.

The story began three hundred miles to the north at about 10:30 p.m. on August 1, when four men boarded a train in the Chicago suburb of Harvey. The Illinois Central's Diamond Special was carrying passengers on an overnight run to St. Louis for the World's Fair.

One of the men put a pistol to the back of the brakeman and walked him through the train as the other three gunmen accosted passengers, some of whom had already gone to bed for the night, ordered the victims to turn over money and jewelry, and beat those who showed hesitation or resistance. Then the brakeman was ordered to stop the train about thirty miles south of Kankakee. The robbers jumped off with their loot in a flour sack and were last seen walking east into woods.

Police determined from passenger descriptions that one of the men was probably "New York" Harry Vaughn, a robber and killer. Vaughn had served a prison term at the Missouri State Penitentiary for a train robbery in 1896. A year before the Illinois Central heist, Vaughn had led a gang on a rampage of post office robberies in which the postal safes were blown open with dynamite. The spree ranged through Tennessee, Georgia, Florida, and Kentucky and ended in a shootout with police in May 1903 in Birmingham, Alabama. Two police officers were killed, two robbers died, and two others were captured—both later said Vaughn had shot the police—but Vaughn escaped.

St. Louis detective Joseph H. James got a tip in October that Vaughn and the other Illinois Central robbers were holed up in the tenement on Pine. He staked out the premises with detective Shea, special officers Dwyer and McCluskey, and Kansas City detective Edward Boyle, on loan to St. Louis for World's Fair security.

Inside the rented room were Vaughn and robbers William Morris and Albert Rosenauer, who used the name "Al Rose." Rose and his common-law wife, Effie Holbert, had rented the first-floor front room of the three-story building, and Vaughn and Morris were living in the back room. Rosenauer had murdered a man at a fish fry on Cherokee Street in 1898 but served only two years in prison before getting a pardon. Morris had written Vaughn two weeks earlier in Pittsburgh to rendezvous in St. Louis at the Pine Street address so the gang could plan its next spate of crimes.

About 4 p.m. on October 21, James told a coroner's jury later, he was standing in front of the address across the street and saw Vaughn leave the house. He could see Morris and Rosenauer inside the apartment. James went into an adjacent saloon, where the other officers were awaiting his instructions. James said he and Dwyer took Vaughn by surprise. While James remained with the captive, Dwyer, Shea, and McCluskey charged into the apartment. Boyle said he went to the other end of the apartment hallway to block off any escape route.

In a matter of seconds, Morris shot Dwyer in the stomach, Shea in the shoulder and head, and McCluskey in the lung and stomach. McCluskey shot Morris in the stomach. Dwyer shot Rosenauer in the head. Boyle, the last man into the room, shot Morris in the jaw. All five of the wounded would die, Shea almost immediately.

At City Hospital, Morris lingered for three days. Doctors decided that drinking water would hurt his chances of survival. The parched killer begged for water from police and got his wishes from Chief of Detectives William Desmond in exchange for a confession. Desmond also brought the conductor, brakeman, and engineer from the Illinois Central to the hospital, and they identified Morris as one of the robbers.

Morris had gotten out of prison in June 1903, he said, after serving a ten-year sentence for a train robbery near Nevada, Missouri. He admitted he was the man who held the Illinois Central brakeman at gunpoint while colleagues Vaughn, Rosenauer, and a man later arrested in Chicago robbed about twenty passengers of more than five hundred dollars.

The outlaw also admitted he had engineered a holdup of a Rock Island train in Iowa in August, but got nothing after blowing up the train's safe. He escaped after uncoupling the engine. Morris, who went by the nickname of "Big Fellow," also robbed a ticket agent in Mattoon, Illinois, and a drugstore in St. Louis in the days leading up to the shootout.

As a police stenographer took down the dying man's statements, Morris told Desmond about the gunfire in the twelve-foot by twelve-foot apartment: "I saw the first that entered reaching for his gun and so I fired. I guess I hit him and when I saw them all shooting at me I just kept on firing. It was my shooting for Rose didn't have a gun on him. I had five shots and I guess I was pretty busy as long as they lasted. My pistol was a .38 caliber and I tell you if I had had another like it, I would have cleaned out the whole damn bunch."

In his statement at the coroner's inquest, Vaughn said he had met both Morris and Rosenauer in the state penitentiary, where Vaughn had been taught the trade of shoemaking. He claimed they had no intentions of any criminal activities in St. Louis. The gang's plan was to scheme here and execute elsewhere, he said.

Effie Holbert, who said she was not really married to Rosenauer because she still had a husband in Illinois, also testified. She had gone to the dentist when the shootout occurred. She knew Vaughn and Morris but denied she knew anything about criminal activities. Police found guns in her trunk and under her bed. She had no comment about either to the coroner's jury.

St. Louisans raised two thousand dollars for the families of Shea, Dwyer, and McCluskey. The funeral Mass for McCluskey was held at St. Kevin's and was attended by fellow members of the Knights of Columbus. Shea was thirty-three and single. McCluskey, forty, lived with a brother and two sisters. Dwyer was the father of two boys.

What to do with Vaughn, who was wanted for crimes in several states? Keep him in St. Louis, authorities decided, but on what charge? He had played no part in the shootout. Prosecutors came up with an innovative solution. They tried Vaughn as an accomplice of Morris in the drugstore holdup.

Shortly before the shootout, Morris had gone into the store of Gustav Selving on Jefferson Avenue and announced a robbery while Vaughn stood lookout in the doorway. Morris got twenty-four dollars from the store and another thirty cents from Selving, while a customer claimed he had no cash at all. As Morris was leaving the store, Vaughn told Morris to club Selving and grab a box of cigars. Morris ignored the former order but followed the latter, and Vaughn got his smokes.

The box of cigars led to a jury conviction on January 27, 1905, and a judge sent Vaughn to the Missouri State Penitentiary to serve a thirty-five-year sentence as a habitual criminal. The other states would have to wait for Vaughn to complete his Missouri time.

But Vaughn had no intention of waiting. With three other inmates on November 24, 1905, he attempted a prison break, in which two guards were killed. For that crime, Vaughn went to the gallows in 1907.

In the aftermath of the shooting, Desmond, the chief of detectives, lauded the police officers who lost their lives and added, "I am thankful for one thing—and the rest I am deeply bereaved—that the country has been ridded of one of the most desperate gangs of train robbers and bandits that have infested this part of the country."

DESPERATE LORD BARRINGTON
1903-04

"The Desperate Lord Barrington" was probably St. Louis's worst villain ever. He had killed a nobleman before he left England for the United States. He had used his wiles and title to marry several women without divorcing any. And he had committed another murder before he even got to St. Louis, where he murdered again. "Desperate Lord Barrington" got his comeuppance in the end, when the body of his St. Louis victim was found near a quarry and he was exposed for the treacherous, murderous cad that he was.

That end was actually act three of a melodrama performed at a St. Louis theater in the fall of 1903 and the winter of 1904 while the real Lord Barrington—if he was, in fact, nobility, as he claimed—huddled in a jail cell in Clayton awaiting trial in a real murder case.

The story of Frederick Seymour Barrington began in late 1902, when he arrived in St. Louis and took a room with Mrs. E. E. Elliott at her home on West Belle Place. Barrington said he had crossed the ocean earlier that year to Halifax, Nova Scotia, and proceeded on to Ottawa to live with a sister. He then made his way to New York, Philadelphia, and Washington, D.C., where he lived with his dying youngest sister.

Elliott's sister, Wilhelmina Grace Cochrane of Kansas City, was also at the Elliott house. After a whirlwind romance of eighteen days, Cochrane became Lady Barrington on January 22, 1903, and the couple moved to the Southern Hotel. Their stay didn't last long, and their marriage lasted not much longer. They were evicted for failure to pay a sixty-nine–dollar bill, and Wilhelmina went home in disgrace to Kansas City. Her brother, James Cochrane, returned to St. Louis in her stead, found Barrington, and beat him up.

Both ended up in court. On February 3, Judge Daniel

O'Connell Tracy sentenced Barrington to the city workhouse. He had admitted that he was an ex-military officer who had perhaps exaggerated his nobility. Tracy fined Cochrane, who was praised in court for defending his sister's honor. The judge added that the case should be a warning that "cultured American girls fall so easy to the wiles and tinkling cymbals of foreign titles."

On what charge Tracy convicted Barrington was still a puzzle to the Missouri Supreme Court several years later. Whatever it was, Barrington got a pardon from the mayor and was promptly hired by a saloonkeeper as a greeter at his tavern, which was quickly renamed Lord Barrington's Saloon. It became an instant success. It also brought to the bar out of curiosity James P. McCann, who showed up in April, felt sorry for Barrington, and gave him fifty dollars. McCann also agreed to hire Barrington as an errand runner and odd-jobs man at the house McCann and his wife were converting at 2901 Franklin Avenue to the Leland Hotel in anticipation of the World's Fair.

McCann, forty-five, was a racehorse owner and racetrack bettor. A Kentucky native, he had married and divorced his first wife in Kentucky and had married his second wife, Jessie, in Chicago in 1900. She ran a matrimonial agency there and opened one here when they moved to St. Louis to open the hotel. They hired Charles and Oney Morrison. Besides Barrington, they took in one boarder, Tom Leonard, on June 11.

On June 18, Jessie complained about a headache, and Barrington said he had one too. McCann said he'd get them some headache powder after he got back with some race returns. Between 7:30 p.m. and 8 p.m., McCann left to buy the medicine. He took Barrington along. He went out the side gate. Jessie gave him five dollars for the powder. McCann said he would be back shortly.

Jessie never saw her husband again. He never returned.

McCann and Barrington caught the 10 p.m. Wellston–St. Charles train at the Wellston station. The conductor saw them get off at the Bonfils Station, a stop in the middle of nowhere, about twelve miles northwest of Wellston. The motorman noticed them walking side by side down a path toward Taussig Avenue. A few minutes later, both the conductor and the motorman heard a shot, then a cry, and then a second shot.

The same two railroad men were aboard the first train the next morning from St. Charles to Wellston and saw Barrington walking near the tracks, about three miles east of Bonfils. His trousers were muddy. The train passed him on several back-and-forth trips that morning, and both men noticed he would try to conceal his identity by turning away or concealing his face with a straw hat. He also carried a cane.

At 9 a.m., Barrington entered the Leland Hotel through the basement door and asked Charles Morrison to "take these clothes and get them off the place, right away." They were wet, spattered with mud, and soaked with blood, Morrison said. When Morrison said he had no place to put them, Barrington told him to wash them with naphtha oil and lye to remove the blood stains.

Morrison saw Barrington with a watch on his bed and placing a revolver in his trunk. Barrington then told Morrison that McCann had cut the throat of a woman they had met with two men and another woman at Suburban Garden, an amusement park. The men heard her scream, knocked McCann down, and knocked Barrington on top of McCann. The men went for a carriage, and McCann fled. "He will never come back. If he does, I will kill him," Morrison was told. McCann has gone to Kentucky, Barrington said.

Jessie, who had been out searching for her husband, got another version from Barrington. In that version, McCann was too ashamed to come home because of something that happened involving the woman at Suburban Garden but would need money later. Barrington said McCann had gone to Centralia, Illinois, and needed three hundred dollars.

Later, Barrington got what he said was a telegram from Centralia with several instructions from McCann and a phone call from a woman in Chicago on McCann's behalf, Barrington told Jessie. Among the instructions: send money and kick Leonard out of the hotel.

On June 25, police questioned Barrington but let him go. The next day, farmer Louis Tucker found a nude body floating in an abandoned, flooded quarry. The quarry was about three hundred yards from Bonfils Station. A postmortem showed two bullet holes to the head. McCann was identified by the general appearance of the body, a chest mole, and the shape of two front teeth.

Jessie ordered Barrington to leave the hotel on June 27, and he hired an expressman to take his trunk to Union Station. Police caught up that day with the suspect and the trunk. In it were a cane and a revolver, both the property of McCann. After Barrington was transferred from one station to another that night, a watch, locket, and ring, also identified as belonging to McCann, were discovered in the paddy wagon. Police confronted Barrington with the railway men, and his story about attacks by strangers switched from Suburban Garden to the Bonfils quarry.

Barrington claimed McCann had arranged to meet someone near the quarry. Two men showed up and confronted and attacked them, and Barrington was knocked unconscious; awakened the next morning and finding no McCann, Barrington assumed he had escaped and fled.

Near the quarry in September, workmen found a coat, a shirt, an undershirt, and gold buttons with the letters "McC." Jessie identified the articles as belonging to her husband.

Barrington was in custody from June 27 until his trial began in February 1904. The newspapers speculated day after day about the lord in the Clayton jail. Among the theories: Barrington had really killed a Lord Barrington and assumed his identity; Barrington was an escaped convict from Newgate prison in England; Barrington had murdered an English army lieutenant named Roby; Barrington was a bigamist with wives in Brooklyn and Philadelphia.

Other possibilities: Barrington also killed a man named John Moog in St. Louis before he killed McCann; Barrington was a notorious English criminal by the name of either Barton or Burgoyne; and finally, Barrington might just be "Jack the Ripper."

Then came the play, with the main actor imitating Barrington's voice and mannerisms. *The Desperate Lord Barrington* was advertised in all of the newspapers. Handbills were posted around town: "The Acme of Sensational Melodrama. A play filled with thrills, throbs, laughter, and tears."

At a preliminary hearing in the fall, onlookers packed the courtroom and applauded whenever a ruling went against Barrington. Barrington's lawyers sought a change of venue and put on three dozen witnesses and exhibits—the flyer from the play, newspaper clippings—to show Barrington could not get a fair trial in St. Louis County. The state, too, put on witnesses, who testified that there had been no excessive publicity in recent weeks, that people did not necessarily believe what they read, that some felt sympathy for the defendant, and that others believed McCann had faked his own death to avoid either bill collectors or a domestic problem. Prosecutors argued also that the Barrington case was well known wherever it would be tried in Missouri.

On January 16, Judge John W. McElhinney overruled the petition for a venue change, and the trial got under way in Clayton on February 23.

Prosecuting Attorney Rowland L. Johnson didn't wait long after jury selection and court instructions to damn Barrington in what were supposed to be opening statements. "In all candor and with due reverence," Johnson told the jury, "I wish to confess to you that during the progress of this trial, my conception of the devil has been materially changed; and if I were to portray him to you now, I would not paint him as hoofed and horned, livid with purgatorial fires, but rather would I picture him to you as arranged in white vest and Prince Albert coat, with a voice as soft as the breath of summer and with a steel gray eye."

Defense Attorney Shelly Grover objected that the argument was improper for an opening statement, and Johnson was reprimanded by the judge.

The circumstantial case against Barrington—no one saw him

shoot McCann or push him into the quarry—had additional twists. In a picture taken at Suburban Garden the night McCann disappeared, McCann is wearing a straw hat and Barrington a black one, their usual attire. But the railroad men distinctly recalled Barrington wearing a straw hat the next morning as he hiked back to St. Louis. The prosecutors also found a friend of the defendant who admitted sending the fake telegram and making the fake phone call. The friend said he had no idea who McCann was at the time.

Barrington testified McCann had given him the hat and cane. He said he walked back because he had no money in his pockets. He stuck to the story of the stranger attacks, saying the two men were chasing him and knocked him down, and McCann had been chasing them, and he called to McCann for help, then heard a shot before he was rendered unconscious.

Over Grover's objections to every question, Johnson then zoomed in on Barrington's background. Where was he from? Where was he born? Was he married to women in Brooklyn or Philadelphia? Who was Lieutenant Roby? What did he do for a living?

The questions were unrelated to any direct testimony and prejudicial, but the judge allowed them and ordered Barrington to answer. Barrington said he was born in India and served in the English military. He was vague about his past and refused to name anyone who could vouch for him, insisting he didn't want his notoriety rubbing off on them. There was no such person as Lieutenant Roby, he said. As to an occupation, Barrington said he had "sufficient line of my own. I had recently left the army where I had been 13 years. . . . I was a war correspondent to South Africa in 1899 when I left Bombay. . . ."

The jury took about three hours to convict Barrington of murder and set his punishment at death. The case went up on appeal to the Missouri Supreme Court, which affirmed the conviction in a five-to-two decision on June 1, 1906. Writing for the majority, Judge James David Fox said the ruling on the change of venue was up to the personal discretion of the trial judge. It was likely that there would have been no difference in the amount of publicity if the case were tried in another jurisdiction, he said.

Dissenting, Judge Leroy B. Valliant flatly declared that "this man did not have a fair trial." Because of *The Desperate Lord Barrington* and extensive newspaper attacks on the defendant's character before trial, Valliant said Barrington had been entitled to a change of venue to a county where his case was least likely to be affected by publicity.

As to the "devil" analogy by Johnson, Valliant said, "It was not proper argument. It was no argument at all. It was a vindictive, passionate, pitiless, cruel denunciation of a prisoner." McElhinney should have set aside the verdict and ordered a new trial, he concluded.

A former prosecutor himself, Governor Joseph Folk probably read the three thousand pages of transcripts before he commuted Barrington's death sentence a year later to life in prison.

Even in prison, Barrington was still playing the aristocracy card. In his autobiography in 1949, Missouri lawyer John T. Barker talked about the Barrington case and agreed with Valliant that Barrington had been denied a fair trial. Barker was on the parole board when Barrington came up several times for parole. Barrington told Barker he was born in India, the son of an English nobleman. Barker said there was speculation that Barrington had been in the United States "on secret work for the British government." Barker said he always voted for Barrington's parole, but he was in the minority. Barrington finally got the votes he needed for parole in December 1918, having spent fifteen years in custody for McCann's murder, and set sail for England on January 4, 1919. He had never been charged with any other crimes.

EDWARD GARNER LEWIS
1905-12

Edward Garner Lewis, the founder of University City, was an entrepreneur, a real estate developer, a builder, a businessman, a publisher, a ceramicist, a salesman extraordinaire, a banker, a visionary, a proponent of equal rights for women even before they got the vote, and a self-promoted potential presidential candidate. Federal and state officials of the 1900s would add another category: conman and crook.

A congressional inquiry into Lewis's dealings ended up in a split decision, a committee majority saying he was a businessman persecuted for his creativity, and a minority accusing him of fraudulent activity. Lewis blamed persecution by the federal government for the downfall of his multifaceted empire, his subsequent bankruptcy, and his departure for California, where he planned another utopia. That, too, failed. Lewis went into bankruptcy again and then to prison in 1928 for fraud. He died in 1950 as he began, penniless.

Lewis was born on March 4, 1869, in Connecticut, the son, grandson, and great-grandson of Episcopal ministers. His father served as rector of St. John's Episcopal Church in Bridgeport. Lewis attended Trinity College in 1886 and in 1888 returned to the school, where he paid his tuition from proceeds he earned as a taxidermist and cigar salesman. Stopping just short of snake oil, Lewis honed his sales skills on such products as a pill that would cure tobacco cravings, a biscuit that would break a cold in an hour, and "Magic Bug Chalk." The pesticide consisted of chalk soaked in evergreen. It repelled cockroaches once it was drawn on a line. It worked for a few hours—until the evergreen evaporated.

In St. Louis in 1899, Lewis bought a magazine called *Winner*, changed its name to *Woman's Magazine*, lowered subscription prices and advertising rates, and soon built up circulation. A year later, the entrepreneur bought a piece of the daily *St. Louis Star*, and later he started a magazine called *Woman's Farm Journal.*

Lewis often told the story how he had canvased the vacant land in the west end of St. Louis and determined there were only six thousand lots remaining and builders were moving westward from hilltop to hilltop at the rate of a thousand lots a year. He said he asked a businessman when St. Louis's westward expansion would reach the city limits. Thirty years, the businessman replied. More like six, Lewis reasoned.

That calculation prompted him to buy in 1902 an eighty-five-acre tract along Delmar Boulevard and to move the headquarters of his publishing business there. Lewis built an octagonal building and annex on Delmar.

During the World's Fair of 1904, NiNi Harris noted in her book, *Legacy of Lions*, that Lewis built a tent city on his property that provided sleeping tents to fairgoers along with a dining tent, nursery, barber shops, a reading room, and showers. It was open on Sundays even though the Fair was closed, and Lewis offered free tours of his magazine buildings. Atop the octagonal building, Lewis installed an eight-ton beacon with a searchlight that was seven feet in diameter, then the world's largest. Harris also noted that Lewis set up the World's Fair Contest Company, where participants were asked to guess the total Fair attendance after buying twenty-five-cent coupons. People debated whether it was a lottery or contest.

Lewis also began plans for the establishment of a new city, with the publishing company, a correspondence university (the People's University), and the People's United States Bank at the core. Outside the core would be University Heights, a seven-stage planned housing community based on the green space theories of Frederick Law Olmstead and the private place design of St. Louisan Julius Pitzman. In 1906, Lewis incorporated University City. He was, of course, its first mayor.

By then, Lewis's far-reaching empire had begun to feel the

pressures of the federal government, perhaps egged on by area newspapers and national magazines unhappy with Lewis's invasion into their advertising revenue and readers.

One boot had fallen when three Post Office Department inspectors were sent to St. Louis by Postmaster General George B. Cortelyou to investigate Lewis. Their recommendation in a report on May 31, 1905: a fraud order be issued against Lewis and the People's United States Bank. Immediately, Missouri Secretary of State John E. Swanger announced that his office would take charge of the bank's affairs and assume control of all the bank's assets. The postal inspectors made several allegations. They said Lewis personally and through his companies had borrowed $411,000 from the bank, with unsecured loans for much of the money. They contended that the board of directors of the bank was selected solely by Lewis from the ranks of employees of the Lewis Publishing Company. The report said, "Lewis obtained money and subscriptions for stock in the bank by exaggerations and misrepresentations of the security, safety, and profits to accrue to subscribers of stock, promising to put in his own funds, dollar for dollar, for every subscriber and then organized the bank so that Edward G. Lewis could and would control it without the voice of the stockholders, and use the funds subscribed or a large portion of them for his own purpose and benefit." Lewis took a salary from the bank from July until November 1904, even though the bank was not officially operating, the report said.

Among representations by Lewis the inspectors argued were untrue: the bank's capital stock would be worth several times par value the day the bank opened; the profits of the bank would be substantially greater and the expenses substantially less than other financial institutions; loans of the bank would be passed on or guaranteed by other banks.

In seizing the bank, Swanger ordered Lewis to pay back the $411,000 he had borrowed. The board of directors would be replaced by one approved by his office, Swanger said.

The postal inspectors' report made no mention of the fact that Lewis's bank by mail was a direct competitor to the Post Office's sale of postal money orders.

Later that year, Lewis was buffeted by two more federal actions: he was charged with fraud, and the Post Office began returning all of the mail of Lewis's holdings stamped "Fraudulent."

Lewis would testify later that his mail often amounted to three thousand to twenty-two thousand pieces a day and that the government's action cost him o$190,000 in advertising revenue alone. Moreover, his credit was cut off.

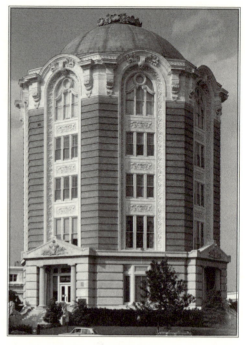

Today, the octogonal Woman's Magazine Building serves as University City's city hall.

The indictment was handed up by a federal grand jury in December 1905, and the case sat before a federal judge, and sat, and sat—continued each term with other criminal cases until November 1907, when Lewis asked that the case be dismissed for lack of a speedy trial. The case was continued anyway until May 1908, when the government decided to drop it. Lewis wanted a ruling from the U.S. Supreme Court that the federal judge should have ruled on his motion to dismiss the case, not the government's decision. He lost. The high court said Lewis had not been "legally aggrieved."

More fraud indictments followed, as did more legal battles.

Meanwhile, Lewis had plunged ahead with his university

project, setting up an Art Academy and bringing in scholars from around the country and Europe to staff it. He and his wife, Mabel, took courses in ceramics and became well versed in the process.

In 1907, Lewis had organized the American Women's League to promote subscriptions to his magazines. Each woman was urged to sell fifty-two dollars in subscriptions; the funds would be paid to the league, and the money would be used for women's education and benefits. Some seven hundred chapters blossomed around the country, with University City as the league's headquarters. The league eventually morphed into the American Women's Republic, aimed at teaching women the ins and outs of politics as part of the suffrage movement. Lewis said he might run for president on a suffrage ticket. One of his platform plans: decentralize the power of the federal government.

Lewis's run was coming to an end. He filed for bankruptcy in early 1911. He moved to California the next year.

The University City Library lists some of his accomplishments on its website. He published newspapers and magazines for a decade. He founded University City and the People's University for which it was named. He built the Woman's Magazine Building, the Press Annex, the Egyptian Temple, and the Art Academy and commissioned the University City Lion Gates—all landmarks today. He served three terms as the city's first mayor and helped establish the University City School District.

Harris summarized the efforts to convict Lewis of wrongdoing in her book. She wrote that more than one dozen indictments were filed against him. He was tried three times, with mistrials in two of the cases and an acquittal in a third. Neither the courts nor Congress were ever able to prove deliberate attempts to defraud on his part.

THEY STOLE THE LOCOMOTIVE
1910

Mail clerk William Pfeiffer had an easy night of it. He was riding an empty mail car back home to St. Louis from the end of his run to Kansas City that afternoon. He had helped the clerks on the eastbound Missouri Pacific sort their mail. And the passenger train with dual mail cars was just thirty miles from Union Station at 9:45 p.m. on January 21, 1910. It had stopped at Pacific for water.

Pfeiffer walked out onto the car platform, and what he saw caused him to retrace his steps into the mail car as fast as he could. Gun-toting robbers were up ahead with engineer George Lutes and fireman William Slocum. Moments later, Pfeiffer heard the train start up again, only to slow down at mile post twenty-eight, just north of Eureka, then stop. Again the train resumed running, only to come to a halt down the track at Castlewood Heights. Pfeiffer looked for a place to hide.

Two men had climbed aboard the train at the Pacific water stop. One of them had a crippled right hand and wore a mask made from a red handkerchief. He was training his pistol on Lutes. The other man, the taller of the two, was wearing a blue bandana for a mask and pointing his gun at Slocum. Lutes was asked the time and then told by the red-masked bandit, "Now you go slow and kill time between here and Eureka. Do as you are told, and you won't get hurt, but if you disobey orders, you will be killed."

When the train reached mile post twenty-eight, Lutes got another order: "Shut off, slow down, and get off." When Lutes was too slow leaping into the darkness from the locomotive, he was shoved off the train, with instructions to "go back west"—opposite the direction the train was heading.

Now it was Slocum's turn to take orders from the robbers. He was told to uncouple the train after the second mail car, then jump off. Slocum did as he was told, and Missouri Pacific No. 8 was split in two, with passenger cars sitting on the track. Passengers were in a panic. Told that a robbery was in progress, they expected holdup men to appear inside their car at any moment. They scurried about the coaches, hiding watches, money, and jewelry in every conceivable nook and cranny, wherever they thought the robbers might not look.

The bandits, however, were miles down the track. They were eastbound in the locomotive with the coal tender and two baggage cars, Pfeiffer hiding in one of them. They stopped the train in what is now Castlewood State Park and began a search for loot in the mail. The pair made only a cursory check of the second baggage car after discovering that it was empty. That worked well for Pfeiffer. They didn't see him. In the other car, they cut open mail sacks and stole all the money they could find. Two thirds of one of the bags that they had sliced open contained nothing more than other mail sacks. They missed the jewelry that filled the rest of the container.

Leaping from the train, the pair headed for the Meramec River, where they climbed into a stolen boat that they then rowed until it stuck in a sandbar about two miles downriver. They walked the rest of the way to St. Louis.

An hour after the holdup, the railroad requisitioned an engine from a freight train on a siding at Eureka. It pushed the passenger cars to Castlewood, where it was met by a special train from St. Louis carrying a posse of railroad detectives, who began the search for the culprits. It took time to get the steam up on the purloined locomotive, and the Missouri Pacific from Kansas City finally rolled into Union Station at 2:35 a.m.

Later that morning, authorities brought from Jefferson City bloodhounds that had been used to trail escaped convicts and more tracking dogs from Sedalia. The scent stopped at the Meramec; the getaway boat had thwarted the trackers.

Both Lutes and Slocum told officials and reporters that the robbers had to be experienced railroad men because they knew what had to be done mechanically every step of the way. But they weren't adept at picking a train to rob, postal inspectors said. The train that left Kansas City at 1:15 p.m. didn't carry that much remittance money in its mail bags, and the same train usually left the Sedalia station before the postmaster had made up the mail to put aboard that train.

Walking along the tracks near Castlewood, *Post-Dispatch* reporter J. R. Groom found a tan felt hat. Tracing the hat, police learned that it had been sold by the firm of Schubert & Lehmann of Giddings, Texas. The search by the posse was unsuccessful, the robbers were long gone from the area, and a tip from a woman that she had seen the robbers turned out to be a false lead; the men she saw were just hobos.

Reading the account that the robbers knew trains, private investigator Thomas Furlong recalled he had recently seen William Lowe in St. Louis. Lowe had once been a railroad engineer and had taken part in a train robbery with Jesse James. Furlong had been a railroad detective for several years. He had worked with police and prosecutors in the Southern Hotel trunk murder in 1885, tracing the train route the killer had taken to San Francisco and providing one of his own men to the circuit attorney's office to go into the jail undercover and get a confession from the murderer.

With the information from Furlong, police determined that Lowe and George Ebeling had been working together in St. Louis selling shares in an Alaskan gold mine. Lowe was arrested about two weeks after the train robbery; Ebeling shortly after that in Hot Springs, Arkansas.

Ebeling wasted little time confessing and giving details about the crime. He said they got about six hundred dollars from the mail bags. He admitted the tan felt hat was his. He described the planning that went into the robbery, and he testified against Lowe at Lowe's trial in May 1910. Ebeling said the pair buried their guns on the bank of the River Des Peres.

Lowe denied any role in the holdup, claiming he was with

his mother that night. She said so, too. But testifying for the prosecution and destroying the alibi defense was Lowe's brother, Jimmie. The jury came back in ten minutes, finding William Lowe guilty of one count of armed robbery and six counts of tampering with the mail. U.S. District Judge David P. Dyer sentenced Lowe to twenty-five years for the robbery and three years each on the mail tampering charges, for a total of forty-three years. For his guilty plea and cooperation, Ebeling got eighteen years.

The day after the trial, Jimmie Lowe showed up in the offices of the U.S. marshal to collect his witness fee of ninety-four dollars. Two city detectives walked into the offices and slapped handcuffs on Jimmie; he had just been charged with murder. Aware Jimmie might testify against him, William Lowe had met with a police officer before his trial and confided that Jimmie had killed a man in a boxcar of the Iron Mountain Railroad on Rutgers Street in 1906. What happened to Jimmie, if anything, could not be determined. Before he left the marshal's office with police, however, he signed over his witness fee check to his mother.

ARSON TRUST
1915

When Julius Bersch and Herbert O. Baker met with Joe C. Christen at his offices in the summer of 1915, they had no idea that their conversations were being recorded—perhaps St. Louis's first wiretap. Baker had paved the way for those meetings when he suggested to Christen that he could provide a dramatic solution for the financial plight of Christen's company. The way out of debt? Insure and burn. Someone phonetically named Christen may have been the wrong man to approach. The owner of a bellows-manufacturing plant on Dock Street bearing his name, Christen wasn't about to get involved in swindles and arson. He talked to police.

Meanwhile, police detective Bart Keaney had been investigating arsonists in St. Louis for six years. Acting at times in an undercover capacity, Keaney was often lunching with Baker, shooting billiards with him, meeting his associates, and listening to his braggadocio. When Keaney's presence was mentioned at one meeting, he heard one of the clique explain to the others, "That old white-haired boob is harmless."

In the summer of 1915, the "white-haired boob" and the bellows maker began working together. Joining the good-guy group was John Leahy, a lawyer representing major insurance companies, and Ben C. Applegate, a private eye also working for the insurers.

If a case ever got to trial, they figured, conversation between Baker and Christen would deteriorate into a "he said, he said" scenario. And Baker had as good a reputation in the community as Christen. He was twenty-eight, the son of a real estate dealer. He lived in Webster Groves and was a member of the First Congregational Church. A bachelor, Baker was often in demand in social circles because he was considered an outstanding dancer. He owned his own business—an insurance brokerage in the Pierce Building downtown.

If Baker brought an associate or superior to a meeting with Christen, the legal dilemma for the prosecutors would be even worse. It would be Christen's word of what transpired versus two or more individuals vouching for each other. The solution, they decided, was a combination of recording and eavesdropping. In Christen's office, they put up a partition adjacent to a wardrobe. Behind the barricade or in the wardrobe were a stenographer, Keaney, and two more police detectives, according to the *Globe-Democrat*. Keaney also had a dictograph, a device invented in 1907 to record conversations. The *Post-Dispatch* in a lengthier article added Leahy as a fifth person hiding in Christen's office but made no mention of the recording device.

At a meeting before the office partition was assembled, Baker had asked Christen how was business, and the executive had told him that "business was very poor," and he said, "Why don't you sell it?"

"I laughed and said I didn't know of anybody I could sell it to as times were bad, and he said, 'Why don't you sell it to the insurance companies?'

"Big men all over the city are doing it every day. The truth is, the insurance companies don't mind a big loss once in awhile. It helps to advertise the business," Christen quoted Baker as saying in their initial talk. The real truth was, the insurance companies minded the heavy losses very much, hence the involvement of Leahy and Applegate in the investigation.

So Baker was back, and with him was Julius Bersch, who owned his own insurance company and had offices, like Baker, in the Pierce Building. Unbeknown to the pair as they discussed the swindle and fire were the four or five people hidden in Christen's office. Baker was actually sitting six inches from the wardrobe with the stenographer and investigators on the other side of it.

They discussed increasing insurance coverage in the bellows company. Baker thought Christen should add a total of fifty thousand dollars more to his existing coverage of forty thousand dollars. Bersch thought the jump would be suspicious and too much. He suggested a twenty-five-thousand–dollar increase. The excess fifty thousand dollars, Baker said, would be split three ways: one share for Baker, one for "his friends," and one for Christen.

The following week, a Saturday, Bersch and Christen met alone in Christen's offices. Bersch said the insurance would be placed with two other companies, not his. Ultimately, fire coverage on the Christen Bellows Manufacturing Company amounted to eighty-five thousand dollars, with the last eleven thousand dollars placed a week before the fire was to take place.

In September, Baker set the burn for a week later on a Saturday. He told Christen to let in four men after his worker left that day. "I let them in, all right, but, as soon as the gate swung shut on them, detectives whom I had tipped off closed in with revolvers and riot guns and arrested them," Christen said.

On September 11, 1915, the four men had driven onto the property in a wagon containing four barrels of gasoline and three hundred feet of tape. They had planned to set up the fire for later that night, but the detectives, led by Keaney, were waiting. Arrested were Max Greenberg, a horse trader; his cousin, Morris Greenberg; Michael "Spit" O'Connor; and Edward Milner, who also went by the name of Ben Miller or Ben Millner. Police found black powder and a flashlight in Milner's pockets. Morris Greenberg had been a suspect in December 1914 in the murder of Sam Mintz, whom police described as an "arch thief and firebug."

Along with two other detectives, Keaney, the "old white-haired boob," got the honor of arresting Baker. It seems the Webster Groves bachelor had money to burn, so to speak. He had recently bought his mother an expensive oil painting and had financed a trip for his sister to San Francisco. And he had purchased four new cars in four years, including his latest, a twelve-cylinder model.

Keaney told the *Globe-Democrat* that Baker, through credit agencies he called in connection with his insurance business, had kept tabs on the financial conditions of companies throughout St. Louis. One of those firms targeted by Baker was the Gilmore-Bonfig Decorating Company at 4455 Olive Street. It was rocked by an explosion and fire on July 24 of that year. Damages to the building and stock exceeded twenty-five thousand dollars.

On September 14, police arrested Harold G. Gilmore in connection with the fire. He had paid $2,750 for property inside the building and had insured it for $35,000, or twelve times its value. Another officer in the company, Harry C. Imel, was also charged. A third figure in that case, Carl Bonfig, wasn't charged. He said he had been a partner for only three months before the fire and had been shut out of several business meetings by Gilmore. Police arrested Bersch, the mastermind of the conspiracy, along with Otto Leman, a partner of Bersch. Leman served as the claims adjuster in the Gilmore-Bonfig fire.

Two businessmen, owners of a printing company and a grocery supply business, respectively, told the *Post-Dispatch* that they, too, had been approached by the arson ring with proposals to burn down their operations. They had refused.

On September 4, another printing company, Nixon-Jones, had burned down. The *Post-Dispatch* reported that the business had been insured for sixty-seven thousand dollars, with thirty thousand dollars taken out after July 1. Firefighters found gasoline in barrels inside the structure at 213 Pine Street.

The St. Louis Fire Department estimated that as many as 70 percent of the city's fires over a two-year period were arson-related. Damages to businesses from fires should have averaged about $750,000 in a normal year. In 1914, damages from such fires totaled $2,139,445, and the figure for the first seven months of 1915 was equally appalling: $961,000.

Cartoons by Jean Knott in the *Post-Dispatch* spoofed both the white-collar and blue-collar members of the arson trust. In one, a woman says to her husband, "John, I Need a Fall Outfit." John replies, "Wait Until After the Fire." In a second cartoon, two women are watching a third, who is all dressed up. One of the women says she certainly has lovely gowns and diamonds. The second replies, "Her Husband Must Be a Torch."

EAST ST. LOUIS RIOTS
1917

After witnessing some of the carnage in East St. Louis and being unable to prevent it, *St. Louis Post-Dispatch* reporter Carlos Hurd hurried to his newsroom and wrote a first-person narrative whose introduction may have summarized the riot of 1917 better than any official report or scholarly study: "For an hour and a half last night, I saw the massacre of helpless negroes at Broadway and Fourth Streets, in East St. Louis, where a black skin was a death warrant."

When the riots of July 2–3, 1917, finally ended, the official death toll listed 39 blacks and nine whites dead, although the unofficial count exceeded 100; 312 houses and buildings in a 40-block area near downtown were destroyed; and thousands of blacks had fled the city. Most would never return.

The *St. Louis Republic* said, "Blood-mad men and women in East St. Louis rose in a mighty mob of more than ten thousand yesterday and wrecked vengeance upon the black population of the city.

"Led, in hundreds of instances, by modern Amazons, this army of fighting citizens avenged the assassination of Police Detective Coppedge in the greatest riot the nation's history has ever recorded."

Take away some of the hyperbole, and the *Republic* was absolutely correct on at least one count—the riot had been the bloodiest in the country's history. It would hold the tragic record of bloodiest, at least by official death count, until the race riots in Los Angeles in 1992, where fifty-five died. Consider the unofficial tally of more than one hundred deaths by East St. Louis police, who did nothing to prevent the street murders, and those bloody days and nights in 1917 might still be the deadliest ever.

National Guard troops had arrived in force, but either they did little or joined in the shootings and beatings while their commander spent hours inside city hall and then had a leisurely lunch at a restaurant within a rock's throw of the brutality.

In 1992, the events of those two days were still seared into the memories of two men who were in East St. Louis seventy-five years ago. Henry Douglas told *Post-Dispatch* reporter Roy Malone that he was nine and living with his parents and two sisters at 1422 Market Street when rioters began shooting into his house, and he heard his father say, "The soldiers were helping kill people." Douglas said the rioters "were like dogs. They were killing all the Negroes they could find. . . . My father had a pistol and was shooting out the window. A bullet hit him in the head, and he fell backwards, right by my bed."

Paul Thebus told Malone he had left work and caught a train on the afternoon of July 2 for his home in Belleville. He was seventeen. He saw a mob chasing a man who was running for the train. They caught him before he could get aboard and threw him to the ground. Thebus recalled, "A woman with short, bobbed hair leaned over him with a pistol. She shot him in the head. The crowd cheered its approval. Yeah! Like cheerleading. A policeman was there but didn't come."

Lena Cook was on her way home on a trolley from a fishing lake outside the city with her husband, son, and daughter when a mob of men stopped the streetcar, pulled her husband by the collar "to the back platform and threw him off and shot him. I saw that," she would later testify.

Another man grabbed her son, dragged him out of the car, and beat him over the head with a revolver, said Cook, who never saw her son, fourteen, alive again. She was next, dragged out of the car, "and men beat me and kicked me and pulled my hair out."

Cook said she crawled to a store, where a man befriended her until an ambulance arrived. Then she saw the bodies of her husband and son in the street. The next day, Cook learned, her daughter had escaped the mob and made it to St. Louis.

The immediate trigger for the riots took place the night of

July 1, when a carload of whites in a Ford fired randomly into a group of black homes along Market Street. Armed blacks retaliated when they saw a similar Ford returning. In it were detectives Samuel Coppedge and Frank Wadley, who were responding to the shootings. Both were shot. Coppedge died instantly; Wadley, the next day.

On the night of May 28, Coppedge and Wadley had been instrumental in stopping a riot and keeping a mob from burning down black homes, wrote Southern Illinois University Professor Elliott M. Rudwick in his book, *Race Riot at East St. Louis, July 2, 1917*. A mob had roamed through downtown May 28 beating up blacks. The same day, union members had gathered downtown to protest the importation of nonunion blacks from the South to East St. Louis to take their jobs.

In the riot of July 2 and 3, witnesses saw whites shoot blacks, beat them, and even stone them with paving blocks. The mob set fire to black homes and then shot blacks as they fled the fire. The rioters included women—hence the *Republic*'s reference to Amazons. In the words of Hurd: "I saw man after man, with his hands raised pleading for his life, surrounded by groups of men . . . who knew nothing about him except that he was black—and saw them administer the historic sentence of intolerance, death by stoning. . . ."

Thousands of blacks managed to get across the two bridges into St. Louis, where city officials provided temporary shelter and food. In the aftermath, several trials were held in the county seat in Belleville, and a federal investigating committee conducted hearings in East St. Louis. Thirteen blacks were charged in the death of Coppedge, and ten were convicted of murder. They were sentenced to a minimum of fourteen years in prison. Two whites got identical sentences for their convictions in the death of an elderly black man.

Then Cook testified in the trial of the two men who killed her husband and son; only John Dow and Charles Hanna were actually on trial for the death of Charles Keyser, a white hardware merchant, who was shot by a stray bullet. In his book on the riot,

Never Been a Time, author Harper Barnes wrote, "The defendants were accused of causing the deaths of three people, not just one. But the prosecution chose to focus on the killing of Keyser almost certainly because he was white, unlike the other two victims, a black father and his black stepson, who were treated in the context of the trial as collateral damage."

The jury found both men guilty and sentenced them to fifteen years in prison. The same day, the House Select Committee began its hearings in a federal courtroom in East St. Louis. One of the ironies of the hearings took place on November 8, Barnes pointed out. Eleven black men testified that they had just arrived in East St. Louis from the South on the promise of two dollars a day plus board. They discovered that the pay was actually $1.40 a day—less than some had made in Jackson, Mississippi—and that the food was bread and molasses. They had to pay for comforters to sleep in a bare railroad car, and they were threatened with jail if they left. Less than four months after the riots, railroad agents were still exploiting blacks, the committee learned.

The committee had less than kind words for the railroads and the Aluminum Ore Company, one of the East Side's major employers. The companies "pitted white labor against black." They "stirred the fires of racial hatred until it finally culminated in bloody, pitiless riot, murder, and wanton arson."

The twenty-four–page report blamed politicians and city officials of both political parties for corruption and dishonesty; it alleged the National Guard leader, Colonel S. O. Tripp, was a "hopeless incompetent"; it stated the state's attorney was "devoid of character"; and it accused the majority of the police force of doing nothing to stop the assaults.

Long before the riot, the committee said, "Sodom and Gomorrah were model Christian communities in comparison."

ROBERT PRAGER LYNCHED AS GERMAN SPY
1918

The afternoon of June 17, 1918, was rainy, and the band of the Great Lakes Naval Training Center of North Chicago had to take shelter under the rotunda of the Madison County courthouse in Edwardsville. The orchestra was in town as a navy recruiting tool for the American effort in World War I, then raging in Europe. Many of those gathered outside the courthouse for the concert also retreated from the stormy weather. They asked the band if it could perform some numbers. The band began, as every military band before or since, with a rendition of "The Star Spangled Banner."

Also in the courthouse that afternoon was a jury of twelve men who had just heard closing arguments in a criminal trial. The jurors were sequestered within earshot of the patriotic band while awaiting final instructions from Judge Louis Bernreuter in the lynching of Robert Paul Prager. He had been accused by a mob of being un-American, disloyal to the war effort, and perhaps a German spy.

Also in the courthouse were eleven of Prager's alleged executioners. One of them, Joseph Riegel, a cobbler and coal miner, was considered a ringleader of the hanging crowd. He burst into tears, witnesses said, as the military band played on.

There was no one in the courtroom that day on Prager's behalf other than prosecutors trying to convict men they said were participants in the lynching two months earlier.

Prager was single and a native of Tresten, Germany. He came to the United States in 1905 and ended up in St. Louis, where he worked as a baker. When the country entered the war in 1917, Prager tried to enlist in the U.S. Navy, but his glass eye meant he couldn't pass the physical.

Prager moved to Collinsville, got a job on the night shift at Donk Brothers Coal Co., and applied for membership in the United Mine Workers. That move may have been a mistake. Wartime hysteria was at a peak, and the loyalty of labor unions had come under scrutiny.

President Woodrow Wilson had created the Committee on Public Information, and, in its zeal to find spies, it urged people to turn in anyone who was disloyal. Anti-German sentiment ran high. An East Alton retailer was beaten because he didn't close his shop during a Liberty Bond rally. In Christopher, Illinois, eighty miles from St. Louis, four men, including a Polish Catholic priest, were tarred and feathered. In St. Louis, Berlin Avenue ceased to exist; it became Pershing, after the American general leading U.S. troops in Europe. In Chicago, socialist leaders were arrested after allegedly subversive material was found in their headquarters.

The Industrial Workers of the World, a labor organization with socialist or communist tendencies, was also headquartered in Chicago. Its members were called "Wobblies." Prosecutors got a grand jury to issue a blanket indictment accusing 166 of its members of hampering the war effort.

Perhaps concerned about infiltration of their local in Collinsville, union officers Moses Johnson and James Farrero expressed suspicions about Prager and asked him to meet them on April 3 at the Madison County sheriff's office. That night, Prager attended a socialist meeting in Maryville. Some of those who were present later told the *Globe-Democrat* that Prager had given a speech disloyal to the country.

The next day, April 4, Prager protested his innocence in the form of a handbill he distributed throughout downtown Collinsville. To members of Local 1802, Prager wrote in that handbill, "In regard to my loyalty, I will state that I am at heart and soul for the good old USA. I am of German birth, which accident I cannot help." Prager added a strange postscript—Farrero could not prove he was a spy.

That night, a crowd—most of whom had been drinking in Collinsville bars—broke into his apartment on Vandalia Street and dragged him to Main Street. Prager was forcibly draped in an American flag, told to kiss it, and ordered to sing American songs. A motorcycle police officer intervened, grabbed Prager, and took him to city hall a block away. The crowd followed.

Mayor John H. Siegel first told the mob that Prager had been taken to East St. Louis. The rioters didn't believe him. Then he said, "We do not want a stigma marking Collinsville, and I implore you to go to your homes and discontinue this demonstration."

Siegel's admonition was partially successful. The rioters dissipated. They headed instead for the taverns. Siegel then closed the saloons at 10:15 p.m. in an effort to get people to go home. Instead, they went back to city hall, forced their way in, and found Prager hiding in the basement.

The mob dragged the immigrant two miles west on St. Louis Road to a hackberry tree atop Bluff Hill. Initially, a fifteen-year-old had been sent for tar. He returned without it. Some said he came back with a rope. Police officers had followed the mob to the hilltop. They said later that they had one purpose only—to make sure whatever happened would happen outside the city limits of Collinsville.

Joseph Riegel said Prager's hands were untied when the crowd tried to hang him the first time and he was able to use his hands to stay alive. He was let down and given a chance to write his parents in Germany and to pray. "I must, on this, the 4th day of April 1918, die. Please pray for me, my dearest parents. This is my last will and testament," wrote Prager in German. He addressed the letter to his father, Carl Henry Prager.

His momentary reprieve over, Prager was strung up again. He died about 12:30 a.m. on April 5 as the crowd watched. He was thirty years old. Prager was buried five days later at St. Mathew's Cemetery in St. Louis by the Odd Fellows, a group in which he was a member. His tombstone said, "The victim of a mob."

Reaction was swift. U.S. Senator Lawrence Sherman called Collinsville and East St. Louis—the scene of a race riot in 1917—"the Sodom and Gomorrah of Illinois." Illinois's reform governor, Frank Lowden, denounced the hanging: "Patriotism will not be permitted to be used as a cloak for crime in Illinois if I can help it. . . . What will it avail us for our soldiers to win victories abroad if self-government breaks down in our very midst?"

Lowden ordered the attorney general to prosecute if local authorities failed. It wasn't necessary. Madison County State's Attorney Joseph Streuber said he would arrest and prosecute the leaders, including Riegel, who had admitted extensive involvement in an interview with the *Post-Dispatch*.

The coroner's jury heard thirty-three witnesses; a grand jury met for two weeks and returned indictments against twelve. And four police officers were charged with misdemeanors for failing to prevent the hanging. Eleven of the twelve, and the four policemen, went on trial in May, a trial that lasted three weeks.

The defense attorneys were dismayed that Judge Bernreuter refused to allow them to refer to Prager as a traitor throughout the trial. Their defense was threefold: the men weren't there; or if they were there, they were mere onlookers at the edge of the crowd; or some unwritten code justified lynching Prager.

Since witnesses neither saw nor heard any evil—even Riegel recanted everything he had told the press—the *Edwardsville Intelligencer* summed up the jury's forty-five–minute verdicts of acquittal for the eleven men on felonies and the four cops on misdemeanors as "no great surprise to most of those who heard the evidence."

On the first ballot, the vote was eleven to one for not guilty; a few minutes later, it was twelve to zero, the newspaper reported. When the verdicts were read in court, "[T]here was wild applauding and cheers from most everyone present. Relatives, friends, and acquaintances rushed toward the bar to shake hands with the defendants."

As the defendants walked from the courthouse, the naval band was marching at the head of a group of recruits playing "Over There."

James O. Monroe, publisher of the hometown *Collinsville Herald*, wrote, "Outside of a few persons who may still harbor Germanic inclinations, the whole city is glad the eleven men indicted for the hanging of Robert P. Prager were acquitted." Of the victim, Monroe said the town "is well convinced that he was disloyal. . . . The city does not miss him." Like the newspapers in St. Louis when Francis McIntosh was burned at the stake in 1836, Monroe wished the whole episode would soon be forgotten.

Monroe's conclusion differed from the governor's. Lowden called the acquittals "a lamentable failure of justice." And Monroe's wish that the story would just go away has never come true. The lynching of the little German baker with the glass eye who tried to enlist in the Navy has been repeated over and over again whenever studies are done about patriotic paranoia. No other individual met the same fate as Robert Paul Prager during World War I.

THE MOB
1920s AND 1930s

The beginning of Prohibition in January 1920 led to bootlegging, lawlessness, and as many as sixty murders in the St. Louis area and southern Illinois over the next dozen years, but two of the six major gangs that participated in the gang slaughter actually predated the ban on booze.

EGAN'S RATS

One gang, Egan's Rats, could trace its ancestry to the 1890s, when Thomas "Snake" Kinney and Thomas Egan organized young hoodlums in Kerry Patch, the Irish enclave northwest of downtown, and used them as roughnecks and intimidators to win Democrat elections for the likes of Democrat boss Ed Butler and his Boodlers.

By 1904, they were the most powerful street gang in the city. Kinney was Egan's brother-in-law, a ward committeeman, and later a state senator. The gang showed its muscle in an attack inside the city courthouse on June 7, 1909. They couldn't wait for a jury verdict. Gang members walked into the building and gunned down Fred "Yellow Kid" Mohrle, who was on trial for the murder of Egan's Rat Sam Young. The Egan gang could count on as many as three to four hundred men between 1913 and 1916 in a war with a rival group, the Bottoms Gang.

Tom Egan died of natural causes in 1919 at the age of forty-five, and brother William T. "Willie" Egan took control until he was fatally shot outside his tavern at Fourteenth and Franklin streets on October 31, 1921.

HOGAN GANG

Willie Egan's death was already the second round in a war with a gang under the command of Edward J. "Jellyroll" Hogan. His forces were rivals of Egan's Rats in the growing field of bootleg liquor. The first round in the battle had been an attack by Egan's Rats on gangster Max Greenberg, who told Willie Egan that a shipload of illegal booze had been lost in a New Orleans barge accident. Egan knew Greenberg was lying and ordered his death. Greenberg, who had switched allegiance to the Hogan gang, survived the downtown shooting on March 11, 1921.

The Hogans were held responsible for Willie Egan's death seven months later. New Rats leader William "Dinty" Colbeck alleged the Hogan gang had paid three men ten thousand dollars each to kill Egan.

In the ensuing shootouts, twenty-three died, Hogan's home on Cass Avenue was shot up, and the gangs even exchanged gunfire in a running battle down Lindell Boulevard. That flareup brought a public outcry and a suggestion by Colbeck publicly that the gangs—at least his gang—would be more careful regarding innocent bystanders. "We are not insensitive to the fact that the public is aroused over what the newspapers have consistently characterized as the violence attending the fights between the Hogan and Egan factions."

The Egans got the better of the battles; Jellyroll retired as head of the clan and ran for public office, and the Hogan gang was no longer a major player in gangdom.

The Rats turned their attention to robberies as well as booze. Between 1919 and 1924, the Rats were credited with stealing as much as $2.5 million. Among the bigger stickups: Granite City National Bank on April 24, 1924, for sixty-three thousand dollars; the Baden Bank of St. Louis on April 10, 1919, for fifty-nine thousand dollars; and the Wellston Trust Company on September 19, 1924, for forty thousand dollars.

An armed robbery of a mail truck in Staunton, Illinois, led to the downfall of the Rats, when gang member Ray Renard turned state's evidence in federal court. Colbeck and nine members of his gang were convicted on November 15, 1924. They got sentences of twenty-five years each in the federal penitentiary. Renard went on to a colorful career as a consultant on gangster movies.

THE GREEN ONES

Like Egan's Rats, the Green Ones predated Prohibition. According to Gary R. Mormino in his book, *Immigrants on the Hill*, the gang's roots can be traced to the arrival in 1910 from Sicily of James Cipolla, Vito Giannola, and Alfonso Palazzollo. They began terrorizing small businessmen in Little Italy—just east of the Irish Kerry Patch—and on the Hill. The gang added bootlegging to its other rackets in the 1920s. The Green Ones, a close-knit organization of Sicilian Americans, had their own St. Louis war in the 1920s. Their opponent gave other nationalities membership in its gang.

THE CUCKOOS

The first reference to this gang showed up in a small *Post-Dispatch* story in 1920, according to Walter M. Fontane in his article, "The Rise and Fall of the Cuckoo Gang," in the Missouri Historical Society's *Gateway*. The *Post* article merely mentions the arrest of five Cuckoos in a jewelry robbery. The gang apparently moved up quickly in the public consciousness. By 1922, the murder of John Pawic prompted a major headline in the *Globe-Democrat*: "Cuckoo Gangster Slain."

Its leaders included Ray Stevenson, a bootlegger who brought booze from New Orleans to St. Louis and also operated stills on the East Side, along with Roy and Herman Tipton.

Like the Rats, the Cuckoos were also into robberies. One aborted attempt on June 10, 1923, of the Telegraph Inn on Telegraph Road in south St. Louis County led to the murder of Edward Griffin, an off-duty St. Louis police officer who had recognized gang members, and John Surgent, former owner of the tavern. One of the gang members, like the Rats' Renard, caved in to authorities and identified the killers and robbers. Three Cuckoos got life sentences; another got twenty years; and another, fifteen years in prison. A sixth member of the gang never spent a day in prison. Tony Massud died in a gun battle with Illinois state police.

In 1926, during the Cuckoo–Green One war, six gangsters burst into the Submarine Bar at Fourteenth and Locust streets and killed its owner and two others. Others were wounded in the shooting. None of the victims were Green Ones, who were the intended targets.

The Green Ones retaliated, but their firepower was no match for the Cuckoos' young guns. Fontane noted that the Green Ones' leader, Vito Giannola, took part in an ambush of Herman Tipton and another Cuckoo, but both escaped, and Giannola was shot in the arm by one of his own men.

Besides the Cuckoos, the Green Ones also had to contend with the Russo Gang or the American Boys, "so named because their members were native-born Italian Americans. They were also fighting a group of disgruntled Green Ones known as the Santino gang," wrote Robbi Courtaway in her exhaustive study of the Prohibition era in Missouri and Illinois, *Wetter Than the Mississippi*. Vito Giannola was later one of the victims of the wars, gunned down by the Russo faction in late 1927.

While the Green Ones and the Cuckoos were fighting for control of the rackets in St. Louis, two gangs were battling it out in southern Illinois.

THE SHELTON GANG

Founded by Carl, Bernie, and Earl Shelton, the gang in the coal fields of southern Illinois was described by the *Saturday Evening Post* in 1950 as "America's Bloodiest Gang." The gang ran a major bootlegging operation during Prohibition from East St. Louis to Cairo.

Its initial war dealt not with a rival gang but with the rise and heavy-handed tactics of a rejuvenated Ku Klux Klan, determined to rid the Bible Belt area of Illinois of booze, gangs, Catholics, Jews, unions, and blacks—in no particular order. The Klan, like the gangs it sought to suppress, was a law unto itself.

The Sheltons were not alone in a war for survival against the Klan.

THE CHARLIE BIRGER GANG

Born Shachna Itzik Birger of Jewish parents in Lithuania, Charlie Birger grew up in St. Louis and Glen Carbon, served a stint in the U.S. Army, and returned to the area to work in coal mines and to open a saloon.

Prohibition gave Birger his start as a bootlegger, and his gang teamed with the Sheltons to go to war against the Klan. The Klan's leader, S. Glenn Young, died in a shootout with a deputy sheriff in Herrin in 1925, and fifteen thousand people turned out for his funeral. A year later, Shelton and Birger gunmen, with Thompson submachine guns, joined forces to battle the Klan in Herrin. By the end of 1926, the Klan was inactive, and the Sheltons and the Birgers were at war over the spoils of bootlegging. Both gangs converted plated cars and turned them into tanks. Ambushes along isolated country roads were common. Both sides claimed alliances with local politicians and law enforcement officials.

Taylor Pensoneau, in his book, *Brothers Notorious: The Sheltons*, provided this picture: "Murder and terrorism were like runaway freight trains in the bottom region of Illinois in the days before Thanksgiving of 1926. Law and order, where the feuding gangsters were concerned, had taken another hiatus. The Shelton and Birger gangs were the law in Williamson County and the surrounding area, and either outfit, if it so pleased, could take control of any number of communities—subject only to interference by the other gang."

West City was one such community. The mayor, Joe Adams, was a Shelton ally and had allowed the Sheltons to house their armored car in his garage. The Sheltons themselves moved their headquarters frequently, from East St. Louis to Fairfield east of Mount Vernon and to Wayne County farms.

Birger, meanwhile, had set up his headquarters at Shady Rest, an abandoned tourist stop on Highway 13 near Crab Orchard Lake in Williamson County. From a gathering place for visiting gangsters, Birger had converted it into a fortress with the barbeque stand at the entrance serving as a twenty-four–hour guard post.

In November 1926, Birger burned Adams's garage, where the armored car was housed. The next month, two men fatally shot the mayor at his front door. Then, in January 1927, Shady Rest blew up and burned down. The Sheltons were accused of the deed, although Birger may have burned down the premises himself. Birger later accused a crooked state trooper of helping the Sheltons to plot an attack on Shady Rest, then he murdered the officer and his wife.

In January and February 1927, the Shelton brothers went on trial in Quincy for a holdup of a mail truck in Collinsville in 1925 in which fifteen thousand dollars in deposits for the Federal Reserve Bank was stolen. Birger was a key witness against his rivals. So, too, were another gangster and a cab driver. All of them said the brothers had plotted and carried out the heist. A jury convicted the trio. A federal judge sentenced the Sheltons to twenty-five years in prison. But the cab driver, in a subsequent interview with a *Post-Dispatch* reporter, admitted he had been forced to lie at the trial by the Birger gang. Suddenly, the Sheltons were out of the Leavenworth penitentiary when the same judge threw out their convictions.

Meanwhile, Birger's date with the law had come. He was arrested for ordering the hit on Adams, convicted of murder, and sentenced to die by hanging—the last public hanging in Illinois—on April 19, 1928.

The Shelton brothers remained the target of law enforcement. They were tried in Taylorville, Illinois, and convicted on January 7, 1928, of a bank holdup in Kinkaid, Illinois, that had taken place four years earlier. Again, their luck held. The Illinois Supreme Court reversed the convictions in October 1928 on the grounds the evidence wasn't strong enough to tie the Sheltons to the bank robbery and shootout.

The Sheltons next moved to recover territory lost to the Cuckoo gang in St. Clair County during the Klan and Birger wars. They used a Cuckoo insider, Tommy Hayes, to wage a civil war against Cuckoo leader Herman Tipton. Hayes succeeded in engineering the war that left several dead on both sides and led to Hayes's own demise in 1932. Hayes's bodyguards in one car were killed when their car was ambushed, and Hayes sped away in a second car. Near Madison, passengers in Hayes's car shot him. Still alive, he crashed the car, got out, and ran. His betrayers followed and finished the job. The execution, experts said, had been arranged by Carl Shelton.

With bootlegging coming to an end in 1933 with the lifting of Prohibition, the Shelton gang in Illinois shifted to racketeering, union infiltration, and gambling during the 1930s. One of their former members, Frank "Buster" Wortman, would successfully challenge them for gang supremacy a decade later.

In St. Louis, the Green Ones and their descendants—aligned with Detroit and Kansas City—would control gambling and racketeering for decades. Remnants of the Cuckoos and the Irish gangs would work for and with the Mafia, particularly in union infiltration, until a gang war broke out in the 1980s.

SHADY REST BOMBING RUN, 1926

Members of the Charlie Birger gang watched the World War I vintage aircraft circle slowly over their compound called Shady Rest on Highway 13 near Crab Orchard Lake in Williamson County. As the plane dipped over them, a package came flying out of the open back cockpit and headed for the property below.

It was a bomb. It was also a dud.

Birger gangsters grabbed their Tommy guns and sent round after round of bullets into the sky as the plane made two more passes over Shady Rest. The second bomb exploded, but no one was injured; the third bomb was also a dud.

Neither the pilot, Elmer Kane, nor the passenger and bombadier, believed to be Shelton gang lieutenant Ray Walker, were injured by the machine gun blasts from below, and Kane navigated the Curtiss Jenny to an airport in DuQuoin to drop off Walker and then flew to another airport, where he met fellow barnstormer Henry Mundale.

In his book *Brothers Notorious*, author Taylor Pensoneau described the run over Shady Rest on November 12, 1926: "Not just a likely first in gang warfare, Kane's sortie may have been the initial civilian bombing raid in the United States."

Kane and Mundale had flown into the Benton airport the day before and were taken to nearby West City and the homes of Mayor Joe Adams and his brother, Gus. They also met the Sheltons, Carl and Bernie, who asked them to bomb Shady Rest and the Birger gang, with whom they were at war. They agreed out of fear for their lives, a thousand dollars, and a car. They watched the gang put together a bomb of dynamite, copper wire, and nitroglycerin. They also ducked for cover in the early hours of November 12 as Birger gunmen drove by and sprayed Gus Adams's house with bullets.

Because there was no room for Mundale in the two-seater, he agreed to meet Kane later. Kane got the thousand dollars; Mundale,

Charlie Birger (center, with vest) and his gang at Shady Rest

the car, which turned out to be stolen.

Pensoneau says local accounts differ on what damage the second bomb caused. Some said it landed in some trees and started a small fire; others said it hit a coop that the Birgers had used for cock- and dog-fighting, killing an eagle and a bulldog.

HONEST UNION LEADER MURDERED BY THE MOB, 1932

Early in the evening of August 10, 1932, a dark sedan crawled east down the 500 block of St. Louis Avenue in East St. Louis and paused when it reached 506. A fusillade of gunshots erupted from the passenger-side window at a man standing next to a parked car. The man was hit twenty-seven times. Two men inside the parked car suffered minor wounds, and two others had ducked quickly and were unharmed. Eleven bullets had hit the car.

Oliver Alden Moore, president of the East St. Louis Central Trades Council and business manager of the boilermakers local, was dead, gunned down outside his union offices. Just forty-five minutes earlier and a short distance away, Moore had given an interview to Carl Baldwin, a reporter with the *St. Louis Post-Dispatch*. Surrounded by bodyguards as he talked to Baldwin, Moore told the reporter, "Sure, I've been threatened. The Shelton gang hasn't been making money out of bootlegging lately. They're trying to make a racket out of labor in East St. Louis." Moore said Carl Shelton had offered him thirty thousand dollars if he would quit the labor movement and leave town. "I turned him down."

"Word has reached me that the Shelton gang is out to get me, that they've imported six carloads of red-hots from Peoria to bump me off. Well, let them try it. They can't intimidate East St. Louis labor."

Moore had planned to meet the next day with an assistant state's attorney to tell him about the meeting with Carl Shelton, head of the East Side gang bearing his name, and what appeared to be both a threat and an attempted bribe. Moore never got to the meeting.

The Sheltons had been hired by Phillips Petroleum as security in its nearly two-year dispute with organized labor over the construction of a $1.5 million pipeline and a terminal just south of East St. Louis. Triggering the labor dispute was a decision by Phillips to subcontract the construction of twenty-four enormous storage tanks to the Chicago Bridge and Iron Company. That company brought in four hundred men from around the country while Depression-ravaged local union workers were unemployed. Several confrontations followed. The outstaters were housed in St. Louis and ferried across the river. Two Phillips service stations in East St. Louis were blown up.

So the company had turned to the muscle of the Mob. The day before Moore died, police had stopped a car in which Carl Shelton and a Phillips watchman were riding and found a pair of

.45-caliber revolvers on the floor. Each said the other owned the weapons. Monroe "Blackie" Armes, a gunman used by the Sheltons in prior gang wars, was also stopped. Police found a submachine gun and a shotgun in his car. He said he was out squirrel hunting.

After Moore's death, a veteran police officer examined the victim's wounds and the close cropping of the shots. "Only one man around here could hold a tommy-gun that steady from a moving automobile," he said. "This was a Blackie Armes job."

The next day, as six hundred union members and mourners marched in Moore's funeral—he was thirty-seven and survived by a wife and two sons, eleven and seven—Phillips Petroleum Company officials, shocked at Moore's death, offered their deepest regrets.

Moore had told Baldwin that the confrontations with Phillips had gone beyond a normal labor dispute. He said four factors were at play: Phillips's tactics; the sheriff's department, which was protecting the unions; the city police department, which had been sitting on the sidelines; and the efforts by the Sheltons to take over unions and to control law enforcement.

Moore's murder fell within the jurisdiction of the East St. Louis Police Department. Its chief, James Leahy, was asked if Carl Shelton was a suspect. "I called Carl. Carl said he didn't do it," was Leahy's answer. No one was ever convicted of the murder.

In an article in 1958 about the labor war and Moore's death, Baldwin wrote, "The lesson of the Ollie Moore case is one all legitimate businessmen should have learned by now. It is. You cannot do business with a professional gangster without sharing his reputation. If he has blood on his hands, some of it may come off on you."

GUNS FOR HIRE

On December 14, 1929, in St. Joseph, Michigan, patrolman Charles Skelly tried to stop a hit-and-run driver and was fatally shot. The shooter's car crashed into a telephone pole, though, and the assailant fled on foot. In the car, police found the name "Fred Dane." That alias led them to a house in St. Joseph where they found $319,830 in stolen bonds and a cache of weapons, including two Thompson submachine guns. They also found shirts with the initials "FRB."

Wanted for murders in Ohio and New York was a man police called the most dangerous in the country. His name? Fred R. Burke. His nickname: "Killer." The two Tommy guns were hand-delivered to Northwestern University's crime laboratory in Evanston, Illinois. Its director, former New York major Calvin H. Goddard, was the foremost expert in the new field of forensic ballistics. He fired the weapons and compared the shells to bullets retrieved from seven Chicago victims. Both weapons were matches, he determined. The bullets, Goddard determined, also matched bullets retrieved from the body of Frankie Yale, a New York crime boss gunned down in 1927.

Fred "Killer" Burke had just become a suspect in the most publicized murder in the annals of organized crime—Chicago's St. Valentine's Day Massacre of February 14, 1929. Five men, two wearing police uniforms, walked into a warehouse at 2122 Clark Street, north of the Loop, and gunned down seven members of the George "Bugs" Moran gang. The hits were believed to be the work of "Outfit" boss Al Capone, who was conveniently vacationing in Florida and thus had an alibi. The victims had gone to the warehouse to unload illegal booze; Moran himself was also supposed to be there, but he was late.

Even before Michigan, Burke had already become one of the prime suspects in the shooting. Burke had used a fake police uniform approach in prior bank robberies. Also, a witness described the driver of what police believed to be the getaway car as missing an upper front tooth, and Burke, too, was minus an incisor.

Authorities finally caught up with Burke on March 26, 1931, in Missouri. He was living in a farmhouse in Sullivan County, outside of St. Joseph. Police and sheriff's deputies awakened him and put him in handcuffs before he could react. He pleaded guilty in the death of the Michigan police officer in April 1931, was sentenced to life in prison, and died in a Michigan cell block nine years later.

Burke was never tried for the St. Valentine's Day Massacre or for other murders in Ohio, Michigan, and New York.

Burke's ties to St. Louis?

Burke had been an Egan's Rat in St. Louis for a decade before the demise of that gang's leaders, and he converted his murderous talents as a gun for hire, working for mobsters in Detroit before hooking up with Capone. He had his own crew of former Rats: Gus Winkler, Bob Carey, and Ray Nugent. They, too, have been mentioned in a long list of suspects in the Chicago attack on the Moran gang. But Burke was the only suspect ever linked officially to the St. Valentine's Day Massacre, wrote John Kobler in his biography *Capone*.

Burke and his crew may have been the most notorious, but other hoodlums from St. Louis tried to make a name for themselves elsewhere. In her book on Prohibition, *Wetter Than the Mississippi*, author Robbi Courtaway said Russo gang or American Boys leader Anthony "Shorty" Russo, along with Vincent Spicuzza, were lured to Chicago for a bootlegging foray; there, two gangsters hired by the rival Green Ones of St. Louis gunned them down on August 9, 1927. A farmer found their bodies along a rural road. The trademark of a St. Louis hatter led to their identification, and Chicago police "recalled the presence recently here of two strange Italians who posed as prizefighters," the *Globe-Democrat* reported. Police also found a railroad receipt for St. Louis to Chicago dated August 6.

In *Capone*, Kobler wrote that the pair had been hired by a Chicago Italian faction offering fifty thousand dollars to anyone who would kill Capone. Obviously, Russo and Spicuzza failed under either theory. Capone allegedly sent ten thousand dollars in flowers to their St. Louis funerals.

More successful in execution but lacking in brain power for its *modus operandi* was the murder of *Chicago Tribune* crime reporter Jake Lingle in a Chicago subway before dozens of witnesses. Performing the murder on June 9, 1930, was Leo Vincent Brothers, another Egan's Rat on loan to Chicago gangsters.

Brothers had been a fugitive from St. Louis, where he had been involved in labor racketeering, arson, robbery, and murder. At his 1931 trial for Lingle's murder, a jury recommended fourteen years in prison—even though the state had sought the death penalty. That meant he would be released in eight years with good behavior. "I can do that standing on my head," Brothers was quoted as saying.

The St. Louis connection didn't end there, though. After the *Chicago Tribune* declared war on the Mob over the death of Lingle, *St. Louis Post-Dispatch* reporter John T. Rogers embarrassed the *Trib* by exposing Lingle as corrupt—a fixer and gambler with a pipeline to Capone. Then, *St. Louis Star* reporter Harry Brundidge investigated other Chicago newspapers and their staffs and found a half-dozen with ties to organized crime.

JACK DANIEL HEIR ACQUITTED OF MURDER
1924

After a bond hearing on March 20, 1924, a *St. Louis Star* reporter wrote that Lemuel Motlow, the heir to the Jack Daniel's Tennessee Whiskey Company, "was a pitiful sight when he walked out of the courtroom in East St. Louis."

"Unshaven since his arrest Monday night (for the murder of train conductor C. H. Pullis), there was nothing about the usually quiet and inoffensive man to indicate the wealth which permitted him to have a corps of expensive lawyers, some of them coming all the way from Lynchburg, Tennessee, to defend him," the *Star* reported.

Motlow claimed he didn't remember what happened on March 17. "Why, I wouldn't hurt a child," the *Star* quoted Motlow. "If I shot Pullis as they say I did, I don't know how it happened. He was one of my best friends, and I have known him for years. My mind is a blank. I have no memory at all. I haven't shot or hurt anyone as far as I know."

It was clear what happened in the mind of Ed Wallace. He was an African American porter on Train No. 53 of the Louisville and Nashville Railroad that Motlow boarded at Union Station. Motlow, a frequent commuter between Lynchburg and St. Louis, was on his way home to Tennessee.

At a coroner's inquest the same day that Motlow walked out of the East St. Louis courtroom on bond for thirty-five thousand dollars, Wallace testified that Motlow's language on March 17, St. Patrick's Day, had been too boisterous, "and his ideas of sleeping car proprieties were not in accordance with common decencies," the *Globe-Democrat* said. Wallace (the *Star*'s spelling) or Wallis (the *Globe*'s version) learned that Motlow had no ticket and asked him to debark and get one. He refused. Motlow was "pugnacious and quarrelsome, loud in his talk and belligerent in his threats," the *Globe* said. Motlow ordered Wallace to remake his bed so he wouldn't have to face backwards and then tipped the porter a quarter.

Motlow also argued with Pullis, the conductor, and his language was exceptionally profane, Wallace said. Motlow struck Wallace. Pullis suggested to Wallace that they put Motlow to bed, an idea the passenger resented. Suddenly, shots were fired. Pullis was hit in the stomach; a second shot passed through Wallace's coat and may or may not have wounded Wallace in the arm. Accounts of the second shot varied.

Joseph Broida, a St. Louis merchant, rushed into the sleeper car after he heard the shots. The shooting had taken place as the train was about to enter the Terminal Railroad tunnel at Eighth Street in St. Louis. As the train crossed the Eads Bridge, Broida helped Wallace disarm Motlow, he told the inquest jurors, and tended to the wounded conductor. In East St. Louis, Pullis was rushed to St. Mary's Hospital, where he died. Police officer James Garvey testified that he found a Smith & Wesson .22-caliber revolver on a seat next to Motlow.

The coroner's jury found probable cause on March 20 to charge Motlow with murder. That afternoon, the *Star* reporter described Motlow's appearance at the bond hearing as "a typical mountaineer, tall, rawboned with drooping mustache and a heavy shock of black hair streaked with gray." One of Motlow's sons told the newspaper that his father wanted someone to "send word" to Pullis's widow "that he didn't know he shot Pullis and he was sorry that he did not shoot himself instead."

The owner of a mill in Union City, Tennessee, and a farm in Lynchburg, where he raised livestock, including mules he bought in Missouri and resold in Tennessee, Motlow had been a member of the St. Louis Merchants' Exchange for thirty years. His friends here, however, told the *Star* that they knew little of his "one bad habit, getting on a periodic spree."

The *Globe* alleged that Pullis was shot by Motlow because the conductor "had dared to resent his rowdy tactics induced by overindulgence in intoxicants."

Prosecutors in both St. Louis and St. Clair County decided that they would try Motlow for murder. In the legal skirmish over jurisdiction—Pullis was shot in Missouri, but died in Illinois—St. Louis Circuit Attorney Howard Sidener won out. He got a grand jury to indict Motlow for murder and sought the death penalty—even though there was no evidence Pullis's death was the result of any premeditation.

Motlow was the nephew of Jasper Newton "Jack" Daniel, who founded the whiskey company in Lynchburg and turned it over to Motlow to run in 1907. In 1910, Tennessee went dry, and Motlow opened distilleries in St. Louis and Birmingham. When Alabama went dry a few years later, St. Louis became the hub for the bonded whiskey until January 16, 1920, when the whole country went dry.

By 1923, bootlegging had become part of the national pastime, and St. Louis was no exception. A target of the bootleggers here was a bonded warehouse the Jack Daniel's Distillery owned at 3960 Duncan Avenue and the 861 barrels of whiskey it contained. That summer, the whiskey was drained from the barrels and replaced with water.

On the same day in 1924 that Motlow made bond on the murder charge, the *Globe* reported that a federal grand jury was investigating the missing liquor. Sale of the stolen whiskey at bootleg prices may have brought as much as $1 million in profits to the thieves, the newspaper speculated. In January 1924, Motlow and his wife consented to a federal lien against the warehouse so taxes on the missing whiskey would be paid eventually by someone. Problems like that could drive a person to drink.

Motlow went on trial in the train shooting later in 1924, with a bevy of Tennessee and St. Louis lawyers putting on a twofold defense. Character witnesses would vouch for Motlow on the one hand, and the lawyers would play the race card, blaming Wallace, the black porter. One of the character witnesses testifying for Motlow in St. Louis was the governor of Tennessee, Austin Peay.

Nashville attorney Frank Bond and St. Louis lawyer Patrick Henry Cullen crossed over the line of even common decency in their denunciation of Wallace, whom they alleged had attacked the defendant, and Motlow had then shot Pullis accidentally. "There are two classes of Negroes in this country. One is the kind that knows its place," said Bond in closing arguments. "These are the Negroes we love, care for, and protect. For these Negroes we are ready to don our helmets and our breastplates and go forth to battle. The other class demands racial and social equality. They want to intermarry with your daughters and mine. They shall not do it. They shall not."

Then Bond predicted class warfare: "When the inevitable conflict comes, we white men will stand together as one and stamp out this evil. This Negro is one of these Negro uplifters. He tells you he belongs to several uplift societies. He was insolent to Motlow because he thought Motlow was poor white trash because Motlow had on an old suit, was minus a necktie, and had no baggage. The human heart is not disclosed by raiment. The depth of the human soul is not gauged or measured by fine fabrics."

Cullen noted that Wallace had filed a personal injury suit against the defendant and argued that, if Wallace won, millionaire Motlow, his wife, and children would somehow go broke. Of Wallace, Cullen added, "And there he will stand, all swelled up with his wealth."

Sidener, the prosecutor, put on a key witness, the Reverend Clinton Cromwell. An Episcopalian minister, Cromwell was in his berth. Just before the shots, he heard Motlow say, "No damn Negro can tell me what to do." Cromwell said he saw Motlow put his hand to his side and pull out a gun. Cromwell heard the shots and Pullis say, "Oh, I am shot." Under cross examination, however, Cromwell admitted he was riding on the train under a false name because he was using a friend's railroad pass.

The jury returned its verdict quickly: not guilty. Motlow turned to his wife and said, "Mother, I guess we can go home."

The jury foreman, Frederick Smith, told the press that jurors believed Wallace had attacked Motlow and Motlow was shooting at Wallace but shot Pullis instead. "Some of us believed Motlow was drunk, and some didn't," said Smith. "A man has just as much right to defend himself when he is drunk as sober."

If all the jurors felt that way, Sidener said later, "It is simply a case of the jury trying to excuse itself for being instrumental in a miscarriage of justice." Sidener said he was unaware before the trial that Cromwell had been traveling under an assumed name, and the testimony hurt the state's case.

In the whiskey theft, Motlow was eventually indicted, but the charge was later thrown out. Back in Tennessee, his Missouri problems behind him, Motlow was elected a judge and later a state senator. In that capacity, he helped Tennessee go wet in 1938. That state had stayed dry when Prohibition ended in 1933.

Lemuel Motlow died in 1947, and his five children took over the company until its sale to Brown-Forman in 1956. His name still appears on the Jack Daniel bottle as "Lem Motlow, Proprietor."

PRETTY BOY FLOYD
1925

When a suspicious deputy sheriff stopped Charles Arthur "Pretty Boy" Floyd and sidekick, Fred Hildebrand, in eastern Oklahoma in September 1925, Hildebrand had cash still in the wrappers of Tower Grove Bank of St. Louis. In all, the deputy found $1,750 in Hildebrand's possession.

Call it a clue. So, too, were the brand-new Studebakers that both Floyd and Hildebrand were driving—and the new clothes they were wearing. The deputy knew the farm boys had left Sallisaw, Oklahoma, about six weeks earlier with virtually nothing to their names.

Floyd and Hildebrand went to jail and then to St. Louis in shackles, accused of a payroll robbery of Kroger grocery headquarters. Floyd was twenty-one; Hildebrand, nineteen. The pair had hopped freights in August to St. Louis, had robbed neighborhood grocers, and had first camped and then found living quarters in Meramec Highlands, a falling-down resort at what is now the western edge of Kirkwood. Their landlord was Joe Hlavaty. Hildebrand checked out Kroger's headquarters and discovered that the payroll was disbursed on Fridays.

On September 11, Floyd, Hildebrand, and Hlavaty walked into second-floor offices of Kroger headquarters on Tiffany Street, west of Grand Boulevard, announced a holdup with a sawed-off shotgun and pistols, and stuffed cash into a bag before running down the stairs and out the front door. A Kroger delivery van driver saw them and gave chase as the trio jumped into a Cadillac they had stolen earlier in the West End.

With the Kroger employee, Louis Vazia, in pursuit, Floyd drove through Tower Grove Park, west on Arsenal Street, southwest on Watson Road, and west again on Scanlan Street to Hlavaty's car.

Then Floyd went one way; Hlavaty, the other. Vazia, meanwhile, picked up a traffic-directing police officer and followed Hlavaty, with the patrolman firing shots out the passenger window. Hlavaty's car went off the road near what is now McCausland Avenue and Interstate 44. As the police officer got out of the van, Floyd barreled down the street in the Cadillac with Hildebrand shooting. Neither Vazia nor the officer nor the trio of robbers were shot.

Vazia's van stalled. The robbers in two cars headed west. Police later found the Cadillac in Webster Groves. At the Highlands, the men divided equally what turned out to be nearly twelve thousand dollars from the holdup. Floyd and Hildebrand were soon on a train to Oklahoma to buy their Studebakers, and Hlavaty had buried his share in Meramec River woods.

In St. Louis after the arrests, Hildebrand identified Hlavaty, and about twenty-three hundred dollars of his buried cache was recovered. Floyd had already picked up in St. Louis the nickname "Pretty Boy," which he allegedly hated. He pleaded guilty of first-degree robbery and on December 18, 1925, arrived at the Missouri State Penitentiary, where he served three years and three months of a five-year sentence.

Soon after his release from the Missouri prison in 1929, Floyd began his spree of bank robberies throughout several states and gradually rose in the rankings of the FBI's most dangerous criminals, until he hit the top with the deadly shootout at Kansas City's Union Station on June 17, 1933. According to the FBI, Floyd, Vernon Miller, and Adam Richetti had planned to free Frank "Jelly" Nash, a bank robber and murderer. Nash was being returned to the federal prison in Leavenworth, Kansas, from which he had escaped in October 1930. He was caught in Hot Springs, Arkansas.

In the ambush outside the station—called the Kansas City Massacre—two

PRETTY BOY FLOYD

Kansas City police detectives, an FBI agent, and a police chief from Oklahoma City were gunned down. Nevertheless, the plan to free Nash failed. He, too, was killed.

The body of Miller was soon found in Michigan. He had been killed by crime figures from New Jersey, the FBI said. The manhunt for "Pretty Boy" Floyd, now Public Enemy No. 1, led to Wellsville, Ohio, where Police Chief J. H. Fultz caught Richetti and wounded Floyd, who escaped. Richetti was executed in Missouri's gas chamber in 1938.

For help in getting Floyd, Fultz called upon Melvin Purvis, Chicago's FBI chief, who had caught bank robber John Dillinger. Purvis and a bevy of FBI agents caught up with Floyd in East Liverpool, Ohio, near the Ohio, Pennsylvania, and West Virginia border, and shot the bandit on October 22, 1934. According to legend, Purvis asked the dying Floyd, "Are you Pretty Boy Floyd?"

"I'm Charles Arthur Floyd," the outlaw said, his last words.

In his biography, *Pretty Boy: The Life and Times of Charles Arthur Floyd*, and in an interview about the book with the *Post-Dispatch*'s Harper Barnes in 1992, St. Louis–born author Michael Wallis says he was convinced that Floyd was telling the truth when the bandit denied any involvement in the Kansas City shootout. Wallis said eyewitnesses gave authorities descriptions that didn't match Floyd. Wallis said Floyd also got blamed for far more bank robberies than he actually committed.

Floyd was a murderer and a robber. His legend was fixed for all time when he became the subject in 1939 of a ballad by folk singer Woody Guthrie:

> If you gather 'round me, children, a story I will tell,
> 'Bout Pretty Boy Floyd, an outlaw. Oklahoma knew him well.

BERTHA GIFFORD, POISONER
1928

At least nine people died in her small home in Catawissa in Franklin County, but no one believed that any foul play could have been involved—not from Bertha Gifford, the kindly, pleasant fifty-six-year-old farmer's wife. She was a woman who helped tend to the sick. She also cooked some of the best meals around those parts.

Gifford had some idiosyncrasies that, in hindsight, may have seemed suspicious. She seemed preoccupied with stories about violence or death, and she always seemed to show up when someone got sick and offer her help.

On November 19, 1928, Gifford walked from her top-tier cell at the Franklin County jail to the courthouse in Union, where more than a thousand people had gathered, packing the courtroom and its hallways and spilling out onto the downtown square. The *Post-Dispatch* reported, "She sits slumped in her chair, but there is no despondency in her attitude. Her hair is black and bobbed with a trace of permanent waving. She is neat in her black coat, not a dowdy farmer wife. . . . Heavily lidded eyes watch the witnesses as they testify against her, persons she has known for years." When she was arrested, neighbors described Gifford to reporters as "a tireless attender of funerals, a visitor of sick persons and a connoisseur of stories dealing with violence, illness, and blood," the newspaper reported.

How many people did Gifford poison? Nine people had died in her home on Bend Road in Catawissa. She was charged with three murders. But some put the death count at eighteen or nineteen.

Gifford was described as a very attractive woman when she married Gene Gifford, a farmer, and moved to Franklin County from Jefferson County. Before that, she had run a hotel near Hillsboro, and her first husband had died under mysterious circumstances.

In an interview with the *Post-Dispatch*'s Bill Smith in 1993, Frank Withington, of Pacific, recalled the woman who treated him kindly and often served him meals as a child. He said Gifford bought the arsenic she used to kill people from a man he identified as "old Doc Powers." "Arsenic to kill rats in her chicken house, she claimed. But that old Doc shouldn't have sold all that arsenic to her," Withington said. "She didn't have that many rats. Well, I think old Doc Powers had a suspicion. A lot of people had a suspicion."

Nothing happened until Edward Brinley died. He was a drinker and suffered a fall in front of the Gifford house. As with so many others before Brinley, Gifford took on the task of nursing him back to health. She fed him stewed tomatoes and lemonade. Brinley died.

Elmer Schamel, seven, died at the Gifford house before Brinley. Six weeks earlier, his older brother, Lloyd, nine, had also died in Gifford's care. Gifford had been helping to care for the boys because their mother had died two months before Lloyd. The string of fatalities was enough to bring in Franklin County authorities, who exhumed all three bodies, discovered organs of all three victims were laced with arsenic, and arrested Gifford. She and her husband, Gene, had moved to Eureka from Catawissa after Brinley's death and the talk and rumors about Bertha's ministering had spread.

Upon her arrest, Gifford said she had given arsenic to all three patients of hers because she wanted to help them. Neighbors began to recall others who had been treated by the sympathetic farm wife. They ranged in age from Bernard Stuhlfelder, who was fifteen months old, to Birdie Unnerstall, who was seventy-two. Others in her care who died included James Gifford, her thirteen-year-old brother-in-law and Withington's childhood friend; her husband's uncle, Sherman Pounds, fifty-three; and the family's hired hand, James Ogle, also fifty-three.

It didn't take much at Gifford's trial for the prosecutor to decide that Gifford suffered from a mental illness. She had confessed to poisoning Brinley and the Schamel boys. A month later, Gifford was committed by a judge to the State Insane Hospital at Farmington. At the announcement on December 18, 1928, that Gifford would be committed the next day by court order, the *Post-Dispatch* reported:

> The element of financial profit, or any other apparent benefit to Mrs. Gifford from the deaths, was absent in most cases, but in a few cases family difficulties have appeared as a possible motive.
>
> "I wanted to help them. I wanted to do good," was her declaration when she finally admitted some of the poison murders. These expressions convinced the prosecutor, as well as the physicians, that the woman was insane.

Bertha Gifford lived for another twenty-three years. She died at the state hospital.

KIDNAPPED: BUSCH FAMILY HEIR
1930-31

Adolphus "Dolph" Busch Orthwein was looking forward to the evening. His grandfather, August A. Busch, Sr., the patriarch of the Busch family and chief executive officer of Anheuser-Busch, had invited Dolph to Grant's Farm to spend New Year's Eve night with him. Dolph had packed his clothes, a pair of skates, and a match case that he intended to give the elder Busch as a present. Dolph, thirteen, then climbed into the family Lincoln sedan with chauffeur Thomas Leroy Yowell at the wheel. Dolph's parents, Percy and Clara Busch Orthwein, were hosting a party that night.

As Yowell drove east down the driveway and then up a hill to Lindbergh Boulevard from the stately home in Huntleigh Village, Dolph saw a man run from a group of trees and leap onto the trunk rack of the Lincoln, then bang on the back window of the sedan and point a handgun at Yowell, who brought the car to a screeching halt.

The attacker leaped from the car and opened the passenger side, where Dolph was sitting. "He reached across my legs and made Roy get out," Dolph would say later in interviews. The man also demanded Yowell's money, and the driver gave him nine dollars as he got out of the car. The man crawled over Dolph, put the car in gear, and sped off south on Lindbergh for a short distance. The kidnapper then drove back north to a driveway that Dolph recognized as the entry to the Duncan Meier house. Dolph was ordered from the car at gunpoint into another vehicle and was told to lie down on the back seat, where the teen was handcuffed. It was 7 p.m., December 31, 1930.

Meanwhile, Yowell raced back to the Orthwein mansion to alert everyone to the kidnapping. Percy Orthwein called police and helped to organize a search. When the Lincoln sedan was discovered nearby, the search focused on the Huntleigh area. Newsmen hearing about the abduction on police radio showed up in force. The Busch family asked radio stations to broadcast a reward. Maplewood Police Chief Joseph Kavanaugh arrived with a pair of bloodhounds, and they raced around in the dark with huffing police, relatives, and reporters giving chase. There was no scent to pick up.

By the time the dogs got to the Orthwein house, Dolph had already been a captive for nearly four hours in a rundown summer house set back about a hundred yards from 715 Bismark Avenue, a dirt lane near the intersection of Berry and Manchester roads in what is now Glendale. The cottage had been part of a former beer garden and dance pavilion. On the three-mile trip from Huntleigh, Dolph had been told to be still. At one point, he asked his abductor what kind of gun he had and was told a .38. "After that, we got to be chummy, and I guess he was a pretty good fellow, because he got to like me," Dolph later told the *St. Louis Star* in an interview from Grant's Farm.

But Dolph was forced to spend the night sitting in a chair in the kitchen with a blanket over his head, shivering in the cold. The kidnapper asked him his name, and Dolph decided he would not say who he was. "You are Percy Orthwein's boy, and I have been trying to get you for three weeks," Dolph was then told.

After the uncomfortable night in the chair, Dolph's captor gave him a slice of bread in the morning and made him some eggs, but Dolph decided "they were so dirty, I couldn't eat them."

That morning, January 1, 1931, St. Louis's major newspapers bannered the kidnapping, wrote about a reward, and quoted one witness as seeing a suspicious green car in the vicinity of the Orthwein house.

That morning, a woman and her seven children left the cottage on Bismark. She told her husband she had heard a commotion in the kitchen all night long and demanded to know what was going on. Before he answered, she told him, "I and the children are going to leave. I'm not going to stay and get mixed up in anything."

Also that morning, a St. Louis real estate developer read about the kidnapping and the green car and knew instinctively, he told the *Star* the next day, the identity of the kidnapper. The real estate developer was Pearl Abernathy, who had his offices at 4323 Enright Avenue. Pearl Abernathy suspected the kidnapper was his own son, Charles Abernathy, and he suspected that Charles had taken the boy to the cottage that the senior Abernathy owned.

"I just put two and two together. I have great powers of intuition," said Pearl Abernathy in the *Star* interview. "As soon as I confirmed what I had feared, I set about to right the wrong my boy had committed." Pearl Abernathy called the Orthweins, told them he had information, and agreed to meet at the sheriff's office in Clayton that afternoon. Percy Orthwein was at the meeting along with his brother-in-law, August A. Busch, Jr., and Clayton lawyer Harry Troll. "I will trade you your boy for mine," Pearl Abernathy said. Percy Orthwein agreed.

At the cottage, Charles Abernathy had given Dolph an orange at lunch, "but before long he took me out of the house and left me in the road, and pretty soon I saw my daddy," Dolph said as his twenty-hour ordeal came to an end about 3 p.m. Soon, he was also reunited at Grant's Farm with his mother, his seven-year-old younger brother, James "Jimmie" Busch Orthwein, and his grandfather.

But where was Charles Abernathy? He had disappeared, and an extensive search in St. Louis by law enforcement failed to locate him. Abernathy had fled to Kansas City, where Harry Brundidge, the *Star*'s top investigative reporter, found him. Abernathy agreed to surrender if Brundidge would tell his story. Brundidge got the abductor's confession, and the *Star* ran verbatim what Abernathy had requested across the top of its front page.

In his own handwriting, signed and dated January 4, Abernathy said, "I want to make this statement. I never had any idea of kidnaping the Orthwein boy, or any other person. I never even dreamed of kidnapping anybody. I have told to Harry T. Brundidge of the *St. Louis Sta*r in the presence of witnesses how the whole thing happened."

Contrary to what he told Dolph about stalking the house for three weeks, Abernathy claimed he took the boy on impulse during a holdup of the chauffeur to get money to feed his kids. "Two years ago, I was worth $30,000. I was a respected businessman. Today I am penniless, a hunted man, wanted by the law for a terrible crime," Brundidge quoted him as saying, adding that Dolph had made quite an impression on the kidnapper in the twenty hours they were together. "I got to love this kid. I would never hurt him." Abernathy said, "There was no food in our kitchen on New Year's Eve. I had exactly fifteen cents in my pocket."

Abernathy blamed his poverty, not specifically on the Depression, but on a bank president whom he claimed had victimized him in a business deal two years earlier. That's why he had a shotgun in the cottage and handcuffs with him the night of the kidnapping, he claimed: to kidnap the banker, not the boy, and get the executive to return the money Abernathy had lost in the deal.

Abernathy, twenty-eight, said he had married young, and the couple had their first child when he was seventeen. After his business failure and several months of unemployment, Abernathy said he, his wife, and seven children were eventually forced to move out of their house on Cote Brilliante to the shack where he took Dolph. Abernathy, Brundidge, and a sheriff's deputy drove back to St. Louis together. Abernathy even shared some of the driving.

Abernathy's claims of poverty, his allegation he never really intended to kidnap the Orthwein youth, and his appeal for sympathy ran against the tide in an era when kidnapping of the well-to-do occurred frequently and stiff penalties were meted out. He was eventually sentenced to fifteen years in prison, serving eight.

August A. Busch, Sr., was also the target of a kidnapping plot that police uncovered about two years later. After that, Busch purchased sixty .32-caliber revolvers and gave them to relatives and wealthy friends whom he thought might also be targets for abduction.

HOMER G. PHILLIPS
1931

When St. Louis Mayor Jim Conway announced the closing of Homer G. Phillips Hospital in 1979, he had unknowingly signed his own political death warrant—even though Conway's announcement of the closing of the venerable institution in North St. Louis made sense economically and politically. For years, the hospital had been a substantial drain on the city's dwindling financial resources. Its ability to provide services had been questioned by some medical experts. Why have two city hospitals, the experts agreed, when one—City Hospital on the South Side—would suffice? But Conway was dealing with more than a building that had outlasted its usefulness. He was dealing with a symbol, with a memory, and with the ghost of Homer G. Phillips himself, perhaps the most revered African American in St. Louis history.

So North St. Louis erupted in anger and protest that year. In winter cold and summer heat, men, women, and children marched in demonstrations against a city hall hierarchy that had taken their dreams lightly. The Reverend Jesse Jackson came. So, too, did activists Dick Gregory and Angela Davis. In 1979 alone, the *Post-Dispatch* ran 281 articles and editorials about the hospital and the efforts to either save or close it—add to that the extensive coverage by the *Globe-Democrat,* the *St. Louis American,* the *St. Louis Argus*, and television and radio stations. The speeches, the marches, the pleas failed. On August 2, 1979, the hospital shutdown began.

Thirty-eight years earlier, Homer G. Phillips and his wife, Ida Pearl, had breakfast together on June 18, 1931. It was a sultry day with the temperature already in the mid-seventies by 8 a.m. as Phillips walked the five blocks from his home at 1121 Aubert Street to Delmar Boulevard to catch the streetcar.

Phillips was fifty-one years old and a successful lawyer with a practice on North Jefferson Avenue. He lived in a predominantly white neighborhood and rode a predominantly white streetcar to work every day. That morning, he had neither fear nor worry, his wife said.

Phillips bought his morning newspaper at a stand. He opened the paper and leaned back against the windowsill of the Rubican Business School while he waited for the streetcar. Two young men suddenly appeared. One of them slapped Phillips, drew a handgun as the lawyer turned to flee, and fired several shots. Phillips died instantly with two bullet wounds to the head and one to the back. The men ran through an alley to the Hodiamont streetcar tracks and disappeared.

HOMER G. PHILLIPS

The police investigation focused initially on a pending perjury case in which Phillips was going to testify as a state's witness. Phillips had represented Hazel Giles in a divorce case. George L. Vaughn had represented high school teacher Walter Giles. At the divorce trial, two women had testified that they had seen Hazel Giles at a rooming house with a young man. Phillips found out that they had lied and had been paid to lie.

By the end of the day that Phillips died, police had already begun to move in a different direction and were focusing their efforts on a family who had reneged on their legal fee to Phillips. The lawyer had successfully represented John McFarland and his family in an estate dispute. He got them an award of three thousand dollars, but they objected to his fee of one thousand dollars. Phillips put the estate funds in an escrow account until the matter could be resolved. The McFarlands had gone to see R. W. Ropiquet, an attorney in East St. Louis. When he told them Phillips had done the right thing, they had gotten angry and threatened Ropiquet.

There had been a witness to the shooting. Abner Parker, a printer, saw the murder. At the coroner's inquest, he identified the assailants as George McFarland, nineteen, and Augustus Brooks, eighteen. George was the son of John McFarland; Brooks, a friend of George. Another witness, George McGuire, also identified Brooks. Brooks, George McFarland, and John McFarland were taken into custody, but the senior McFarland was soon released from jail for lack of evidence.

When the case went to trial in February 1932, Parker and McGuire identified George McFarland as the shooter and Brooks as his sidekick. But the defense put on three alibi witnesses who claimed McFarland was two miles away when the murder took place. Brooks said he was at a pool hall. The jury acquitted both men.

None of the major newspaper editorial writers eulogized Phillips in the days after his death. It remained for police reporters to give readers a brief history of the victim and to get quotes from city officials, who called Phillips a crusader. Phillips was described as an effective speaker in campaigns and the courtroom; a man who could control elections through his ability to get out the black vote for candidates and causes he backed; an unsuccessful candidate for the Republican nomination for Congress in 1926; and a leader in decades-long efforts to get a decent hospital for St. Louis's African Americans.

As a lawyer, Phillips made legal history when he won a one-hundred-thousand–dollar case for Fisk University of Nashville. Phillips represented the school in an estate dispute. He had argued successfully that a carbon copy of the will of Dr. John W. McClellan was a legal document in the absence of the original and should have been admitted in Probate Court.

Born in Sedalia, Missouri, Phillips was the son of a Methodist minister, but his parents died when he was young, and he was raised by an aunt. Phillips graduated as valedictorian in 1900 from George R. Smith College in Sedalia. From there, it was on to Washington, D.C., where Phillips got his law degree from Howard University.

He worked as a student in the Justice Department.

Phillips arrived in St. Louis in 1915, just as the city was embarking on one of its most racially divisive eras. In 1910, Baltimore city officials had passed a residential segregation law. Since 1911, white neighborhood associations had lobbied for a similar law in St. Louis, but the Municipal Assembly had rejected it. In 1915, neighborhood groups got enough petitions to force a vote on the matter. The measure said no person of any race could move to a block where 75 percent of the residents were a different color. The proposal also called for separate churches and dance halls—no mixing of the races, hymn to hymn, or cheek to cheek.

To block a vote for February 29, 1916, Charles Pitman of the NAACP sued. Phillips was one of the lawyers drafting and filing the suit. They lost. Along with Roger Baldwin of the American Civil Liberties Union, Phillips then headed the campaign against the proposed ordinance. Also opposing it were the *Post*, *Globe*, and *Argus*, as well as Mayor Henry Kiel and twenty-three of twenty-eight aldermen. Neighborhood groups, real estate developers, and the city's upper social echelon favored it. Many ministers and priests sat on the sidelines.

The proposal passed 52,220 to 17,877, but Pitman and Phillips wasted little time going back to court and getting a restraining order from a federal judge. Then the U.S. Supreme Court, in a case out of Louisville, Kentucky, ruled a similar residential segregation ordinance unconstitutional. At Phillips's request, the federal judge here made permanent his order barring the measure from taking effect. The new law was dead.

Phillips soon turned his attention to healthcare and the deplorable conditions that blacks faced in St. Louis. Black doctors had long lobbied for a city-funded hospital for blacks and finally got their wish. The facility opened in 1919 in a building vacated by Barnes Hospital. The 177-bed facility was soon overcrowded.

By the early 1920s, St. Louis civic leaders had decided the city had fallen behind other metropolitan areas and was badly in need of new hospitals and many other facilities. Voters had shown in the past a reluctance to pass bond issues. Without the black vote, the leaders felt, they had no chance of passing the bond issue and rebuilding St. Louis.

Enter Homer Phillips to the negotiations. In a series of meetings, Phillips promised to deliver the black vote in exchange for a hospital in the black wards. Mayor Henry Kiel and Board President Louis P. Aloe agreed. In 1923, a bond issue totaling $87.4 million—the largest bond issue ever approved by a city at the time—won voter approval. All twenty-one proposals passed in the black wards. Twenty of them passed citywide. The measures would have gotten approval without the black wards, but they may have never reached the ballot without the assurances of Phillips.

Of the $87.4 million, $4.5 million went to build hospitals—first City Hospital on the near South Side, then finally the hospital in North St. Louis at 2601 Whittier Avenue. Groundbreaking began in 1933, and the hospital opened in 1937, six years after Phillips was murdered. Closed in 1979, the six-story Art Deco complex was renovated and reopened in 2004 as the Homer G. Phillips Dignity House, a 220-unit residence for seniors.

The hospitals weren't the only things St. Louis built with the bond issue Phillips helped pass. A water plant went up on the Missouri River. The River Des Peres was extended and improved. The Soldier's Memorial and Kiel Auditorium were built. The city also spent money on parks, paved streets, and added new fire stations. And perhaps on a cool spring morning, you can imagine a tall, well-dressed lawyer walking briskly past the Carl Milles "The Wedding of the Rivers" sculpture at Aloe Plaza to the Egyptian-style courthouse at Tucker and Market streets. The fountain and the courthouse are as much a legacy of Phillips as they are of Kiel and Aloe, even though he never got to see the play of the water in the sun or try a case in the mahogany courtrooms.

NELLIE TIPTON MUENCH
1930s

Born in Odessa, Missouri, and raised in Columbia, Nelle Tipton Muench was the daughter of William Ross Tipton, a Confederate Army veteran and a Baptist minister with a large following in mid-Missouri. Her brother, Ernest "Tip" Tipton, was a star quarterback at the University of Missouri, a football and baseball coach at Westminster College, a partner in a Kansas City law firm, and finally a judge of the Missouri Supreme Court. Nelle Tipton attended Stephens College in Columbia, where she met Ludwig Muench, a premed student at Mizzou from Washington, Missouri. They eloped in 1912 and moved to St. Louis, where her husband got his medical license after studying at Washington University and then began a lucrative career with New York Life as a medical examiner. Nelle became "Nellie" in St. Louis, where the couple lived on Westminster Place in the fashionable Central West End.

Music lovers, Ludwig played cello to Nellie's grand piano accompanied by musicians of the St. Louis Symphony, who were frequent visitors to their home. Nellie opened Mitzi's, a boutique dress shop on Euclid Avenue for the wealthy and the mighty. The couple's out-state Missouri background, however, kept them from reaching the highest levels of St. Louis society—they weren't "old money."

That was the way Nellie Muench appeared to most St. Louisans in the 1920s. But by the end of 1936, after a series of sensational trials—for kidnapping, child custody, and fraud—St. Louisans and indeed most of the country saw a different Nellie Muench as she sobbed in a courtroom for a final time and U.S. District Judge George H. Moore sent her to the women's prison at Alderson, West Virginia, to serve a ten-year sentence.

An article in the January 4, 1937, edition of *Time* magazine said, "In St. Louis no local woman has been the subject of more newspaper columns or more shocked social chitchat than lively, red-haired Mrs. Nellie Tipton Muench." In hindsight, *Time* and the newspapers found what they considered evidence that Nellie's life as a socialite was a facade as early as 1919, when her name showed up on a police blotter as a suspect in a theft of jewelry from a hotel room. No charges were filed.

The next year, Nellie submitted a bill to an estate lawyer claiming his wealthy client had died owing her seventeen thousand dollars. The lawyer argued that the businessman's signatures on the notes were fraudulent. Nellie sued, then dropped her suit, saying her lawyer had lost her evidence.

In 1923, Nellie opened Mitzi's to cater to the well-to-do on Euclid Avenue in the Central West End. She often borrowed jewelry from jewelers so customers could try on her clothes with the proper accessories. In August 1925, Nellie made the papers again as the heroine in a theft of her dress shop. She told police a man entered her shop and stole about $12,200 worth of the borrowed jewelry before she bopped him on the head with her purse as he fled with the loot. Police hauled in a man she identified. He argued indignantly that he had never seen the lady before she fingered him. He was released; the jewelry was never recovered.

Three years later, Mitzi's was in financial trouble, and Nellie filed for bankruptcy, claiming net debts of $77,000. At a court hearing, she blamed her financial woes on a lender who lied to her, she said, about his rates and then charged her excessive interest on her loans. Her creditors got fifteen cents on the dollar.

A reporter painted a word picture of Nellie, circa 1928: "She is about five feet two inches tall and rather plump. Her hair is dark red, her eyes brown and vivacious, and she has an animated, dynamic personality. She complained she was on the verge of a nervous breakdown as a result of her troubles, which she claimed stemmed from a usurious interest rate of forty-six percent she was charged on a ten thousand–dollar loan." Nellie managed to maintain her community image—most of the 1920s escapades had been minor in nature but would come to the fore later.

The next major event in the Nellie Muench saga began about 10 p.m. on April 20, 1931, when Dr. Isaac D. Kelley and his wife were interrupted from their reading in the library of their Portland Place mansion. The phone rang. A hysterical parent pleaded with Kelley, an ear, nose, and throat specialist, to come to Davis Place in Clayton to treat his son's severe earache. Kelley was recommended by a doctor in Chicago who was going to perform a mastoid operation. After a second call an hour later, Kelley agreed.

The doctor never got to treat an earache. Two men kidnapped him on Hanley Road in Clayton and took him first to a farm in St. Charles County and then to a series of hideouts in St. Clair County in Illinois. Police found his car the next day in Jennings. Kelley was a natural target in a decade when kidnapping became the in-crime for gangs and independents alike. Kelley's wife was the daughter of William McBride, an oil millionaire. But the kidnappers acted like amateurs, Kelley decided. They had difficulty agreeing on how much to collect: from $250,000 initially, down to $50,000, and they argued over who to use as a go-between, even asking the doctor at one point if he could recommend someone. During their arguments, one of the men complained, "Where the hell is Goldie?"

After seven days of transferring Kelley from one East Side location to another, the hoodlums gave up. They called John Rogers, a prize-winning reporter for the *Post-Dispatch*, and told him to come to a roadside location in St. Clair County. In the middle of the night, seven days after he was abducted, a bedraggled but healthy Kelley was rescued along the rural road by Rogers, who returned him to his family after conducting a lengthy and exclusive interview. For his enterprise, Rogers got a bonus of a year's pay from Joseph Pulitzer II. Kelley, however, was unable to identify his abductors, and police came up empty-handed. The case languished until February 1934, when Adolph Fiedler, a 515-pound former justice of the peace, approached the *Post-Dispatch* and offered a story for pay. St. Louis County Prosecuting Attorney C. Arthur Anderson was informed of the story that Fiedler was peddling. Fiedler ran the Arcade Country Club, a pool hall, bar, and hangout for hoods on Olive Boulevard in University City.

Fiedler claimed the kidnapping of Kelley involved a half-dozen men, and the head of the gang was none other than red-haired, social swirl Nellie Tipton Muench. It was Nellie, Fiedler said, who chose Kelley as the victim because of his rich father-in-law. It was Nellie, Fiedler said, who chose the story to lure Kelley to Clayton and even wrote the script, adding that no one else had any idea what a mastoid operation was. And it was Nellie whom the gang called "Goldie."

Nellie was quite indignant when police showed up on Westminster Place. "You can't possibly imagine my mental state when the detectives came and told me I was wanted for questioning in the Kelley kidnap case," she said. "To be arrested and taken from my home and booked as a kidnapper on the word of a man I don't know and have never seen in my life. I didn't know a living man would have so little character as to do such a despicable thing."

The arrest was also poor timing for Nellie. She just had begun a love affair with Dr. Marsh Pitzman, an associate of her husband who lived on Kingsbury Place. The year before, Nellie had been nursing at her home Carl Auer, a German-born symphony musician, who suffered from deteriorating leg tissue caused by World War I wounds. Nellie dressed and bathed Auer's legs. Pitzman was the treating physician, and he was impressed with Nellie's devotion to his patient.

Pitzman, fifty-one, was a bachelor, a Harvard graduate, and the son of Julius Pitzman, who had laid out the plans for such private St. Louis subdivisions as Compton Heights and Portland Place.

The affair, a prosecutor later told a jury, began on Christmas Day of 1933, when Marsh kissed Nellie under the mistletoe. By the time of her arrest, the affair had reached torrid stages and had prompted Pitzman to write his lover, "No one knows better than I that you are the sweetest, most honorable woman alive."

Among those charged along with the "honorable woman" were

Felix McDonald, already serving a prison sentence for an attempted kidnapping of shoe manufacturer Oscar Johnson; Bart Davit, acquitted in the same case for which McDonald went to prison; hoodlum Angelo Rosegrant; Tommy Wilders, a gangster hiding out in Florida; and John C. Johnson, whose farm in St. Charles County the kidnappers had used the first night of Kelley's abduction.

Because she had a brother on the Supreme Court and a socialite husband, more than a dozen lawyers offered Nellie their legal services for free. One account put the number at twenty-two. Nellie's trial was continued several times and moved to Mexico, Missouri, on a change of venue because of the publicity. The choice could not have been better. Mexico in Audrain County is part of Little Dixie, a conservative Democrat, Bible Belt half-moon of Missouri that leaned toward Southern politics. Boone and Callaway counties, where William Ross Tipton had preached, Nellie had grown up and gone to college, and "Tip" Tipton had gone to school and coached, were also part of Little Dixie.

While Nellie was awaiting trial, several developments took place. On May 12, 1934, Johnson was in hiding in St. Louis County after turning state's evidence. He was killed with machine-gun blasts. In October, Rosegrant was convicted and sentenced to twenty years in prison. McDonald got a sixty-year sentence in January 1935.

As the alleged leader of the gang, Nellie Muench was facing some serious prison time if she were convicted. Her trial in Mexico was set to open in October. That May, Nellie and Ludwig Muench announced that Nellie was pregnant. They said it was "a gift of God." On August 18, 1935, they announced the birth of a son. She had been childless for twenty-three years of marriage.

Nellie went to trial for kidnapping Kelley on October 3 of that year. One of her attorneys, Press Cross, talked about the wicked city and the simple daughter from a rural community. Her brother, the Supreme Court judge, sat beside her. Her husband, Ludwig, exchanged pleasantries with townsfolk outside the Audrain County Courthouse.

Fiedler was the main prosecution witness and outlined the plot to kidnap Kelley. Nellie was called Goldie by the gang because she was more greedy than other members, he told the jury. She rehearsed the script she had written for the call to Kelley with the gangster who made it, he added. Fiedler's veracity was an issue the defense pursued. He denied he had been prosecuted for perjury seven times. "Only four," he said. And he claimed for a home address, "Anywhere it's healthy."

Nellie denied knowing Fiedler or McDonald or Davit and met Rosegrant once when he paid a medical bill. Kelley's wife said she had seen Nellie dancing with Rosegrant at the Coronado Hotel. A Westminster neighbor said she had seen Rosegrant at the Muench house. Fiedler testified gang members went to the Coronado with "Goldie" so she could point Kelley out to them. Kelley testified about a woman named Goldie whom the kidnappers had mentioned. Prosecutors brought in a county officer, William Niland, who said he stopped Nellie in a car with Davit in 1933 on Woodson Road. Niland testified he asked her what she was doing with the hoodlum. "She said she was out to have a good time."

The trial lasted three days. The jury was out about five hours. The verdict? Not guilty. Nellie could go home to her husband and her "gift from God," her two-month-old baby. But trouble was brewing for Nellie on that front. A young woman named Anna Ware now claimed the baby was hers—and Nellie was again in a denial mode, calling the claims by the nineteen-year-old maid from Philadelphia preposterous. Anna had come to St. Louis to have her baby and had given the child up for adoption. She determined from newspaper accounts of Nellie's legal problems that Nellie's new baby and her own were one and the same. She had given her infant to Wilford Jones, a lawyer. She questioned him, but he assured her that her baby had actually gone to a nice couple in Tennessee. Anna told her story and suspicions to the *Star-Times*.

The *Post-Dispatch* reported that the child of an unwed mother from Minnesota had been transferred in July to the Muench home from City Hospital, but that boy was sickly and died. Anna's baby was a late substitute. Jones claimed the first baby was also destined for the Tennessee couple and had been taken to Dr. Muench for an examination. Anna said her baby had dark hair; Nellie claimed her infant had red hair. Nellie's maid had purchased hair dye at a local pharmacy, the *Post-Dispatch* found. Later that October, a judge ordered the baby taken to Children's Hospital while the who's-the-mother scenario played out. Nellie didn't like the ruling at all, screaming at the judge, banging the table, and being dragged out of court.

Attorney Rush H. Limbaugh of Cape Girardeau was then appointed a special commissioner. He was the father of Stephen H. Limbaugh, a federal judge in St. Louis for more than thirty years, and the grandfather of both Stephen H. Limbaugh, Jr., a former judge of the Missouri Supreme Court and now a federal judge in St. Louis, and Rush Limbaugh, the conservative talk-show host. Limbaugh heard testimony from eighty-six witnesses, including neighbors who thought Nellie looked more pregnant on different days and saw Nellie sunbathing with only a small bulge in her midriff. He ruled that Nellie had obtained Ware's baby to influence jurors in Mexico. He ordered the infant returned to Anna.

The testimony before Limbaugh led to the next trial, in Kahoka, Missouri, in April 1936 because of publicity. The charge: taking a child without the consent of the juvenile court, a misdemeanor. On trial were Nellie and Ludwig Muench, Wilford Jones, and Helen Berroyer, a friend of Nellie who had wholeheartedly supported her contentions the baby was Nellie's. A mistrial was declared when a juror claimed he had been the subject of a bribery attempt. A second trial got under way, and Nellie steadfastly insisted she had given birth. She claimed she had been attended by Dr. Ralph Williams, but the only Ralph Williams with a medical license in Missouri had been dead for fourteen years. One of the state's witnesses was Pitzman, who said he thought he was the father and had paid sixteen thousand dollars to Nellie. "One side of her was attractive. The other side I feared," he said. "I am now completely confident I was fooled."

That jury convicted all four defendants, and it wasn't long that the federal government indicted the same quartet on fraud charges relating to Dr. Pitzman's losses. The indictment was returned the same summer day that Franklin Delano Roosevelt was nominated for a second term as president. Nellie got better play in the area newspapers than FDR.

At the trial in November 1936, the defense argued that "every dime that Dr. Pitzman gave her, he gave her out of love. When she wrote letters to him for money, she told him exactly what they were for. There was no fraud in that." Prosecutor Herbert H. Freer saw it differently. The plan to bilk Pitzman of as much as two hundred thousand dollars by pretending that Anna's baby was his amounted to fraud, he argued, and he added, "A more ingenuous scheme was never conceived in the mind of any woman in the U.S." The jury convicted all four. Besides the ten years meted out to Nellie, Jones got ten years, and Ludwig Muench eight years. Both men would serve their sentences at Leavenworth, Kansas, and Berroyer joined Nellie at Alderson to serve five years.

Pressed by *Post-Dispatch* reporter Spencer McCullough, Nellie wrote her own confession. It ran in the December 23, 1936, edition of the *Post-Dispatch*:

> And so I come to the end. I make this confession but for one purpose, to do some good, if that is possible at this late date, for the only innocent person convicted in this so-called conspiracy—my devoted husband. I repeat, I alone am to blame. Dr. Muench is innocent. I ask for nothing for myself.
>
> I have disgraced my brother and ruined my husband. If I had not been such a hussy, none of the things I am about to relate could have happened.

Nellie moved to Kansas City after she got out of prison. Ludwig had divorced her while she was still in custody. Research by *Post-Dispatch* writer Tim O'Neil for *Mobs, Mayhem and Murder* found that she died there on August 28, 1982, at the age of ninety-one.

AUGUST LUER KIDNAPPING, ALTON
1933

When FBI Director J. Edgar Hoover announced the capture in May 1935 of "Irish" O'Malley in Kansas City without a shot being fired, the arrest brought to seven the number of kidnappers in jail or prison for the botched abduction of wealthy Alton banker and businessman August Luer. Only Vivian Chase remained at large after Hoover's troops caught O'Malley. "He was one of the ringleaders in the Luer kidnapping, and our men have been hunting him for two years," said publicity-hound Hoover.

It was O'Malley, known to his gang as Walter Holland, and Chase who had banged on the door of the Luer residence at 9 p.m. on July 10, 1933, and told Helena Luer that they needed to use her telephone. Once inside the Luer home at 759 Washington Avenue, O'Malley grabbed August Luer, and Chase cut the telephone lines. A third man, entering on their heels, pushed Helena Luer into the parlor, knocking her to the floor. Shoving August Luer into a car parked in the driveway, the kidnappers drove off. "Carl, they've stolen papa," screamed Helena Luer to her son, Carl Luer, who lived across the street.

August Luer was an inviting target. He was seventy-seven years old, frail, retired, and rich. He was president of Alton Banking and Trust Co. Born in Germany, he and his brother, Herman, had opened a meatpacking company in Alton in 1881 and had turned the Luer Packing and Ice Company into a major financial success.

Helena and Carl Luer were worried about August because of his heart condition—an illness that may have actually saved his life. His eyes were sealed with tape as he lay on the car floor. When he said he had a heart ailment, he was allowed to sit up. Three times, he was transferred to different cars. At one point, he heard a train so close that he thought he would be thrown under it. After what seemed about three hours, Luer was forced out of the car and walked barefoot between two men on a gravel bed, then marched down a flight of stairs and placed on a slab. When he complained he couldn't sleep without a pillow, he got a sack filled with weeds.

Luer's kidnappers put their victim in still another car, took him to yet another location, and forced him into a cellar passageway so low his head would hit the ceiling without bending over. Then he was forced to crawl through a trapdoor in a floor to a lower level. He ended up in a damp, chilly cellar four feet square and four feet high. His guards got him sandwiches and medicine for his heart condition when he told them about it. On the second day after the kidnapping, Luer was forced to write a note to his family. One of his abductors complained that he hadn't known Luer's age or health. If he had, Luer would not have been a target.

Because he was a former member of both the board of education and the city council, Luer's abduction prompted an immediate all-points alert in Madison County and four surrounding Illinois counties. Executives of the bank and the packing house—Lawrence Keller, Jr., and Orville S. Catt, respectively—were appointed by the Luer family to deal with whatever demands the kidnappers made and with the press. Helena Luer made a public appeal to the abductors. She asked them to let her know that her husband of fifty-six years was still alive.

Carl Luer got a letter from the kidnappers, postmarked from St. Louis. It was delivered at 5 a.m. on Wednesday. Luer had been taken from his home about 9 p.m. on Monday. The second missive arrived in a roundabout manner at 5 p.m. on Thursday. It was a special delivery from East St. Louis to the Mineral Springs Hotel in Alton, a well-known spa. Inside that envelope was another one to deliver to the Luer family. The third message—with the instructions for the ransom negotiations—also contained the note written by Luer: "Dear Mamma, I thought I would be home before this."

But the instructions had called for negotiations on Friday night. To their horror, the Luers didn't get the message until Saturday morning. It had been placed in a flower bed next to the Fairy Inn, a restaurant in East Alton. It was addressed to a family relative, telling him to take it to the Luers. He didn't find it until Saturday morning, a piece of paper tied with a string to a fence.

The Luers prepared a statement for the press to run in the St. Louis Sunday papers. They were asking the kidnappers to resume negotiations.

By that time Saturday, the abductors had apparently become frustrated and were concerned about Luer's health. Two men came to the cellar for their captive, put him in the front seat of a car between them, and forced him to keep his head down. They drove to an isolated area, then told him to get out and to wait twenty minutes before uncovering his eyes. It was early Sunday morning, and Luer saw a light, toward which he walked. It turned out to be a roadhouse three miles from Collinsville. At the door, Luer blurted out, "Please, ma'am, I'm August Luer. The kidnappers pushed me out of a car on a dirt road two miles over the hill. Can I come in?" From the roadhouse, Luer called home and told his family he was free and unharmed.

While Luer was being reunited with his family, a Madison police officer, George Miller, had a hunch. He suspected one or more of the gang was part of a group rounded up by police after a bank robbery in the city of Madison three years earlier. Miller took mug shots of the gang members to County Sheriff Peter Fitzgerald, and he, in turn, showed the photos to Helena Luer. She identified Percy "Dice Box Kid" Fitzgerald as the ruffian who had knocked her down when her husband was dragged from their house. Percy Fitzgerald, no relation to the sheriff, immediately confessed, "I'm right for this job. You've got me."

Other gang members were soon identified. They were Nameoki township bondsman Eugene Norvell; Mike Musiala, a tenant operator of the farm where Luer was held captive; Christ Gitcho of Madison; Charles and Lillian Chessen of East Alton; "Irish" O'Malley;

and Vivian Chase. Only O'Malley and Chase were at large.

Kidnapping was a capital offense in 1933, and Madison County State's Attorney M. L. Geers sought death in the electric chair in a trial in Edwardsville that ended on September 30, 1933. Testimony disclosed that the gang had considered other potential victims, including John and Spencer Olin of Alton, owners of the firearms and ammunition manufacturer of that name. Luer, they had decided, was an easier target.

Police testified that they had found the location where Luer was held. In a toolshed on a farm north of East St. Louis, they found shiny new screws in the floorboard. Ripping up the boards, they discovered a pit, a tunnel, and the cellar or cave that had held the captive banker.

The jury deliberated a total of twenty-four hours and rejected the death penalty. The jurors set the penalties of life in prison for Fitzgerald, Norvill, and Lillian Chessen; twenty years for Musiala; and five years each for Gitcho and Charles Chessen.

After O'Malley was caught by the FBI in May 1935, he went on trial a month later in Edwardsville for the Luer kidnapping—he had also been a suspect in a pair of bank robberies in Oklahoma. Helena Luer took the stand. She said O'Malley was the man who dragged her husband out of the house. O'Malley quickly changed his plea to guilty and was sentenced to life in prison.

Chase was the only abductor who avoided prison—the hard way. She was found in a parked car at Kansas City's St. Luke's Hospital, a bullet wound in her neck, on November 3, 1935. She had been dead about two hours. Victims of a series of drugstore robberies by a man and a woman earlier that year in Kansas City identified photographs of Chase as the female robber.

Both August and Helena Luer are buried in Alton Cemetery. She died in February 1939 at the age of eighty. Despite his heart ailment or perhaps because of it, August lived until September 22, 1942—more than nine years after the infamous kidnapping. He was eighty-six when he died.

KELLAR'S LAST SUPPER
1933

Spencer Tracy was starring in *Face in the Sky* at the Fox Theater; Joan Blondell was featured in *Central Park* at the Hi-Pointe; and Randolph Scott was shooting bad guys in *Wild Horse Mesa* at the Tivoli. Old Judge Coffee was selling for a dollar for a three-pound can at Tom Boy's, and A&P was featuring eggs at nineteen cents a dozen. Famous-Barr advertised two trouser suits for $31.50. Brentwood businessman Denver Wright had imported a pair of African lions and had turned them loose on Wolf Island in the Mississippi River so he could teach his son the thrills and dangers of big-game hunting. Alas, the lions didn't want to leave their cages. They were shot anyway. So, too, was ex-convict Oliver Holland, who survived three bullet wounds from Leo Cusey but refused to squeal on the gangster. The Japanese began their expansionist conquests with an attack on the Chinese in Manchuria. Unemployed workers rioted in Chicago. "The Kingfish," Senator Huey Long of Louisiana, paid a visit to President-elect Franklin Delano Roosevelt.

Sharing the news that third week of January in 1933 was the death of James Kellar. No one knew it then, but Kellar would be the last man hanged in St. Louis County.

Kellar was thirty years old the night of January 21, when he granted an interview to a young *Post-Dispatch* reporter, Asa Bryan. Later that evening, he wrote farewell letters to his father and wife. "We will soon meet up yonder and go through eternity together hand in hand," he told his wife. "With that thought in mind I am perfectly at ease and ready to go any time."

Kellar ate his last meal of two ham-and-egg sandwiches, coffee, and a whole cherry pie. Then, with time on his hands until dawn, he whiled away the hours playing cards with his guards and Bryan, whom Kellar had asked to play.

At 6 a.m., Kellar walked to the gallows on a drawbridge between the old county jail and the courthouse with Reverend Albert Kervis of the Bethel Lutheran Church of Clayton. Kellar had converted a week earlier. The minister sang "Rock of Ages" as they walked with a ten-officer escort. Kellar wore a brown suit, a tan shirt, and house slippers. As the group approached the gallows, Constable Rudy Baumer placed a black cap over the condemned man's head and asked him if he had any final words. "No, I will see you all up there," Kellar said.

The sheriff sprang the trap, and Kellar dropped below as fifty people watched. Outside the county jail on Forsyth Boulevard, two hundred people had gathered but saw nothing. Three loud clangs from the bell of "the dinky"—the streetcar that ran through Clayton into Ladue—told residents the deed was done. Kellar was pronounced dead at 6:21 a.m. One of the witnesses was R. R. Corson, the victim's brother-in-law. The victim's husband, Louis Sauer, didn't attend.

Sauer had employed Kellar at his machine shop in Maplewood but had let him go in January 1932. Four days later, Kellar showed up at Sauer's house on Walter Avenue in Maplewood and demanded money from Sauer's wife, Etta, to send his own wife back to California, but Etta refused to provide any financial help. Kellar grabbed an iron pipe, beat her to death, took twenty-two dollars from a pocketbook, and fled. Two of Etta Sauer's three children found their mother's body when they got home from school. Police focused on the fired machinist, particularly after they learned the unemployed Kellar had purchased a new hat. In custody, Kellar confessed.

Kellar's lawyer, James E. McClellan, asked for an evaluation of his client, a request that was denied. Kellar pleaded guilty, and Judge Robert McElhinney sentenced the defendant to death. The Missouri Supreme Court affirmed the conviction. Governor Guy Park refused to commute Kellar's sentence, and Kellar became the last to die in St. Louis County at the end of a noose.

Missouri subsequently changed the law that had been in effect since territorial days: the law that said each county was to execute its own murderers. In 1937, the legislature mandated the use of the gas chamber, setting it up in a separate building at the Missouri State Penitentiary. Its first customers a year later were two murderers from Kansas City, and its last of thirty-nine in 1965 was the killer of a St. Louis drugstore deliveryman.

Asa Bryan never forgot James Kellar over the next thirty-nine years as a reporter covering courts and government in St. Louis County. After his retirement from the newspaper, he moved into a county government office, where he worked for a succession of county executives.

THE STRANGE CASE OF MARY CATHERINE REARDON
1947

J. Vincent Reardon had just turned onto Clayton Road from Lindbergh Boulevard at the border of Ladue and Frontenac. It was 8 a.m. on February 8, 1947. Reardon was not in a good mood. He had been searching all night for his daughter, Mary, and her boyfriend, Michael D'Arcy. He had finally found them at the Travelers Auto Court at Highways 40 and 61 in Wentzville, where they had spent the night. He had learned from a cab driver who had driven them to the nearby Southern Air Restaurant that they had been necking in the back seat of the cab on the trip to Wentzville from Union Station.

The owner of a paint-manufacturing company bearing his name, Reardon, fifty-eight, of Ladue, was particularly disappointed in his daughter. He had doted on Mary, he had taken her on trips with him, and he always had set aside time to be with her.

Mary, fourteen, was in the back seat behind her father. She had been humiliated when he showed up at the tourist cabin that morning, rousted them out of the motel room, and told them to get in the car. And she was worried about what would happen next. She was afraid her father would become very strict, take her out of the ninth grade at Wydown School in Clayton, and send her to an all-girls school. Her father's arrival that morning also had ended her plans to run away; she had planned to go to New York or Chicago to work as a waitress.

Michael D'Arcy, thirteen, was on the passenger side in the back seat. He, too, had been humiliated by Reardon's arrival at the tourist cabin where he and Mary had stayed overnight. They had played hooky Friday and had gone to Union Station. Mary skipped school a lot, but it was Michael's first time. He knew the school would have called his parents in Clayton, so he had called home from Union Station and admitted he had not gone to Wydown that day. His mother told him to come home, that they could work it out. He said he would, but he went to Wentzville with Mary instead. They had pretended to be brother and sister and told the auto court owner that they had just arrived from New York, that their father was on his way, and that he would pay the bill when he arrived. That he was nearly five feet ten inches tall at the age of thirteen and Mary was also a tall, heavyset girl helped to convince the owner to give them a cabin. Twice on the way home, Michael had asked Reardon what he was going to do to him. Reardon was silent the first time. The second time, he said he was taking Michael home, and Michael could do his own explaining to Mr. and Mrs. Martin D'Arcy.

As Reardon drove east on Clayton nearing Warson Road, there were gunshots, Reardon lost control of his car, and it plunged down a ten-foot embankment. Reardon died. Michael was thrown from the back seat of the car and suffered a fractured skull and broken neck. He died eight hours later. Mary suffered seemingly minor injuries. "How is the young guy? Is the old man dead?" she asked Ladue Police Inspector H. E. Weiland, one of the first officers to reach the grizzly scene. Mary was sitting calmly on the back seat. Police found a gun in the car, an automatic pistol.

By the time Michael died that afternoon, Mary had made several statements to many people and had agreed to give newspaper interviews. When she learned that Michael had died, she was combing her hair in front of a mirror in preparation for a newspaper photographer, said Deputy Sheriff Harold Hoeh, adding that the teen didn't miss a brush stroke as she told Hoeh, "Of course, I wanted to know."

"I just got to thinking what might happen to me if I had to go back home," she told *Globe-Democrat* reporter Charles Fackler as they rode together. "So I asked Mike for his gun and pointed it at the back of my father's head."

At St. Louis County Hospital, where she was treated about 9 a.m., she told Vera Kelly, an attendant, "I shot my father, at least, I think I did. I put the gun to his head, and I fired, at least, I think I fired." Kelly told a supervisor, who directed that Reardon's body be checked again. Authorities had been unaware that Reardon had been shot. Examiners then found the small entry wound in the back of Reardon's neck. The bullet had traveled forward and lodged in his right cheekbone. The wound wasn't fatal; injuries in the crash were. By the time Mary ended up in jail that day and was later transferred to a detention facility for minors, she had also confessed to another reporter, to a Clayton police officer, to a deputy sheriff, and to St. Louis County coroner Arnold Willmann.

Prosecuting Attorney Stanley Wallach said charges would be brought against the teen, perhaps even murder in her father's death and manslaughter in Michael's demise. Wallach said he asked Mary if she knew what might happen to her. "Well, I might be executed—or again, I might be sent to reform school. But that might not be so bad, because I understand they have lots of books at reform school, and I like to read."

The newspapers played the story on the front page and concluded that Mary was guilty beyond any doubt. The *Globe-Democrat* lead of February 9 by Marguerite Shepard said, "Mary Reardon, fourteen, shot and killed her father, J. Vincent Reardon, well-to-do paint manufacturer, and, in doing so, indirectly killed her thirteen-year-old sweetheart, Michael D'Arcy, with whom she had spent Friday night in a tourist cabin."

While Mary was sent to a detention home to await trial on March 24 in St. Louis County Juvenile Court, her mother, Leona, was declared of unsound mind because of alcoholism and involuntarily committed by court order to McMillan Hospital.

Terms of J. Vincent Reardon's will showed that Mary would inherit 40 percent of the stock in the Reardon Company, Leona would get 50 percent, and 10 percent would be divided between three sisters of the deceased. The preliminary figure of the estate, including the family house on Price Road in Ladue, was placed in excess of one hundred thousand dollars. Then and now, Missouri law barred a recipient of an estate from collecting his or her share if that person was responsible for the death.

Mary went on trial in Clayton, charged under the juvenile code with delinquency by reason of murder. If the jury of seven women and five men found her guilty, the worst punishment she faced would be incarceration at the Industrial Home for Girls in Chillicothe, Missouri, until she was twenty-one. She was represented by criminal defense attorneys Henry G. Morris and Frank Williams. Wallach was assisted in the prosecution by William Hough.

The state put on a half-dozen witnesses. Kelly and others repeated Mary's confession. One of the prosecution witnesses was Dr. J. O. Beley, a pathologist. He was questioned at length on cross-examination about bullet trajectories by Morris, who produced stifled guffaws from a crowd of more than one hundred when he used a toy pistol to suggest the shot might have been fired from the passenger side of the back seat.

On March 26, 1947, the same day more than one hundred workers died in a coal mine disaster in Centralia, Illinois, Morris proclaimed that Mary was innocent of shooting her father and causing the crash that took the life of Reardon and Michael D'Arcy. The *Globe* reported the next morning that "the strange case of Mary Catherine Reardon became stranger yesterday . . ."

Dr. Victor J. Meinhardt was the key defense witness. A traumatic-surgery specialist, Meinhardt testified that what had appeared to be three superficial wounds Mary had suffered from the car crash had actually been caused by a bullet. Meinhardt showed the jury that the bullet had entered the outside of her upper arm, had exited the underside of the arm, had entered her body at her armpit, and had lodged in fleshy tissue in her back. He called it a superficial but peculiar wound. Meinhardt said he had X-rayed Mary on February 13—five days after the crash.

Meinhardt was full of surprises—his physical examination of

the defendant disclosed that she had never had physical relations with Michael or any boy; she was still a virgin.

Mary then walked in front of the jury, rolled up her sweater, and showed three scars to the jury. Mary let the jurors feel a lump in her back. Some of the jurors nodded their heads. The bullet wounds had been missed by hospital personnel. Meinhardt said the scars the jurors saw were the healed bullet wounds. In his opening statement to the jury, Morris said the hospital had X-rayed Mary's arm but not her back, where the bullet had lodged. Morris said the gun had gone off in a struggle between Mary and Michael, and Mary was shot. After fighting off Mary, it was Michael who shot Reardon. Dr. Paul F. Titterington supported Meinhardt's bullet-wound testimony. He, too, X-rayed Mary at the request of her attorneys. He, too, found a bullet in her back, he said. He took the X-rays on February 17, four days after Meinhardt.

Also testifying for the defense were Lee Muzzy of Fenton and Marcellus Bax, a Chesterfield farmer. They were the first passersby at the crash site. Contrary to the prosecution's witnesses, Mary was not sitting on the back seat immediately after the crash. In fact, she was on the floor of the car, and the seat had lodged on top of her. They said they tried to make her as comfortable as possible by putting the seat back where it was supposed to be and placing her on it. Both said she seemed dazed, she was shivering, and her hands were trembling, all possible signs that she was in shock.

Family witnesses said Mary loved and adored the father she was accused of shooting. Her uncle testified that Leona Reardon had been "drinking excessively and almost continuously for the last five or six years."

A pathologist called by the defense said the coat Mary wore that morning showed powder burns and blood stains.

Two classmates at Wydown testified that Michael had boasted of knowing Al Capone, an indication that the young teen was into guns and gangster lore.

Morris suggested several reasons for his client's multiple confessions, the linchpin of the state's case. Mary was in shock, or she was confused, or she was in some way trying to protect Michael, or she was "too numb mentally to realize what she was saying." Testifying for the defense, a psychiatrist said her failure to remember the confessions was due to shock from the crash and bullet wound.

The last day of the trial was Mary's turn. She didn't do it, she said. "I was looking more or less straight ahead, and I happened to glance at Michael and saw him raise his hand with the pistol in it and seemingly point it at my father," she told the jury. "I reached over with my left hand, pulled his hand toward me and heard a shot fired. He shoved my hand away and fired again."

Hough cross-examined the teen for fifty-one minutes. She said she didn't remember any of the confessions she made. She did recall riding with Fackler, the *Globe* reporter, in a sheriff's car, but couldn't remember talking to him.

The jurors got the case the same day Mary testified, March 29. They took one hour and thirty minutes to acquit her. After the verdict was announced, Mary was told by Judge John A. Witthaus that she was a fortunate young woman. The judge told her to stay out of trouble. Mary then turned to the jury box: "Thank you, ladies and gentlemen, I was sure that justice would be done, and I couldn't possibly be convicted of something I hadn't done."

Because her mother was confined in a mental hospital, Mary needed a legal guardian. She chose Frank Williams, her co-defense counsel. She went home that night to her house on Price Road to live with relatives.

A bit grandiosely, Morris told newspaper and radio reporters that, if not for the X-rayed bullet, "one of the worst miscarriages of justice in the history of jurisprudence might have happened."

THE KEFAUVER COMMITTEE
1951

THREE BLIND MICE

John English was the city commissioner in charge of the East St. Louis Police Department. Adolph Fischer had been the sheriff of St. Clair County from 1946 to 1950, and Dallas Harrell had been Fischer's counterpart in Madison County in the same period. With their shared law enforcement background, they knew one another. They had something else in common, too. All three were derided and made to look, at best, like buffoons and, at worst, like crooks before a million people—local viewers of that new gizmo called television. They tuned in at home or watched in taverns or stood on the street in front of appliance stores. U.S. Senator Estes Kefauver, a Tennessee Democrat, and his staff of probing attorneys and untouchable investigators brought their televised investigation of corruption to St. Louis in February 1951.

The three lawmen-politicians weren't willing witnesses before the bright lights; they had been subpoenaed to testify. They underwent sharp and often sarcastic questioning. Their answers

SENATOR ESTES KEFAUVER

bordered on the ridiculous and, at times, even went beyond the ridiculous. Meanwhile, more people in St. Louis watched the Special Committee to Investigate Organized Crime in Interstate Commerce than the 1950 World Series between Joe Dimaggio's New York Yankees and the Philadelphia Phillies' Whiz Kids.

St. Louis was one of fourteen cities on the committee's cross-country road show, and the trio numbered among more than six hundred witnesses the committee heard. Yet the committee's reports singled them out for their ineptitude, their corruption, or both.

JOHN ENGLISH

Under the heading "Official Corruption" in its Second Interim Report dated February 28, 1951, the committee stated that English could not explain his one hundred thousand–dollar summer house, his interest in real estate, and his part ownership of a restaurant and a gas station, "all on a salary of forty-five hundred to six thousand dollars. The fact that the city was wide open for years and only two or three gambling arrests were made in 1950 may have some relation to the commissioner's wealth."

At the hearing in the St. Louis federal courthouse, the committee had asked English about his assets, and he had refused to provide any details. That prompted a comment by the questioner, John L. Burling, associate committee counsel: "It's a strange situation when a police commissioner who receives one hundred thousand dollars in political payoffs refuses to testify about his income." English was also treasurer of the Democrat Party in St. Clair County. The committee noted he had paid taxes on $131,409 he supposedly received in the form of political contributions in 1948 and 1949.

In its Third Interim Report, the committee said that English's comments that he had found no major law violations in East St. Louis "verge on the incredible," when two of the largest handbooks in the United States were operating downtown. He said he had first heard of one of the bookie joints by reading about it in a newspaper.

Jimmy Carroll was then considered the dean of the bookmakers. Incredibly, English said he believed Carroll was violating no federal or Illinois law. Asked also what he knew about area crime boss Frank "Buster" Wortman and his gang, who got their start in his city in the days of bootlegging, English drew a blank, testifying he knew nothing about the Al Capone–linked Wortman or his lieutenants.

ADOLPH FISCHER

Like English, Fischer testified he had little or no knowledge of gambling operations in East St. Louis. Two local handbooks, C. J. Rich & Co. and Carroll-Moody, had combined gross revenue in 1950 of $7 million, based on testimony by Harry C. Vermillion, superintendent of the St. Louis Western Union office. The committee figures were much higher than Vermillion's for Carroll-Moody. It ranked as the third largest horse race gambling house in the country, with an annual volume of $20 million in bets.

But Fischer testified he didn't know about any of it. He was asked how many gaming houses or casinos he had closed in his four-year term.

"None," he said. "Didn't know of any."

An exasperated Kefauver then showed Fischer Bureau of Internal Revenue records listing the excise taxes that had been paid the year before on 1,850 slot machines in St. Clair and Madison counties. The records failed to refresh Fischer's memory about gambling in his county.

DALLAS HARRELL

Harrell had been embarrassed the year before the hearings, when Governor Adlai Stevenson ordered a raid of two casinos in Madison County, the Hyde Park in Venice and the 200 Club in Madison. About seven hundred patrons were in the gambling meccas when state police burst in. The betting parlors and casinos had operated for years under Harrell's nose. Stevenson said he had tried to get Harrell to close Hyde Park before the state police raid. Harrell denied it in his testimony at the hearings.

Regarding the 200 Club in Madison, Harrell admitted he knew it was in operation. He said he had raided it once after the home of the state's attorney had been bombed, the club had been shot up, and a newspaper editor had been threatened. The former sheriff didn't elaborate on the seemingly mob-related violence, nor did he ever take any further action.

Harrell also blamed local officials for local problems. "If the mayor and the chief of police and the citizens of Madison, the city of Madison, were satisfied with it [the gambling den], it suited me," Harrell told the astonished committee and staff.

At first, the ex-sheriff claimed there had been no commercial slot machines in Madison County. Then he was shown St. Louis newspaper articles that listed the persons who had paid the hundred dollars a year federal tax for the establishments where slots were kept. Harrell changed his testimony, admitting he had known about the slot machines and conceding he had taken no action. The committee wanted to know specifically about the slot machines in the Red Rooster tavern on Collinsville Road that East Side crime boss Frank "Buster" Wortman owned. Harrell had a ready answer for that one. He, in effect, blamed Fischer. The tavern literally straddled the Madison–St. Clair County border. The slot machines were on the St. Clair County side of the saloon, and therefore, they were not his responsibility.

CONCLUSION

In its Third Interim Report of May 1, 1951, the committee summarized its view of the three lawmen and others: "There is little doubt in the minds of the committee that 'wide open' conditions were flourishing in Madison and St. Clair counties because of protection and payoffs."

NO TV FOR ME

When the Kefauver Committee convened in a St. Louis courtroom on February 23, 1951, its members intended to grill Jimmy Carroll, the self-proclaimed national betting czar. Carroll, after all, often set the odds nationwide for races, boxing matches, basketball games, and other sporting events. The *Globe-Democrat* described Carroll as an affable man who "dressed like a banker—a gentleman gambler, an oddsmaker and not a common bookie."

The courtroom was packed for the afternoon testimony by "the kingpin of the nation's betting commissioners," according to another *Globe* description. But Jimmy was absent, and in his place sat St. Louis criminal defense lawyer Morris Shenker. "Since we want some testimony from Mr. Carroll, whom you represent, we would like to hear testimony from you first," Senator Estes Kefauver told Shenker. Shenker said Carroll had testified at a prior hearing of a different Senate committee in Washington, D.C., and had described himself as "a betting commissioner." Shenker said Carroll was vacationing in Florida.

"You knew this committee was particularly interested in illegal gambling and interstate commerce, didn't you, and interested in hearing from Carroll?" John Burling, associate committee counsel, asked. Shenker said he was unaware until six weeks earlier that Carroll had been subpoenaed. He told the committee that he didn't think Carroll could offer much information.

The exchange angered Kefauver, who declared the committee would take steps to charge Carroll with contempt of Congress.

By the next day, Carroll had arrived, but nothing went smoothly for the committee. The "gambling kingpin" gave his age as sixty-four and his address as 4605 Lindell Boulevard; he then told the government he would not testify as long as the hearing was being televised. "I have no intention of being the object of ridicule," Carroll told Kefauver, who replied that Carroll's stance marked "the first time any witness refused to say his piece over television." (St. Louis had but one TV station at the time, KSD.)

Kefauver: "I cannot understand why you should be shown any special privileges, Mr. Carroll."

Carroll: "The whole proceeding outrages my sense of propriety, Senator. I simply will not testify before television."

He didn't. And his refusal threw the final phase of the committee hearing into confusion. Kefauver said he "would move with all vigor" to have the recalcitrant witness cited for contempt.

The following week, Carroll told the *Post-Dispatch*, "I have nothing to hide. I have a little hypertension, and an appearance before television is a big dose of excitement. As long as there is no television, I would be all right, but with excitement, I might black out." Shenker contended that forcing Carroll or any witness to testify before a television audience was a privacy violation.

Not surprisingly, in subsequent hearings of the Kefauver committee, New York gangsters invoked the same argument that Carroll had used about television to avoid testifying, which sounded better than invoking the Fifth Amendment against self-incrimination.

Meanwhile, Carroll submitted a letter to the committee—emphasized in the committee's reports—that he was closing up shop—no more oddsmaking, no more bookie joints. His East St. Louis establishment had already been raided, and it was shut down.

The St. Louis gambler was to learn that jousting with politicians usually meant the politicians got the last word. In its Third Interim Report, the committee noted sarcastically that Carroll was called the "Betting Commissioner." "The term was intended to signify some sort of respectability," the report said. "The committee found him to be an ordinary bookie operating clandestinely behind locked doors, which had to be broken down, in order to gain entry to the premises in broad daylight when many employees cringed behind the locked barrier."

MADISON COUNTY RAIDS

On the afternoon of May 12, 1950, customers of the 200 Club in Madison were worried. Uniformed men had burst into the gambling den and ordered everyone to stay in place. Police had never before entered the club at 200 State Street in Madison to make an arrest. And none of the officers were known to the patrons. Many of the customers feared the worst as they lined up in accordance with the orders of the men in uniform—they thought the officers were hoodlums wearing bogus outfits as a ruse for robbery.

Surprise. The officers were really Illinois state troopers and honest ones at that—and none of them were from the counties of Madison or St. Clair, home to major gambling dens for decades.

That morning, police had been summoned from all over Illinois to meet in Springfield at 11 a.m. They were told they were about to take part in raids; they were not told where.

At 3 p.m., fifty troopers descended in what the *St. Louis Post-Dispatch* called "spectacular raids on the notorious Hyde Park Club and the 200 Club on the East Side." At Hyde Park, police found about five hundred customers listening to national race results on a public address system, watching results posted on a blackboard, placing bets, tearing up losing tabs, cashing in winners at cashiers' cages, or playing blackjack or slot machines. Another three hundred had gathered for the same late-day gambling at the 200 Club in Madison when the raid took place. Roulette wheels, dice games, and poker tables had been shut down the year before because they weren't bringing in enough revenue.

The troopers had arrived in unmarked cars and vans. As they entered the casino, they told customers not to move until their names and addresses could be taken down. Then customers were ordered outside as police began making arrests based on "John Doe" warrants obtained by state officials from an Alton justice of the peace.

Alton became the first stop for a convoy of prisoners, later transferred to the Madison County jail in Edwardsville. The arrests totaled fifty-one: forty-eight clerks and cashiers, plus three owners—Gregory E. "Red" Moore, a close associate of Metro East crime boss Frank "Buster" Wortman; Louis "Murphy" Calcaterra, a co-owner with Moore in Hyde Park; and Henry Wrest, a co-owner of the 200 Club. As they were being taken away, Moore told employees not to worry.

Then authorities began loading vans with seized gambling paraphernalia and equipment, including betting stubs, the public address system, printed cards and tabs, even the comfortable armchairs customers would use while awaiting race results. Not all of it fit in the vans. Newspaper photographs show officials smashing gaming equipment with the heavy metal base of a hatrack. The operation continued into the night, with police cutting up and destroying hundreds of feet of uncut betting tabs. Besides equipment, police seized $22,663 in cash, three revolvers and a pistol from Hyde Park, and three revolvers and brass knuckles from the 200 Club.

The raids had been ordered by Governor Adlai Stevenson, who had campaigned in 1948 on a pledge to clean up gambling. For Governor Dwight Green's two terms, Illinois had been wide open; scandals had rocked his Republican administration, ranging from crooked cops and sheriffs to newspapermen on his payroll. Stevenson won the election by a half-million votes. Stevenson and Illinois Attorney General Ivan Elliott, also a reform candidate in 1948, were determined to turn things around. They lobbied, with some success, to close down handbooks and gambling establishments in other areas of Illinois.

After the raids, Stevenson commented that Madison County officials had ignored repeated calls from him to act. Neither Sheriff Dallas Harrell nor States Attorney Austin Lewis had been told of the raids beforehand. "I have stated repeatedly that the state would intervene if necessary in cases where commercialized gambling persists in spite of all our efforts," Stevenson said. He would later order raids of bookie joints in neighboring St. Clair County, in Lake County north of Chicago, and in central Illinois.

The raids were the death knell for the 200 Club and Hyde Park—a blow to the revenue stream of organized crime—despite a ruling by a friendly Madison County judge, who concluded the state had no authority to make the raids in the first place and ordered all the equipment returned to its owners.

"Red" Moore was right in telling his employees not to worry. By the time the state police had finished seizing some equipment and destroying the rest of it the night of the raid, all fifty-one suspects had been bailed out of jail.

KEFAUVER COMES, CLUB 45 GOES

The night before the U.S. Senate's Special Committee to Investigate Organized Crime in Interstate Commerce brought its traveling road show to St. Louis for hearings in February 1951, organized crime locally decided to shut down a casino it was operating in Jefferson County. The names of the Club 45's owners read like a Who's Who of both 1951 and future crime leaders of the St. Louis area, topped by East Side crime boss Frank "Buster" Wortman. He would be a no-show during the two days of hearings run by Senator Estes Kefauver.

Club 45 was a gambling resort located in a remote area on the Meramec River, about fifteen miles south of St. Louis. Patrons were driven there by men called "steerers," who would pick up gamblers at three locations: Third Street and Washington Avenue, the Statler Hotel downtown, as well as the Chase Park Plaza in the Central West End. For their pleasure at the Club 45, patrons could choose among dice games such as roulette and card games like blackjack and poker, as well as a bank of slot machines. Wortman had financed the casino along with Chicagoans and a former employee of late Kansas City mob boss Charles Binaggio, whose name would come up frequently during the Kefauver hearings.

"Operating the joint," as the *Post-Dispatch* put it, were the men who would run the Mob in St. Louis for the next three decades, while Wortman ran organized crime on the East Side until he died of natural causes in 1968. Those men were identified as "Tony Giordano, Ralph Calico, John Vitale, and Tony Lopiparo, all notorious St. Louis hoodlums."

The Club 45 closed, the newspaper said, "in deference to the Senate Crime Committee, which opened hearings here today."

St. Louis was one of more than twenty cities the Kefauver Committee visited in 1950 and 1951. Because many of its sessions were televised, the committee estimated that 30 million people, including 1 million in St. Louis, got to hear firsthand about illegal gambling operations from coast to coast, about gangsters who rose to power as bootleggers in the 1920s and remained in power, and about politicians the criminals paid off.

By the time Kefauver opened the hearings here—he was the only one of five senators to attend the St. Louis session—four of the biggest gambling dens in the area had already been shut down by a combination of state and federal intervention.

All four of the gaming houses and casinos came in for

substantial scrutiny by the committee for the way they operated, the size of their operations, their links to a national race wire, and the connections between the gamblers and organized crime on the one hand and local politicians and law enforcement on the other. The quartet were C. J. Rich & Co., also known as Rich-Wyman; the Carroll-Mooney betting parlor of East St. Louis; the Hyde Park Club of Venice; and the 200 Club of Madison.

Three other major issues on the minds of Kefauver, his battery of attorneys, and his team of investigators were the alleged attempt to fix the Missouri governor's race in 1948; the murders of Binaggio and an associate in Kansas City; and the links of St. Louis factions to a national racing wire that was run, the committee claimed, by the successors to Al Capone in Chicago.

Among local mobsters who failed to respond to subpoenas were Wortman, whom the *Globe-Democrat* and committee staff simply called the Capone syndicate's area director, and his lieutenants, Elmer "Dutch" Dowling, a North St. Louis gangster during Prohibition, and Louis "Red" Smith, once an Egan's Rat. One of the men the *Post-Dispatch* had described as a "notorious St. Louis hoodlum," Anthony Lopiparo, did testify. He provided spectators and television viewers with some comic relief, albeit unintentionally.

Kefauver demanded that Lopiparo testify about an alleged meeting of Mafia bosses in Tijuana, Mexico, that Lopiparo supposedly attended. The theory of committee investigators: Lopiparo and other Mafia leaders were involved in the murder of Kansas City crime boss Charles Binaggio. Lopiparo refused to answer questions about Binaggio or Tijuana. Kefauver persisted with the questioning.

"What's the matter? Haven't I got a Constitution?" Lopiparo wanted to know.

Kefauver replied to the hulking Lopiparo, "You seem to have a good constitution."

Lopiparo finally admitted he knew Binaggio—but that was all he admitted. He also conceded he had made two trips to Tijuana, but they were health-related, he claimed.

Binaggio's murder on April 6, 1950, along with that of Charles Gargotta, may have been linked, the committee said in its Third Interim Report, to allegations that Binaggio and other Kansas City crime figures had backed Forrest Smith for governor in 1948 and had bragged that Smith would open Kansas City and St. Louis to crime elements. In St. Louis, gambler William Molasky contributed twenty-five hundred dollars to Smith's campaign in hopes that Smith would appoint criminal defense lawyer Morris Shenker to the St. Louis Police Board. No evidence showed Smith providing any favors for the Mob in either city. Instead of Shenker, Smith had appointed to the St. Louis Police Board William L Holzhausen, an anti-gambling witness before the committee.

"Did Binaggio and his group ever try to operate here?" Kefauver wanted to know. "As far as I know, they did not," Holzhausen said. About efforts by organized crime to obtain police influence, Holzhausen said, "No one ever approached me. Governor Forrest Smith instructed the police board to see that all laws, state and city, were enforced."

His failure to open up Missouri to vice was Binaggio's downfall, and crime leaders from Chicago and St. Louis had actually plotted Binaggio's murder, according to investigators, at the Hyde Park Club in Venice two weeks before his death and a month before Illinois Governor Adlai Stevenson raided and closed down the betting parlor and casino.

At the hearings in St. Louis, Kansas City, Washington, D.C., and Miami, the committee spent considerable time investigating national and regional racing wire services. Binaggio had run the regional racing wire distributorship in Kansas City. In St. Louis, the regional racing wire, *Pioneer News*, traced its roots to the 1920s, when it was run by William "Bev" Brown and Gully Owens, who were also the primary bail bondsmen in St. Louis. In 1938, Chicago crime figures muscled their way into the picture. Three Chicagoans, who were involved in a nationwide racing wire headquartered in Chicago, took over 50 percent of the stock. While the Bureau of Internal Revenue was looking at his taxes, Chicagoan Moses Annenberg then sold his share of *Pioneer* to St. Louisan Molasky for one dollar.

In subsequent years, Bev Brown and his son, William P. Brown, were back at *Pioneer*. Binaggio had taken over the regional racing wire in Kansas City, and others with ties to the Capone Mob took over in Florida. *Pioneer* would charge some bookies one hundred dollars a week for its services, William Brown had testified at an earlier hearing. Others would be charged three hundred dollars for the results and horse information. Brown could not explain why one bookie paid less and another more for the same services.

Molasky was questioned by Harvard-trained associate committee counsel John Burling, who asked if Molasky knew gambling was illegal in Missouri and Illinois. "No sir, I didn't know it was illegal," said Molasky, whose reply stunned even his lawyer, Shenker, sitting at his side.

Burling asked Molasky if he had ties to the Chicago Mob. "Who is the Chicago Mob?" Molasky replied. Under further questioning, the committee learned that Molasky was doing well financially; he owned eighteen thousand shares of Western Union stock, worth eight hundred thousand dollars in 1951. Molasky's ownership of Western Union stock led the committee to suggest that he had influenced local officials of that company, particularly in their dealings with C. J. Rich & Co.

Before the government raid on June 26, 1950, the company "grossed about $4.5 million a year and used Western Union telegrams, money orders, and Western Union agents to carry on operations," the committee noted in its Third Interim Report.

The bookmaker operated in East St. Louis, where it received bets, which were then messengered to the corporate headquarters at 7203 St. Charles Rock Road in St. Louis County. Most of the bets came from more than 150 miles from St. Louis. Western Union agents were used as runners and solicitors for bets. They were paid a percentage of winnings for their services or commissions, as much as 25 percent, the committee was told. In addition, they often got cash or gifts from Rich & Co. In one month alone, the company's telegraph bill was $26,700. The committee said it was clear that "Western Union aided and abetted the violation of gambling laws of the state because it was profitable to do so."

After the raid, Western Union closed down all of Rich's accounts. "One wonders whether the Western Union's obliviousness to its public responsibility not to permit the facilities to be used in violation of state law was in part due to the fact that William Molasky of St. Louis, a well-known gambler, is one of its outstanding stockholders," the committee reported. The St. Louis prosecuting attorney (noting that Rich & Co. took in from $150,000 to $300,000 a month) and the city police board's Holzhausen urged Congress to bar the transmission of gambling and racing news by telegraph.

Despite the high numbers, Rich & Co. may not have been the biggest bookmaker in East St. Louis. The gambling den run by Jimmy Carroll and John Mooney operated with impunity and immunity in downtown East St. Louis until a raid in 1950 by state officials and federal investigators. It took in about sixteen thousand dollars a day, according to one of its former employees. The committee eventually ranked Carroll-Mooney as the third largest gaming center in the United States, behind only a Los Angeles bookmaker and a Miami gambling operation.

Also high on the bet-taking list before their demise were the Hyde Park Club in Madison and the 200 Club in Venice. All four, plus independent area bookies whose numbers may have exceeded one hundred, were part of a nationwide pattern in the early 1950s that the Kefauver Committee succeeded in changing.

In off-track betting, illegal in every state except Nevada, the committee estimated that $20 billion changed hands every year. The numbers racket accounted for another $150 million in illegal wagering, and slot machines took in $540 million nationwide.

J. EDGAR HOOVER

Some of the illegal earnings by crime figures often went to corrupt law enforcement officers and venal politicians. Crusaders like newspaper publishers Paul Simon of the *Troy Tribune* and James O. Monroe of the *Collinsville Herald* testified the system was often self-perpetuating. Illegal funds were used to buy off politicians and police, who would look the other way so criminals could continue their operations.

In the wake of the Kefauver hearings, Congress changed the laws on the use of telephone and telegraph wires; grand juries began racketeering investigations throughout the country; incompetent or corrupt officials were voted out of office; racket squads in the Treasury Department focused once again on mobsters' tax returns, as they did in the days of Al Capone; and even FBI Director J. Edgar Hoover had to admit there was a national crime syndicate.

After documenting how organized crime switched to gambling and vice once its bootlegging days ended, the committee predicted in its final report, "The organized gangster syndicate will unquestionably turn to the sale of narcotic drugs when they are driven out of the presently lucrative field of gambling."

The committee was right on.

POPULAR POL, CORRUPTION
1951-52

As the jury verdicts were read in U.S. District Court on the night of March 15, 1952, former revenue collector James P. Finnegan covered his face with his hands as he heard that he now faced prison time after convictions for two counts of misconduct in office. His hands fell away as a deputy marshal intoned not-guilty verdicts on three additional counts of accepting bribes. But the jovial extrovert was in no mood to talk to reporters or joke with friends or flash his politician's smile as he walked from the courtroom with his wife, Eve, and headed for his home in St. Louis Hills. Earlier that day as the jury was deliberating for eight hours, Finnegan had joked with a reporter that the slight limp in his gait was an old injury from his football-playing days at Saint Louis University "kicking up again." Too many hours of sitting during ten days of trial had kept him from stretching it out, he explained.

The trip home was only temporary. He was free on bond until his sentencing on March 24. Federal Judge Rubey M. Hulen then imposed two years in prison on the two misconduct counts, and Finnegan was on his way to the U.S. Penitentiary in Terre Haute, Indiana, where he would eventually be released after eighteen months.

Just a year earlier, there had even been speculation that the affable friend of President Harry S. Truman would be a good candidate for mayor. There had also been speculation about widespread corruption in the federal Bureau of Internal Revenue, the predecessor to the Internal Revenue Service.

Enter stage right the conservative federal Judge George H. Moore, who had suspicions of a failure by the government to prosecute tax cheats. Moore raised the issue with local prosecutors and directly by telephone with the attorney general of the United States, J. Howard McGrath, who told Moore to go through normal channels. Moore contended the normal channels—going through Finnegan's office—were clogged. Ironically, Moore had sworn in Finnegan as collector of revenue for the St. Louis District after Finnegan's appointment in 1944 by President Franklin Delano Roosevelt. McGrath told Moore he would get back to him. When Moore heard nothing from the Justice Department, he decided on his own to convene a federal grand jury to investigate. Local prosecutors were suddenly ordered to assist, and the grand jury returned a report indicting seven for criminal tax fraud but declaring there was no evidence of "influence lawyers." Moore was shocked. The shock turned to outrage when U.S. Attorney Drake Watson—in ill health, he would die two months later—told the judge that the language exhonerating the "influence lawyers" had been drafted in his offices at the instructions from Washington and read to higher-ups in the Justice Department before the grand jurors ever saw it or voted on it. Moore declared a whitewash and ordered the grand jury back in session to do some serious investigation.

Enter the *Post-Dispatch* stage left. The liberal *Post*—never a Truman supporter—and its bulldog of an investigative reporter, Ted Link, were looking at a specific company, American Lithofold, and its ability to get $565,000 in loans from an agency called the Reconstruction Finance Corp. Three times Lithofold applied for loans; three times Charles Alexander, RFC's local manager, turned it down. Higher-ups in Washington also said no. Then came early 1949 and a loan from RFC to Lithofold for $80,000 and another loan in September, bringing the total to Lithofold to $465,000 and finally another $100,000 two months later. When government agents began to look into it in 1950, Lithofold paid back the loan.

What connection did Lithofold have to Finnegan? About forty-five thousand dollars' worth, or the total amount of money the company had paid Finnegan for so-called legal services. In 1949, Finnegan was on the company books for one thousand dollars a month. The company also paid five hundred dollars a month in early 1949 to Bill Boyle, chairman of the Democratic National Committee. He dropped off the payroll in April. His office said he got a total of fifteen hundred dollars; the *Post-Dispatch* reported a total of eight thousand dollars. Boyle gave up his Lithofold funding, but his partner, Max Siskind, was added to the payroll for an eventual total of thirteen thousand dollars.

Boyle stepped down as party chairman. Finnegan resigned in April 1951 amidst the *Post* disclosures and the grand jury investigation. The president said he accepted the resignation with deep regrets. *Time* magazine said Truman had asked Finnegan to resign.

In October, Finnegan was indicted on the five counts, for which he stood trial the following March. The grand jurors accused Finnegan of violating the law that prohibits a government employee from receiving pay for services in which the government was an interested party. Finnegan violated that ban when he got a $3,000 payment from Lithofold in helping it get the $565,000 from RFC. Alexander, its local head, said he would see Finnegan at meetings, and Finnegan would ask about American Lithofold. Alexander would say some of its business practices were unsound, and Finnegan would agree, but "he would inevitably ask at each meeting, 'How's the loan coming, Charlie?'"

Finnegan also was accused of accepting three thousand dollars from the Warwick Hotel Company for helping its owner collect a forty thousand–dollar claim against the Coast Guard.

Both counts, for which Finnegan was eventually convicted, amounted to misconduct in office, violating the statute barring influence peddling by a government official.

The other three counts involved a St. Louis dressmaker called Karol Kell Garments. Prosecutors alleged Finnegan took two bribes of $250 each and $641 in furniture for giving Karol Kell easy terms for payment of $36,000 in delinquent taxes and helping the dressmaker get a loan from RFC.

In September 1951, Finnegan had been forced to testify before a Senate subcommittee in Washington. He was questioned sharply by Senators Karl Mundt, R-South Dakota, and Richard M. Nixon, R-California, about the forty-five thousand dollars he got from Lithofold. Mundt wanted to know how he spent the money. "I could take you or Senator Nixon out on a party at the Shoreham Hotel, and I could spend eight hundred dollars so fast you wouldn't know it was gone."

Two weeks later, it was a House committee delving into the corruption cases. Once again, Finnegan was on the carpet, and he admitted he spent just two to four hours a day at his job at the collector's office. "Sometimes more," he added.

"And sometimes less?" asked counsel Adrian DeWind.

"And sometimes less," Finnegan conceded.

The House subcommittee also alleged that Finnegan had sent the names of suspected tax evaders to an insurance company that then investigated and split the profits with Finnegan.

After his conviction, the *Post-Dispatch* noted that the $45,000 he got from Lithofold, coupled with $30,000 he got in legal fees from other outside sources, was far more profitable than the $10,500 a year he got as collector.

Before his federal appointment in 1944, Finnegan had served as a municipal judge and a prosecutor. He was a third-generation public servant. His grandfather had been a fireman; so, too, his father and a brother, William. He chose law after his undergraduate days at Saint Louis University, where he was captain of the football and track teams. He regaled friends later with reminiscences about the Saint Louis–Notre Dame game of 1922 and legendary Knute Rockne. The Billikens lost 26–0.

Finnegan's convictions were among the first in an ever-widening probe of the Bureau of Internal Revenue. *Time* reported in July 1954 that 213 federal employees and their friends had been indicted. Besides Finnegan, the list included a former head of the bureau and an assistant commissioner.

A bad year for St. Louis's Finnegan, 1952 was a good year for the city's newspapers. Link and the *Post-Dispatch* won the Pulitzer Prize for the corruption stories. Louis LaCoss, sixty-two, a veteran *Globe-Democrat* editorial writer, won the Pulitzer Prize for an editorial, "The Low Estate of Public Morals."

That senator from California took the high road. Richard M. Nixon publicly praised the *Post-Dispatch*. Years later, it would make Nixon's enemies list.

Finnegan was pardoned by President Lyndon Johnson in 1967 and died five months later.

THE AMMONIA BOMB HOLDUP
1952

The holdup of an armored car outside the Mound City Trust Company in North St. Louis on November 22, 1952, provided plenty of speculation. Both the background of the robber and the method of the robbery—fitting neither the profile of a holdup man nor the usual gun-in-your-face methodology—stunned authorities.

That Friday morning, a Guarantee Service Company armored car pulled up in front of the bank at Natural Bridge and Newstead avenues, and two guards carried sacks of cash into the bank as part of a routine delivery. Guard Thomas Doerflinger remained in the back of the armored car. Suddenly, a man carrying a brown bag jumped into the truck's cab. He pulled from the bag a long tube and a canister. He placed the tube into a hole between the cab and the money compartment. He yelled to Doerflinger, "Hey, look this way." Then he squeezed the canister. That sent a stream of suffocating ammonia gas into the back of the truck, blinding and disabling the guard. Before he passed out, the twenty-four-year-old Doerflinger was able to draw his Luger and get off several shots at his assailant. One hit the holdup man in the left leg, another in the left arm, and a shot that proved fatal struck the robber in the neck.

Passersby ran into the bank and told Doerflinger's colleagues what had happened. They rushed out and helped pedestrians pull the two men from the armored car. The robber was dead on arrival at City Hospital; Doerflinger died a few days later.

Police found no identification on the robber but did find a pair of car keys in his pocket. Officers tried the keys on cars parked near the bank and found a match in a late-model Chevy. The car held a hacksaw, chisel, hammer, and screwdriver. Police decided that the robber had intended to drive the armored car away—the keys were in it—and then use the tools to pry open the money compartment.

So who was the inventive if unsuccessful robber? The license plates of the Chevy were registered to Reed Ice Cream Stores, which had one of its outlets a few blocks from Mound City Trust. The owner of the company was listed as Jacob Katz, who lived in an affluent neighborhood of University City. Katz was forty-five. He owned ice cream franchises. He was the father of three. His wife told police that her husband had left the house that morning and had not returned. Orville Richardson, then an attorney and later a county judge, knew Katz, went with police to the city morgue, and identified the robber as his friend.

Before World War II, Katz had operated a stone quarry and had been a homebuilder in Fort Dodge, Iowa. He shut down the businesses during the war and worked in an aircraft factory in Omaha.

Katz came to St. Louis in 1945, bought a Reed Ice Cream Store, and later expanded the business to five shops. By 1952, however, Katz was deep in debt. He told a friend on the Wednesday before the ammonia bomb holdup, "If someone shoots me, my wife will be in good condition." Katz had sixty-five thousand dollars in life insurance.

A few weeks before his death, Katz had applied at Mound City Trust for a loan of three thousand dollars, offering property as collateral.

The bank turned him down.

THE GREAT ST. LOUIS BANK ROBBERY
1953

The Great St. Louis Bank Robbery of April 24, 1953, was anything but great, nor was it really a robbery. Call it an attempted holdup. It lasted just fifteen minutes. But the bold, mid-morning attempt to rob the age-old Southwest Bank at the corner of Southwest Avenue and Kingshighway was the kind of event in someone's lifetime that brings the response: Oh, yeah, I remember that.

At 10:20 a.m. that day, cashier Arthur Zinselmeyer was working behind his cage. Joe Bauer was repairing a Southwestern Bell telephone line. The bank's board of directors was meeting. I. A. Long, a vice president at rival Mercantile Bank and the police board president, was visiting downtown police headquarters. Zinselmeyer described what happened. A man walked in a side door of the bank. He wore a tan mask, and he carried a sawed-off shotgun. He yelled, "This is a holdup."

On cue, two other gunmen charged in the front door of the bank. Moving quickly, the robbers gathered up $141,000 into a zippered bag. A fourth man waited outside in a getaway car. A teller immediately hit the alarm button. At the same time, Bauer saw the armed men and reported the holdup in progress from the phone he had hooked up. Police began responding from every direction. Long jumped into a patrolman's car and raced to the crime scene. So, too, did Chief Joe Casey and the police department brass.

Corporal Robert Heitz and officer Melburn Stein were within a few blocks of the bank. Heitz burst through the side door and began exchanging gunfire with the robbers. Two robbers fell. A third came up from a crouch behind a teller's cage and shot Heitz.

Myrtle Howard was about to go into the bank when she saw the robbers. She kept other passersby from entering before more police arrived. A member of Southwest's board of directors opened a door of the boardroom, saw the robbery in progress, and slammed the door shut. Board members ducked under desks.

About one hundred police officers responded to the alarm and converged on the bank. In the gun battle, police and robbers exchanged about forty shots. Then police fired canisters of tear gas into the building. During the din, about twenty employees and customers made it to the safety of the bank's basement. But one of the robbers grabbed Eva Hamilton as a shield. Police yelled to Hamilton to drop to the ground. As she fell, the forty-two-year-old secretary broke both her wrists, but Stein and others shot the gunman who had been holding her.

When the shooting finally stopped, the score read: one robber, Fred Bowerman, fatally wounded by police; another, William Scholl, shot and wounded; a third, Frank Vito, shot in the head by his own gun; and the getaway driver captured later. The money was recovered intact. Heitz survived wounds to his head and neck.

St. Louis lawyer Raymond Bruntrager was first assistant circuit attorney in 1953. One of the robbers, Scholl, told the prosecutor that Bowerman had cased the bank, and the gang had met daily at Tower Grove Park to plan and plot. They had worked out such small details as using different first names during the robbery and carrying ignition cables in their pockets in case they got separated. The robbery planning originated in Chicago and shifted to St. Louis, where one of the gang had rented an apartment in the 3500 block of Forest Park Boulevard. Police later recovered a cache of weapons and ammunition at that address.

Vito, the robber who shot himself, had served prison terms for hijacking and faced a potential sentence of life in prison. Bowerman was on the FBI's "Ten Most Wanted" list for the robbery of a bank in South Bend, Indiana, in September 1952.

The failed robbery became the subject of the movie *The Great St. Louis Bank Robbery* by United Artists in 1959. In a year in which Hollywood produced such classics as *Ben-Hur* with Charlton Heston, *On the Beach* with Gregory Peck, *North by Northwest* starring Cary Grant and Eva Marie Saint, *The Mouse That Roared* with Peter Sellers, and *Anatomy of a Murder* with James Stewart, the robbery movie was lost in the shuffle. Produced and directed by Charles Guggenheim, the film featured unknowns David Clarke, James Dukas, and Molly McCarthy. Another unknown played the getaway driver. His name? Steve McQueen. One reviewer called it "an attempt to create a realistic depiction of scheming and a bank heist that is a failure. . . . The long drawn-out expose of four men going through routine tasks gets to be boring."

Three months after the holdup, Long, the police board president, and two other major investors bought Southwest Bank. Long built the bank's assets to $110 million from $20 million over the next thirty years. Long developed such an uncanny knack for cutting interest rates before his big-city brethren could act that his bank garnered attention over the years from as far away as London and Bangkok.

GREENLEASE KIDNAPPING
1953

Nine years after Bonnie Heady and Carl Austin Hall were executed for the kidnapping and murder of six-year-old Bobby Greenlease, ex–St. Louis patrolman Elmer Dolan met secretly with the FBI in Washington, D.C., at the behest of Attorney General Bobby Kennedy. Dolan disclosed his involvement in three hundred thousand dollars in missing ransom money. He told FBI agents that he had told no one else—not his wife, not his family—and they thought he was an innocent man who wrongly went to prison. He asked the FBI to keep his sworn testimony confidential. FBI Director J. Edgar Hoover said there would be no deals. But the agency agreed that it had no reason to reveal any of Dolan's secrets unless someone else would be prosecuted some day, and that seemed highly unlikely.

Of the main characters involved in the nationally publicized case of the little boy kidnapped from a school in Kansas City on September 28, 1953, Dolan may have been the least culpable. Giving him the benefit of the doubt, his actions could have been those of a prudent man faced with the possibility of his own death or the murder of his wife, Mary, if he talked. In the FBI interviews, Dolan may have been too hard on himself when he said he should have arrested a superior officer and a hoodlum instead of silently going along with their plot to steal half the ransom money.

Dolan had been the driver for St. Louis Lieutenant Louis Shoulders on the night of October 6, 1953, when they arrived at Hall's apartment at 5316 Pershing Avenue. The officers were initially unaware that the man they were taking into custody was the subject of a nationwide manhunt unequaled since the days of the Charles Lindbergh baby kidnapping in 1932.

On September 28, Hall and Heady and Heady's dog, Doc, a boxer, had driven to Kansas City from St. Joseph with one stop in between, at a tavern to fortify themselves. They got to the French Institute of Notre Dame de Sion in time to watch Robert Greenlease drop off Bobby at 8:50 a.m. Heady got out of their 1953 Plymouth station wagon a few blocks away and got a cab. At 10:55 a.m., Heady told the driver to take her to the school and wait for her. Heady told a sister that she was Bobby's aunt and that Bobby's mother had had a heart attack at Country Club Plaza. Without any apparent suspicion, Bobby joined Heady, and the cab driver dropped them off at a drugstore at 40th and Main Street, where they got into the Plymouth. The wagon sped off.

Carl Austin Hall had just carried out the first part of his plan to make a bundle that would keep him in money, booze, and pills for the rest of his life. But Hall had about as much talent for crime as he had in almost every other aspect of his life—little or none. He wasn't a down-and-out bad guy from an abusive family background. He couldn't blame childhood poverty or a lack of opportunity or even a low IQ. He was thirty-four years old, with a bad complexion, a heavy face, and too many pounds on his six-foot frame. He chain-smoked, drank whiskey by the fifths per day, and added Benzedrine to the mix. He was born in 1919 in Pleasanton, Kansas, the son of a lawyer, who died when Carl was thirteen, and a mother who was the daughter of a judge. Zelba sent her son to a military academy in Missouri for three years of high school. After graduating in Pleasanton, Hall joined the Marines, served a four-year hitch, and reenlisted for another four. He served in the South Pacific with the First Marine Division, facing disciplinary action six times for drunken sprees. Back in civilian life in 1946, Hall managed to squander an inheritance of two hundred thousand dollars from the death of his mother. He got married and divorced; failed as a crop duster; failed as a music store owner; and failed in attempting to operate liquor stores.

By 1951, he was a vagrant under arrest in Milwaukee. He was arrested for a robbery in Kansas. He pleaded guilty of robbing eight cab drivers in Kansas City out of a total of thirty-three dollars and was sentenced to five years in the state penitentiary, serving one year and three months. Hall had failed as a used car salesman and insurance agent in St. Joseph when he met Bonnie Brown Heady at the Hotel Robidoux bar. She was in her cups; so was he.

At forty-one, Bonnie was seven years older than Carl. She had been in a state of perpetual drunkenness since her divorce a year earlier from Ellis Heady, to whom she had been married for twenty years. She was born on a farm in northwest Missouri, graduated from high school, and attended Northeast Missouri State (now Truman State University), before marrying Heady, a livestock merchant. She showed horses and raised championship dogs. In the divorce, Bonnie got the house in St. Joseph. She also inherited forty-four thousand dollars from her late father. At five feet one inch, she had heavy breasts and was overweight. That didn't keep a steady stream of men from visiting her bungalow. She drank heavily. She turned tricks, and she had lived with another ex-con before Hall came along.

That was the couple with whom Bobby Greenlease was riding the morning of September 28. Hall had no intention of sparing the child. He had already dug Bobby's grave in the backyard in St. Joseph. Bobby was the son of a doting father who was sixty-five when Bobby was born in 1947. His sister, Virginia Sue, whom the kidnappers had once considered abducting, was five years older. They lived in Mission Hills, a fashionable suburb in Kansas. The elder Greenlease had parlayed the growth of the automobile industry into a series of Cadillac and Oldsmobile distributorships.

Hall drove his Plymouth to a field in Kansas, where he first tried to strangle Bobby, failed, and fired two shots, one missing the boy, the other killing him. Back in St. Joseph, Bobby was dumped into the grave that awaited him. Then the calls to the family for six hundred thousand dollars in ransom began, with Hall assuring Virginia Greenlease that her son was still alive. In one conversation, Hall told the Greenleases that Bobby "says his parrot whistles. Lady, he is driving us nuts. We have earned this money."

A week after the abduction, the Greenleases placed a bulky bag with tens and twenties totaling six hundred thousand dollars at an overpass of Highway 40, the predecessor to Interstate 70, and the kidnappers headed for St. Louis with the loot. They got to St. Louis on October 5, drank at several bars, and rented an apartment on Arsenal Street in South St. Louis, where Heady drank herself into oblivion while Hall hit scores of taverns and eventually hired John Hager, a driver for Ace Cab Company, to drive him around. One of the stops was Room 49a of the Art Deco and private garage-to-room Coral Courts Motel on Watson Road in Marlborough, where Hager brought a prostitute, Sandra June O'Day. She complained later that Hall was unable to perform. Hall moved from the motel to the Town House Apartments in the 5300 block of Pershing Avenue.

Hager told his boss, Joseph Costello, owner of the taxi company, about his rider. Costello contacted his police buddy, Louis Shoulders.

In his secret confession to the FBI in 1962, Officer Dolan picks up the story. He was the lieutenant's driver. After roll call on October 6, Dolan drove Shoulders to the back of the tavern in the 4900 block of Delmar Boulevard, where he saw but couldn't hear Shoulders talking to Costello. They then drove to 5316 Pershing Avenue, where Hager pointed out Hall's apartment. The cops knocked. Hall answered and was met with a drawn weapon. The FBI report says, "Shoulders took two suitcases of ransom money and passed them out the apartment door to Joe Costello. He (Dolan) emphasized that he did not see this occur because Shoulders was not in his vision."

Dolan and Shoulders took Hall to the Deer Street station and booked him. Then Dolan and Shoulders disappeared for more than an hour. Dolan told the FBI nine years later they went to Costello's house. "This is the first time I have ever been in Joseph Costello's house. When I entered the house, it was dark. I followed Costello or Shoulders down some stairs to a rathskeller in the basement.... On what appeared to be a coffee table, I observed two large trunks, one black and one green, which were opened and contained a large amount of money. In addition, there were large stacks of currency on the table outside the trunks," Dolan recalled. "At the time, the thought went through my mind that this was just a hell of a lot of money. . . . Shoulders, Costello, and I were the only ones in the basement."

Dolan said Shoulders told him he had just made fifty thousand dollars, but Dolan refused. "I next recall Shoulders saying we are going to take the money (half) back to the station house in the suitcases. I asked him not to take any of the money because he couldn't get away with it. . . . I recall that as we drove from Costello's house to the police station Shoulders appeared happy over making some money while I, in turn, tried to tell him it was a mistake and I was apprehensive over the whole situation."

The pair parked in a lot in an alley off the back of the station, carried the luggage into the station, and put it in a captain's office. Hall confessed to the kidnapping that night, later to the murder. Police picked up Heady at the apartment on Arsenal Street. Authorities learned that Bobby, for whom the FBI and every police agency in the country were searching, had been dead for ten days. They dug up the remains in Heady's backyard.

Hall and Heady were indicted by a federal grand jury on October 30, 1953; tried in U.S. District Court in Kansas City on November 16; convicted in one hour and eight minutes; and sentenced to die.

About 8 p.m. on December 17, the pair supped on fried chicken, mashed potatoes and gravy, a salad with Roquefort dressing, and orange sherbet. Hall wore olive twill trousers; Heady, a green cotton dress and slippers. At 12:04 a.m., sodium cyanide powder was dropped into vats of sulfuric acid. Hall died at 12:12 a.m. in Missouri's gas chamber. Heady died two minutes later. Neither had offered a final word. Just eighty-one days had passed since they snatched Bobby and killed him.

At the police station the night Hall was arrested, Dolan and four detectives counted $288,510 in ransom money. FBI Agent John H. Poelker, a future mayor of St. Louis, and three others counted again, found some small amounts the first counters had missed, and came up with a total of $295,790.

St. Louis was embarrassed. Hall claimed he was certain there was $570,000 in two suitcases and $20,000 in a briefcase when he was arrested by Shoulders and Dolan. He said he saw a man in the hallway that night. Shoulders suggested mobsters had robbed Hall at the Coral Court. Both Shoulders and Dolan stuck to the story that they had brought all the money to the station with Hall. Seven witnesses at the station, including two women there to see boyfriends who had been arrested, said there were no suitcases accompanying Hall.

Shoulders and Dolan were charged in Kansas City with perjury and convicted of the crime. Shoulders got a three-year sentence; Dolan, two years. The search for the missing money involved one hundred FBI agents. All 40,000 bills had been recorded. Over the years, only $2,255 of the ransom money was ever recovered. A favorite St. Louis pastime was speculating on where the money went: it was buried on a bank of the Meramec River near Fenton, where Hall had gone briefly; it was hidden in a wall at the Coral Courts, since torn down with no money found; Sandra O'Day stole it; the cabbie took it.

Some of the bills showed up in the Chicago area, and others in Michigan. One theory had East St. Louis crime boss Frank "Buster" Wortman disposing of it through Chicago mob connections; another theory—one espoused by Bobby Kennedy when he was chief counsel of the Senate Rackets Committee—had the Teamsters Union involved in distributing the ransom. Kennedy quizzed Dolan, but the ex-cop wasn't talking.

When Kennedy became attorney general, he asked the FBI to question Dolan. In 1962, both Shoulders and Costello died, and Dolan agreed to secret meetings in Washington, D.C. Dolan said he eventually agreed to take fifteen hundred dollars from Shoulders after he got out of prison because he felt he had served prison time for Shoulders. He used it to buy Christmas presents for his family and for living expenses, he told the FBI.

Dolan said Costello once told him that the money was buried on the farm of a relative. Another time, Costello mentioned John Vitale, the St. Louis crime boss. On a third occasion, Costello talked about the Teamsters Union, Dolan said. Then there was a mystery man in the hallway the night Shoulders turned the money over to Costello. Dolan couldn't see who it was. Could it have been crime boss Vitale? An organized crime figure? Or maybe it was just Hager, the cabbie, helping his own boss carry the money away. The FBI never found out.

Dolan was pardoned by President Lyndon Johnson in 1965. He died of a heart attack in 1973. The public would never have known about the confession by Dolan if not for the reporting on October 7, 1982, of Sue Ann Wood, *Globe-Democrat* assistant managing editor, and Edward O'Brien, the paper's Washington bureau chief. They obtained the FBI files, thousands of pages including all of Dolan's transcripts of his secret confession—nearly sixty years after the crimes—as part of a Freedom of Information Act demand.

It included an FBI memo of March 24, 1970, saying the Greenlease kidnapping case should be officially closed because the statute of limitations had run out on prosecution over the missing money.

The file also contained Dolan's feelings about his own role. Dolan blamed himself for failing to arrest Shoulders and Costello when he saw the stash of cash in Costello's basement and learned they were going to steal half of it.

STALKING THE STALKER: THE NORTH COUNTY RAPIST
1957

St. Louis patrolman Chester Voelpel probably had second thoughts about the man he had pulled over on Riverview Boulevard near Chain of Rocks Park at dusk on November 12, 1957. Wearing a plaid flannel shirt, the mild-mannered man behind the wheel looked anything but a serial rapist. He was slightly built and stared at Voelpel with that open what-did-I-do-wrong look. He was a good four inches shorter than the police officer. And George Henry Frangel, Jr., twenty-seven, was married, the father of four. He owned a house in Glasgow Village. He worked as a route clerk for a trucking company in East St. Louis. He appeared to be the epitome of 1950s middle-class living.

A week before, a motorist had stopped the car of a woman from Roxana by driving alongside her and yelling that her car was on fire. After she stopped, the man approached, pointed a pistol at her, and showed her a badge, saying he was a police officer, then forcing her into his car. He drove into a secluded area of the park. As he began his sexual assault, the victim grabbed the aggressor's car keys and threw them into the street. The diversion worked. As the rapist went to retrieve his keys, the woman ran about 150 yards, then spotted a parked patrol car and an officer standing in front of it. She ran into Voelpel's consoling arms.

So Voelpel began to stalk the stalker, driving the streets near Chain of Rocks every evening on the hunch the rapist would return to familiar haunts. On his front seat, Voelpel had a composite sketch of the attacker, whom the newspapers were calling "the North County Rapist." He knew also that the attacker was driving a 1953 Chevy with a burnt-out headlight.

As he drove along Riverview about 6:55 p.m. on November 12, a car matching that description passed him in the other direction. Voelpel pulled over the Chevy. When he looked inside, the officer spotted what appeared to be a toy pistol on the back seat. That find, plus the driver's resemblance to the victims' sketch, was enough evidence, despite Frangel's denials, to take the suspect to the Ruskin Avenue police station.

It didn't take long for Frangel to admit he had tried to rape the woman from Roxana the week before. He also readily confessed to six other sexual attacks between July and November, including one the night before involving a woman, forty-one, from Florissant. Frangel told detectives that the badge he used as a ploy had belonged to a lieutenant in an Illinois volunteer fire department and that Frangel found it in a friend's car. He said he had once seen an automobile on fire, and that gave him the idea of yelling fire to get his targets to stop. Frangel admitted he had taken some of his victims to a secluded area near the Missouri River. In another case, he told police he had walked nude into the home of a woman in Bel-Ridge and threatened her son with a knife if she tried to resist him.

As the attacks throughout north St. Louis County mounted that summer and fall before the suspect's arrest, city, county, Jennings, and Moline Acres police had beefed up patrols in their search for the rapist. Moline Acres Police Chief Arthur Hannebrink had come close. He suspected Frangel because of the car description and kept the man's Glasgow Village house under surveillance for several days. But nothing happened while Frangel was being watched.

In January 1960, Frangel cut a deal with prosecutors, pleading guilty to four felonies and withdrawing his appeal of a rape conviction returned by a jury a year earlier. In sentencing Frangel to a total of eighteen years in prison—he got out in nine—the judge said he thought Frangel "was in need of psychiatric treatment."

In today's world, Frangel's actions would have merited four or more life sentences. His punishment in 1960 reflected the popular thinking of the time. People viewed a rapist as a man overcome by sexual desire. Still others tended to blame the victim, suggesting somehow that she was at fault. But study after study has shown that rape is a crime of violence—not sex but domination, not desire but humiliation and hurt.

NOT GUILTY: AN INSANITY PLEA
1959

Sam Iaconetti got the meeting he wanted with W. Victor Weir on November 19, 1959, at Weir's private office at 8390 Delmar Boulevard in University City. Iaconetti brought a nephew with him to help him plead the family's case and to ask Weir to hold off on foreclosure. Iaconetti was the owner of a nightclub at 6600 Delmar in the University City Loop. He had purchased the property from the St. Louis County Water Company, and he had spent thirty-five thousand dollars converting it into Club Variety, but he had fallen behind in mortgage payments. He owed the water company sixty-five thousand dollars. The company was threatening to foreclose.

Weir was president and chief executive of the company, as well as a mover and shaker in the St. Louis area. He had been national president of the American Water Works Association in 1950. Six years later, he was the Founder's Day speaker at Washington University.

At the meeting that day, Iaconetti begged Weir to hold off on foreclosure. Weir reportedly replied, "Other people go broke, why not you?"

Iaconetti then pulled out a handgun and shot Weir in the head. Then he turned the gun on himself and pulled the trigger. Iaconetti survived; Weir didn't.

Iaconetti went on trial in March 1960, but it ended in a mistrial because a juror fell ill. The second trial began in June, with the defendant claiming innocence by reason of insanity. The trial pitted two unrelated and antagonistic Shaws. At one point, William Shaw, the prosecutor, accused Charles M. Shaw, the defense attorney, of being a communist, and the latter responded by physically attacking the former as the jury watched. Trying to avoid a second mistrial, Judge Robert G. J. Hoester restored order, told William Shaw to apologize for the commie comment, and moved on.

As his star witness, Charles Shaw called Dr. Paul T. Hartman, who testified that Iaconetti was "not of sound mind" when he shot Weir. Hartman said that the accused suffered from schizophrenia, that he had been mentally ill for at least twenty years, and that there was little hope for recovery. A second psychiatrist testified for the defense that Iaconetti could not distinguish right from wrong when he fired the fatal shot. But William Shaw countered with mental health experts of his own. Two psychiatrists from Fulton State Mental Hospital, where Iaconetti had been examined before trial, told the jury that Iaconetti knew what he was doing and knew it was wrong to shoot Weir. From any legal standpoint, Iaconetti was sane at the time of the killing, they said.

Iaconetti took the witness stand and described the shooting. He then launched into a diatribe against Sheriff Orion Litzinger, accusing the sheriff of offering Iaconetti a pistol to commit suicide. Litzinger testified that Iaconetti said something to him about his gun, "and I said to him maybe you'd like to finish the job you started a couple of months ago." The sheriff said he was referring to a previous suicide attempt by Iaconetti.

William Shaw asked Iaconetti if he had confessed to Litzinger that he would still kill Weir if he had to relive that November day. "I said that if the sheriff did to me what Weir did to me, make me lose my mind where I had to kill myself, I would kill him to," was Iaconetti's disjointed answer.

In his closing arguments, William Shaw portrayed Iaconetti as a cold-blooded killer motivated by revenge for his own financial mistakes. Charles Shaw portrayed his client as "a desperate man, crushed by water company officials." In the packed courtroom in Clayton on June 11, the jury found Iaconetti not guilty by reason of insanity. Iaconetti gave his lawyer a bear hug. Iaconetti's wife, Jean, embraced her husband, and then she, too, hugged Charles

Shaw. Iaconetti had just got away with what many people would have called murder. But the case was nowhere near over.

Instead of facing prison bars at the Missouri State Penitentiary, Iaconetti caught a bus to a building that housed the criminally insane at Fulton State Hospital. Once psychiatrists determined that Iaconetti was a threat neither to himself nor to society, he could go home to Jean in University City and try to get his life back in order.

Just thirty days after his arrival in Fulton, Charles Shaw petitioned for Iaconetti's release. Missouri law required the superintendent at Fulton to decide if a patient was sane. And two Fulton psychiatrists, Shaw argued in a petition in Callaway County Circuit Court, had so determined at Iaconetti's trial in Clayton. Now it was the state's turn to flip-flop. The two defense psychiatrists who took the stand at Iaconetti's trial were called to repeat their testimony that Iaconetti was crazy. They said so again. He was crazy last month; he's still crazy. Caught between his own psychiatrists and public sentiment, the Fulton superintendent played for time. He said Iaconetti should be confined for more study—and still more study and again more study.

Meanwhile, the Missouri legislature began work on a new law: custody releases of the criminally insane would require court approval as well as the okay of mental health officials. That is still the law today. Three times Iaconetti petitioned a judge in St. Louis County under the new law to set him free. Three times he was denied.

On January 29, 1966, the former nightclub owner hanged himself with a belt from a clothing rack in the laundry room at the state hospital. He was fifty-five.

Hoester served another thirty years as a judge in St. Louis County before taking senior status in 1990. Charles M. Shaw continued an illustrious career as a criminal defense attorney. William Shaw switched sides a few years later to become St. Louis County's first public defender, a post he held for more than two decades.

Every year since 1968, the Missouri Water and Waste Water Conference chooses an individual in the waterworks field throughout the state to honor with the W. Victor Weir Award for his or her high professional and moral attributes.

Research by this writer involving interviews with judges, prosecutors, defense attorneys, court personnel, psychiatrists, and psychologists—and this writer has so testified in a deposition in a murder trial—has shown that no murder suspect since Sam Iaconetti in June 1960 ever got a not-guilty verdict from a jury in St. Louis County on the grounds of insanity. That's forty-nine years and counting.

PULITZER PRIZE-WINNING REPORTER SHOOTS HANDYMAN
1960

Jacob H. "Jake" Wolf, Jr., got the call in the early afternoon of July 11, 1960. City Editor John Bell, Sr., told Wolf to head for St. Albans in Franklin County immediately. A reporter and friend who sat next to Wolf in the newsroom had just shot a handyman at his farm, Bell said. The shooter was legendary journalist Theodore "Ted" Link, a *St. Louis Post-Dispatch* reporter who had won the Pulitzer Prize for exposing fraud in the Internal Revenue Bureau—the predecessor to the IRS.

Wolf drove to Link's farm near the picaresque village of St. Albans on the banks of the Missouri River. When Wolf arrived, he recalled nearly fifty years later, the body of odd-jobs employee Clarence Calvin was still there. Calvin was lying on his back, uncovered, near a cement picnic bench. It appeared that Calvin had been sitting on the bench at one point, smoking a pipe, before he was shot. Wolf talked to Lieutenant Vince E. Maxey of the Missouri State Highway Patrol about what happened and to Link, whom Wolf quoted that day in the newspaper: "It was either him or me."

Link told Wolf his version of what took place, a story Link would repeat to Maxey, to Franklin County Sheriff H. Ben Miller, to a grand jury in July 1960, and, with greater detail, at a trial in Hermann, Missouri, in January 1961. Link had learned on July 8 during a business trip to New York that the ancestral farm home that he used on weekends and in summers had burned down. The next day, Link toured the ruins. He found a quart oil can that was scorched and smelled of kerosene or some accelerant. On July 10, Link was able to telephone Calvin, thirty-five, a sometime-employee who lived about a mile from Link's farm, but Calvin's answers to

Link's questions were so vague that he fired the handyman.

About 10:30 a.m. on July 11, Link and his son, Theodore Link, Jr.—"Buddy" to family and friends—got to St. Albans and began looking for Calvin in caves near the property. When they returned to the house, they found Calvin digging in the ruins with a hoe. Link invited Calvin to sit down at the picnic bench and began questioning him about the fire and his whereabouts that day. When Calvin gave several different answers and finally told Link that he had been in New Madrid, Illinois, Link said there was no such town and accused Calvin of setting the fire.

Calvin got up, started to open a switchblade knife, and grabbed the hoe. Link said he ran to a tree where he had propped up a shotgun. "My first shot from about twenty feet away struck him in the abdomen," Link told Wolf. "He kept coming, and I shot him in the chest. He was still on his feet, and I shot him with a .38-caliber revolver which I had in my pocket."

With the story in hand, Wolf raced into St. Albans to find a phone so he could call it in to a rewrite man at the newspaper. He found Mae Head's general store, but all it had was a crank phone, an instrument Wolf had never used. The young reporter had to ask the owner for help in cranking it. As he dictated the story, Wolf could hear numerous clicks on the line as people began to listen in to the St. Albans story of the day—perhaps the century—on the multiparty phone line. Then Wolf heard a woman's voice cutting in. "This is Clarence's mother," the woman told Wolf. "I have been looking for him. I am going up there."

Uncertain what she might do when she found her son's body, Wolf hurried back to the farm and found Maxey. They looked around, but Link had wandered off. As Wolf told Maxey about the telephone conversation, both men heard several shots from the woods and ran in that direction, fearing the worst. What they found? Link taking target practice.

Franklin County Prosecuting Attorney Charles Hansen wasn't sold on Link's self-defense claims. For one thing, Link had bought the shotgun that morning at a store in Grover (now Wildwood) on his way to St. Albans. There were also discrepancies between the statements of Link and Buddy, Hansen claimed. And then there were the five shots Link had used to bring down Calvin.

Hansen took the case to a grand jury in July, and it indicted Link, fifty-five, of Kingsbury Place in St. Louis's Central West End, on a charge of first-degree murder. Link now faced the possibility not only of jail but also of the death penalty. A judge let him go free on a twenty-five thousand–dollar bond. The bond was put up by twenty-five St. Albans landowners, Link's rural neighbors.

Because of all the publicity, the case was moved to Gasconade County, and the trial opened on January 16, 1961, in Hermann, with Judge Joseph T. Tate presiding.

Hansen had not run for reelection. The new prosecuting attorney for Franklin County was Charles P. Moll. Hansen served as Moll's assistant and conducted much of the four-day trial. Also assisting Moll was Fred L. Howard, an assistant attorney general. Hansen had asked Governor James T. Blair to order the Missouri attorney general to send Moll, a veteran trial lawyer, to help with the prosecution.

Defending Link were two of the top criminal lawyers of the day: Henry Morris and William Wessel. They had a hard time keeping their client in check, Wolf recalled. In the old-fashioned courtroom, prosecution and defense shared a table, and Link, once a Marine sergeant in the South Pacific, often glared and glowered at the opposition—not the image his lawyers wanted to present to the jury of a man facing the death penalty.

Maxey testified, and so did Miller, the sheriff. Under questioning by the defense, Miller said that Calvin had threatened him two years earlier after a traffic stop. On another occasion the same year, Calvin's parents called Miller to come to their farm because they were being threatened by their son. Miller found Calvin sitting up in a bed with a shotgun in one hand and a pistol in the other. Miller had also been called to the farm of Marion Thebes, who accused Calvin of firing a shot at him while he was getting his mail. At the crime scene, Miller testified, he found a partially opened switchblade and a hoe near the body. Prosecutor Hansen alleged in his questioning that Link shot the handyman while the latter was seated at the picnic bench.

Link testified on his own behalf, telling the jury he had in fact purchased the shotgun at the store in Grover for protection. He said, "Calvin tried to pull a knife, and I let him have it. I thought he had a gun." Link was asked at one point how long he had known Calvin. "Since the day he was born," he answered.

Although he was endorsed as a prosecution witness, Hansen never called Link's son, Buddy, to the stand. For the defense, Thebes testified that Calvin had told him earlier in 1960 that he was "going to get" Link because Link had searched Calvin's house and had accused Calvin of breaking into Link's farmhouse and taking things.

In closing arguments, Link's attorney, Morris, cited Link's ties to St. Albans and "the many happy hours" Link had spent at his weekend and summer retreat. The Link family had owned land in Franklin County for three generations, Morris said, going back to Link's grandfather, his namesake. That Theodore Link was the well-known architect who designed scores of St. Louis buildings, including landmark Union Station.

Hansen had conceded in his close that Calvin was a troublemaker, but "that does not give a reporter for the *Post-Dispatch* the right to come out here from St. Louis and kill somebody. Link took it upon himself to be judge, jury, and executioner."

Co-counsel William Wessel countered that Link was on his own property and had shot a trespasser in defense of himself and his son. "The only dissenting opinion comes from Mr. Charles E. Hansen, the Franklin County prosecutor who doesn't like Mr. Link and doesn't like the *Post-Dispatch*," Wessel said.

The jury had the options of convicting Link of first-degree murder with punishment of death or life in prison; of second-degree murder with a range of punishment of ten years in prison to life; or of manslaughter with a range of three months in jail to ten years in prison. Or the jury could acquit the defendant.

In his instructions, Judge Tate told jurors that they should acquit Link on the grounds of self-defense if Link acted because he had reasonable cause to believe he or his son were in danger. On the night of January 19, 1961, the jury deliberated for two and a half hours before acquitting the defendant. In the first row of the courtroom when the jury came back were his wife, Ruth, Buddy, and his daughter, Virginia, eighteen. The jury foreman, Raymond Engelbrecht, said the jurors agreed that "if they had been in his position, they would have done the same thing he did."

The indictment of Link for the shooting of Calvin wasn't the first time Link had faced serious prison time. In 1948, Link and three members of the Shelton gang had been indicted for kidnapping—accused of abducting a man in Peoria. The Shelton gang had run gambling for two decades throughout southern Illinois and were major bootleggers before that. The so-called victim, according to the indictment, was Peter Petrakos, a Peoria lowlife, and Link had lured him to Link's ninth-floor room of the Pere Marquette Hotel. The Shelton gang had gotten the word that Petrakos was involved in the murder in July of that year of Bernie Shelton. Older brother Carl had been gunned down nine months earlier. Besides Petrakos, Link, "Big Earl" Shelton, and gang members Roy Walker and Jack Ashby were in the room. Petrakos was questioned by the group for four hours. He later alleged that Big Earl wanted to wrap him in a sheet and hold him out the window until he talked. (About twenty years later, a former member of the Shelton gang working as a bartender in Wood River told this writer that Link himself had actually held Petrakos out the window by his ankles until he was convinced that Petrakos was telling the truth.)

After Bernie's death, the Shelton gang had been holed up, and Link had been holed up with them. They had decided their days were numbered, and they began to recount to Link payoffs to state and local politicians and vice and gambling and corruption that reached into the Republican administration of Governor Dwight Green. Under a barrage of unfavorable publicity from Link and other *Post-Dispatch* reporters, Green and Attorney General George F. Barrett empanelled grand juries in Springfield and Peoria to make a pretense of an investigation. Instead of looking at the graft and payoffs, Barrett's special prosecutor, James A. Howe, steered the Peoria grand jury away from corruption and onto the Petrakos matter, which resulted in the grand jury indictment of the newsman and a public outcry against the Green machine throughout Illinois.

The attack on Link and the *Post-Dispatch* backfired. Adlai Stevenson defeated Green by a half-million votes. In his book about the Sheltons, *Brothers Notorious*, Taylor Pensoneau makes the case that the spurious indictment of Link may even have resulted in the election of Harry S. Truman as president. Truman needed Illinois to defeat Republican Thomas Dewey. Before the Peoria indictment that engendered widespread publicity, Truman had been trailing Dewey. That November, Truman eked out a thirty-three thousand–vote margin in Illinois.

The indictment alleging that the questioning of Petrakos by Link and the others amounted to "kidnapping, conspiracy, and intimidation" was dropped the next year.

Link went on to write the stories about federal tax fraud that won him and the *Post-Dispatch* a Pulitzer Prize. He had joined the *Post* staff in 1939, after beginning his newspaper career fifteen years earlier with the *St. Louis Star*. His career was sidetracked by World War II, when he served as a Marine and was wounded in the South Pacific. Link continued to cover crime, mobsters, and corruption for the *Post-Dispatch* until his death from a heart attack in 1974 at the age of sixty-nine. He was a legendary figure in the newsroom when this writer joined the newspaper in 1973 and took part in the daily ritual of watching Link arrive for work. It would be a good day if Link took his gun out of his holster, placed it in a desk drawer, and locked the drawer.

Wolf, Link's friend and the *Post-Dispatch* reporter at the St. Albans crime scene, described Link as a person who was "quiet and friendly and soft-spoken." After the trial in Hermann, Link rebuilt the farmhouse. Wolf was among a number of guests at St. Albans for a barbeque. As they walked along, Link turned to Wolf and said, "I guess you haven't been out here since I shot the piss out of Clarence."

(Michael W. Lhotka interviewed Jacob H. Wolf, Jr., in Jefferson City on April 29, 2009, for this story.)

FRANK "BUSTER" WORTMAN, CRIME BOSS
1960s

The last Prohibition-era gangster to reach the heights of area crime boss was Frank "Buster" Wortman, who ran gambling and vice in southern Illinois for more than two decades—until his death during throat cancer surgery in 1968. Son of an East St. Louis fire captain, Wortman began his criminal career in the mid-1920s as a gopher, runner, and small-time hood in the Shelton gang that controlled Illinois vice from Mount Vernon, Herrin, and Cairo to East St. Louis and Madison County and eventually as far north as Peoria.

Wortman wouldn't be around for much of that time. In 1933, federal agents raided a Shelton-operated still near Collinsville. Wortman and two others intervened, attacking the agents, beating them, and driving them off. For that, Wortman—who had been arrested numerous times before, primarily for burglary and robbery—was convicted and sentenced to ten years in prison. Wortman spent the next eight years in Leavenworth, according to some accounts, although newspaper biographies also stated he spent time in Alcatraz, where he got to know the dean of crime bosses, Al Capone.

Released in 1941, Wortman used his influence with the Chicago Mob to muscle his way into the rackets in his hometown, East St. Louis. Just as the Shelton gang had turned Cuckoos against Cuckoos a decade earlier, Wortman lured to his side two of the Sheltons' onetime machine gunners, Monroe "Blackie" Armes and Black Charley Harris. He also added to his own gang Elmer "Dutch" Dowling and Louis "Red" Smith, both former Egan's Rats.

With the help of Chicago Mob money and a takeover of *Pioneer*

News, Wortman moved into the lucrative field of providing racing news results to bookies. He and his brother, Ted, had also set up the Plaza Amusement Company to push slot machines and jukeboxes to Illinois tavern owners.

Carl Shelton was gunned down on a rural road near his Fairfield home on October 23, 1947. Black Charley Harris was the suspected killer. Nine months later, a sniper fatally shot Bernie Shelton outside his tavern in Peoria. Wortman had become the undisputed mob leader on the East Side.

Gambling was wide open at betting parlors throughout Illinois. The Hyde Park Club in Venice grossed more than $6 million in one year; the 200 Club in neighboring Venice, $1.5 million. Wortman got his share. He also got his cut from gambling dens in East St. Louis. But the wide-open nature of the gambling business would not last long under Wortman's reign. In 1950, state raids shut down Hyde Park and the 200 Club, along with bookie operations at major clubs in East St. Louis.

The Kefauver Committee had declared war on organized gambling in 1950 and 1951, and Wortman, who failed to show up to testify, felt the pinch financially. He still operated upscale, behind-closed-doors, illegal casinos just outside East St. Louis on Collinsville Road. A *Post-Dispatch* reporter with phony credentials got past security at the Corona Club—the other gambling operation was the Club Prevue—and described dealers in tuxedos and gamblers with women dressed in mink playing the games.

The Kefauver directives included using racket squads within the Treasury Department to hound gangsters, to monitor every dollar of income they reported, and to look for every dollar of income they didn't report. Wortman was a target, and for nearly a decade, he fought off one federal investigation after another.

One Internal Revenue Department agent assigned to the Wortman case was Frank Hudak, who became a Collinsville attorney after retiring from the federal government. In an interview several years ago with this writer, Hudak told the following Buster Wortman story:

Tired of constant surveillance by federal agents, Wortman, with friends, hopped a St. Louis train bound for Los Angeles and, with a big grin, waved goodbye to the agents following him. The agents caught the next L.A. flight out of Lambert Field, however, and waited at the station when Wortman's train arrived. The gangster had taken only a few steps off the train when he saw the waiting party. With a glare, the crime boss retraced his steps and got back on the train for a return trip to St. Louis.

The IRS investigations caught up with Wortman in 1962, and he was convicted of income tax evasion. Although sentenced to five years in prison, he never served a day—an appeals court set aside the conviction.

In March 1963, his chief underboss, Dowling, and a bodyguard were shot to death near Belleville. The murder, like most gangland killings over the decades, was never solved.

BIBLIOGRAPHY

DUELS
Baker, Jean H. *Mary Todd Lincoln*. New York: W. W. Norton & Co., 1987.
Darby, John F. *Personal Recollections of John F. Darby*. St. Louis: Hawthorn Publishing Co., Reprint of 1880.
Goodwin, Doris Kearns. *Team of Rivals*. New York: Simon Schuster Paperbacks, 2006.
Historical Encyclopedia of Illinois and History of St. Clair County, Vol. 1. Chicago: Munsell Publishing Co.,1907, Rice–Jones; Bennett–Stewart.
History of St. Clair County. Belleville: Advocate Steam Printing House, 1876.
Howard, Robert P. *Illinois: A History of the Prairie State*. Grand Rapids, Mich.: William B. Eerdmans Publishing Co., 1972.
Letters of Abraham Lincoln to Joshua Speed, 1842.
Primm, James Neal. *Lion of the Valley*, 3d Ed. St. Louis: Missouri Historical Society Press, 1998.
Stevens, Walter Barlow. *Centennial History of Missouri*. St. Louis: The S. J. Clarke Publishing Co., 1921.
Steward, Dick. *Frontier Swashbuckler: The Life and Legend of John Smith T.* Columbia: University of Missouri Press, 2000.
Wikipedia, James Shields; Thomas Hart Benton.

CHIEF PONTIAC, 1769
Allen, John W. *Legends and Lore of Southern Illinois*. Carbondale: Southern Illinois University Press, 1963.
American Monthly Magazine. Washington, D.C., July 1901.
Baldwin, Carl. *Echoes of Their Voices*. St. Louis: Hawthorn Publishing Co., 1978.
Brennan, Charlie, Garwitz, Bridget and Lattal, Joe. *Here's Where: A Guide to Illustrious St. Louis*. St. Louis: Missouri Historical Society Press, 2006.
Historical Encyclopedia of Illinois, Pontiac; Starved Rock.
Wikipedia, Pontiac; Illiniwek Confederation; French and Indian War.

SLAVES EXECUTED FOR MURDER, CAHOKIA, 1779
Cahokia Records, 1778–1790. Collection of the Illinois State Historical Library. Vol. 2. Virginia Series, Vol. 1. Springfield, Ill., 1907.

DANIEL BOONE MAKES AN ARREST, 1804
Bryan, William S. and Rose, Robert. *A History of Pioneer Families of Missouri.* St. Louis: Bryan, Brand & Co., 1876.
Historic Daniel Boone Home & Bloomfield Village, Lindenwood University.
Missouri Historical Review, April 1909.
Missouri Life, February 2004.
Morgan, Robert. *Boone: A Biography.* Chapel Hill, N.C.: Algonquin Books of Chapel Hill, 2007.
Primm, *Lion of the Valley.*

MANUEL LISA'S EXPEDITION AND FRONTIER JUSTICE, 1807
Douglas, Walter B. *Manuel Lisa.* Vol. 3, nos. 3 and 4, Missouri Historical Collection, 1911.
Missouri Gazette, September, October 1808.
Morris, Larry E. *The Fate of the Corps.* New Haven, Conn.: Yale University Press, 2004.
Shepley, Carol Ferring. *Tales from Bellefontaine Cemetery.* St. Louis: Missouri Historical Society Press, 2008.

THE IOWAS WENT THAT AWAY, 1808
Missouri Gazette, July 26, 1808; August 2, 1808; August 10, 1808; August 17, 1808; July 19, 1809.
Wikipedia, Iowa Indians.

ST. LOUIS'S FIRST CONVICTED MURDERER, 1809
Frazier, Harriet C. *Slavery and Crime in Missouri, 1773-1865.* Jefferson, N.C.: McFarland & Co., Inc., pending publication.
Missouri Gazette, August, September 1809.
McCullough, John A. "Launched Into Eternity," *Gateway,* summer 2005.
Primm, *Lion of the Valley.*

A RARIFIED MURDER, THE STEPHENSON HOUSE, 1825
Darby, *Personal Recollections.*
Edwardsville Intelligencer, November 1, 2002; November 14, 2002.
Mateyka, Karen Campe. *Henry the Stephenson House Mouse: A Diary.* St. Louis: Reedy Press, 2007.
The 1820 Colonel Benjamin Stephenson House.
Wikipedia, Benjamin Stephenson; Ninian Edwards.

FRANCIS MCINTOSH, ELIJAH LOVEJOY, 1836-37

Allen, *Legends and Lore.*
Alton Telegraph, November 1982.
Darby, *Personal Recollections.*
Dilliard, Irvin. *Quill.* October 1952. (Reprinted in the *Alton Telegraph*, 1987)
Dillon, Merton L. *Elijah P. Lovejoy, Abolitionist Editor.* Champaign: University of Illinois Press, 1962.
Faherty, William Barnaby. *The St. Louis Portrait.* Tulsa, Okla.: Continental Heritage Inc., 1978.
Historical Encyclopedia of Illinois.
O'Neil, Tim. *Mobs, Mayhem and Murder.* St. Louis: St. Louis Post-Dispatch Books, 2008.
Primm, *Lion of the Valley.*
Sidel, Doug. Research on the statute of limitations for murder. Assisted by Mary Dahm and Bernard Lewandowski, law librarians.
St. Louis Post-Dispatch, February 11, 1960; January 14, 1962.
St. Louis Star-Times, January 20, 1937; October 24, 1937.

BEAUMONT AND GEYER: A CASE OF MALPRACTICE, 1840

Bay, William Van Ness. *Reminiscences of the Bench and Bar of St. Louis.* St. Louis: 1878.
Darby, *Personal Recollections.*
Missouri Historical Review, October 1964.
Primm, *Lion of the Valley.*
St. Louis Post-Dispatch, April 27, 1958.
Stevens, Walter Barlow. *St. Louis: The Fourth City.* St. Louis: The S. J. Clarke Publishing Co., 1911.
Wikipedia, William Beaumont; Henry S. Geyer.

GIVING THE FRENCH A BAD NAME, 1849

Howard Louis, Conard, ed. *Encyclopedia of the History of Missouri.* Louisville and St. Louis: Southern History Company of New York, 1901.
O'Neil, *Mobs, Mayhem and Murder.*
Primm, *Lion of the Valley.*
Stevens, *Centennial History of Missouri.*

JOSEPH CHARLESS, JR., 1859
St. Louis Democrat, June, September, and November 1859.
Stadler, Frances Hurd. *St. Louis: Day by Day.* St. Louis: Patrice Press, 1989.
Wikipedia, Joseph Charless; Charlotte Charless; Taylor Blow.

JAMES UTZ, CONFEDERATE SPY, 1864
Hazelwood Park and Recreation Department.
Missouri Division, Sons of Confederate Veterans. Florissant, Mo.: Major James Morgan Utz Camp #1815.
Missouri Life. "Five Famous Generals," April 2007.
Winter, William C. *The Civil War in St. Louis: A Guided Tour.* St. Louis: Missouri Historical Society Press, 1995.

THE WHISKEY RING, 1875
Historical Register and Dictionary of the U. S. Army, Orville Babcock.
McFeely, William S. *Grant.* New York: W. W. Norton & Co., 1982.
New York Times, November 27, 1875; February 1876; May 1, 1876; August 15, 1877.
Primm, *Lion of the Valley.*
Rives, Timothy. "Grant, Babcock and the Whiskey Ring," *Prologue Magazine.* The National Archives. Fall 2000.
Wikipedia, Whiskey Ring; Benjamin Bristow; Orville Babcock.

THE *POST-DISPATCH* NEWSROOM SHOOTING, 1882
O'Neil, *Mobs, Mayhem and Murder.*
St. Louis Post-Dispatch, October 1882.
St. Louis Globe-Democrat, October 1882.
Swanberg, W. A. *Pulitzer.* New York: Charles Scribner & Sons, 1967.
Wilensky, Harry, *The Story of the Post-Dispatch.* St. Louis: St. Louis Post-Dispatch, 1981.

SOUTHERN HOTEL TRUNK MURDER, 1885
O'Neil, *Mobs, Mayhem and Murder.*
St. Louis Globe-Democrat, April–May, August 1885; May–June 1886; August 1888.
St. Louis Post-Dispatch, April–May, August 1885; May–June 1886; August 1888.
Smith, Sharon and Johnson, Donn, Missouri History Museum, information on trunk murder displays.

Wagner, Allen E., *Good Order and Safety: A History of the St. Louis Metropolitan Police Department, 1861-1906.* St. Louis: Missouri Historical Society Press, 2008.

MARION THE OUTLAW, 1891

Legends of America. On-Line at legendsofamerica.com.
Patterson, Richard M. *Train Robbery: The Birth, Flowering and Decline of a Nortorious Western Enterprise.* Boulder, Colo.: Johnson Books, 1981.
St. Louis Globe-Democrat, December 2, 1891; January 4, 1910.
St. Louis Post-Dispatch, December 1, 1891; November 23, 1893; January 4, 1910.
San Francisco Chronicle, December 28, 1891.
Sifakis, Carl. *Encyclopedia of Crime.* New York: Facts on File Inc., 1982.

A CLAYTON COURTHOUSE CONFRONTATION, 1892

Dahm, Mary and Lewandowski, Bernard. *Mount Olive to Carondolet.* Clayton: St. Louis County Law Library, 2006.
Litz, Arthur. "Killed in Court," *Missouri Bar Journal,* fall 1978.
St. Louis Globe-Democrat, July 1892; May 6, 1893.
St. Louis Post-Dispatch, July 1892; May 5, 1893.
Terry, Dickson, *Clayton: A History.* City of Clayton, 1976.

BALLAD OF FRANKIE AND JOHNNY, 1899

Burton, Jack. *The Blue Book of Tin Pan Alley.* New York: Century House, 1962.
Hagen, Harry. *This Is Our St. Louis.* St. Louis: Knight Publishing Co., 1970.
Harris, Ellen. "They Done Her Wrong," *St. Louis Magazine*, November 1999.
O'Neil. *Mobs, Mayhem and Murder.*
St. Louis Life, June 1995.
St. Louis Globe-Democrat, October 1899.
St. Louis Post-Dispatch, October 1899.

THE BOODLERS, 1901-02

Kaplan, Justin. *Lincoln Steffens: A Biography.* New York: Simon & Schuster, 1974.
Kirschten, Ernest. *Catfish and Crystal.* New York: Doubleday & Co., 1960.
O'Neil, *Mobs, Mayhem and Murder.*
Primm, *Lion of the Valley.*
St. Louis Globe-Democrat, November 1902; October 11, 1975.
St. Louis Post-Dispatch, November 1902; November 20, 1904.

Shepley, *Tales from Bellefontaine Cemetery*.
Thurmann Jr., A. L. "Joseph Wingate Folk," *Missouri Historical Review*, Vol. 59.
Wagner, *Good Order and Safety*.

BELLEVILLE LYNCHING, 1903
Historical Encyclopedia of Illinois, Belleville lynching.
St. Louis Post-Dispatch, June 1903.

DOWNTOWN ST. LOUIS SHOOTOUT, 1904
O'Neil, *Mobs, Mayhem and Murder*.
St. Louis Globe-Democrat, October 21–29, 1904; November 21, 1904
St. Louis Post-Dispatch, October 21–29, 1904.
State vs. Harry Vaughn.
Wagner, *Good Order and Safety*.

DESPERATE LORD BARRINGTON, 1903-04
Barker, John T. *Missouri Lawyer*. Philadelphia: Dorrance Co., 1949.
State of Missouri vs. Barrington. Missouri Supreme Court, June 1, 1906.
O'Neil, *Mobs, Mayhem and Murder*.

EDWARD GARNER LEWIS, 1905-12
Harris, NiNi. *Legacy of Lions*. St. Louis: Historical Society of University City, 1981.
Morse, Sidney. *The Siege of University City*. St. Louis: University City Publishing Co., 1912.
New York Times, June 1, 1905; November 26, 1911; April 9, 1912.
St. Louis Post-Dispatch, October 10, 1958.
Wikipedia, Edward G. Lewis; U.S. People's Bank.

THEY STOLE THE LOCOMOTIVE, 1910
O'Neil, *Mobs, Mayhem and Murder*.
St. Louis Globe-Democrat, January 1910; May 10, 1910.
St. Louis Post-Dispatch, January 1910.

ARSON TRUST, 1915
St. Louis Globe-Democrat, September 1915.
St. Louis Post-Dispatch, September 1915.

EAST ST. LOUIS RIOTS, 1917

Barnes, Harper. *Never Been a Time: The 1917 Race Riot That Sparked the Civil Rights Movement.* New York: Walker & Co., 2008.
O'Neil, *Mobs, Mayhem and Murder.*
Primm, *Lion of the Valley.*
Rudwick, Elliott. *Race Riot at East St. Louis, July 2, 1917.* Carbondale: Southern Illinois University Press, 1964.
St. Louis Post-Dispatch, May–July 1917; May 7, 1992; July 2, 1992.
St. Louis Republic, July 3, 1917.

ROBERT PRAGER LYNCHED AS GERMAN SPY, 1918

Edwardsville Intelligencer, June 15, 1918.
Howard, *Illinois: A History.*
O'Neil, *Mobs, Mayhem and Murder.*
St. Louis Globe-Democrat, April 1918.
St. Louis Post-Dispatch, April 1918; April 5, 1993.
Schwartz, E. A. "The Lynching of Robert Prager, the United Mine Workers and the Problem of Patriotism in 1918," *Journal of the Illinois State Historical Society*, winter 2003.

THE MOB, 1920s AND 30s

Courtaway, Robbi. *Wetter Than the Mississippi: Prohibition in St. Louis and Beyond.* St. Louis: Reedy Press, 2008.
Fontane, Walter M., "Baseball to Bullets," *Gateway*, 2007.
Kirschten, *Catfish and Crystal.*
Kobler, John. *Capone.* Greenwich, Conn.: Fawcett Publications Inc., 1971.
Mormino, Gary Ross. *Immigrants on the Hill.* Champaign: University of Illinois Press, 1986.
O'Neil, *Mobs, Mayhem and Murder.*
Pensoneau, Taylor. *Brothers Notorious: The Sheltons.* New Berlin, Ill.: Downstate Publications, 2002.
St. Louis Globe-Democrat, August 11–12, 1928.
St. Louis Post-Dispatch, January 1, 1910; August 10, 1932; November 3–4, 1947; May 21, 1958.
Wikipedia, Egan's Rats; Fred "Killer" Burke; Leo Vincent brothers; Charles Birger.

JACK DANIEL HEIR ACQUITTED OF MURDER, 1924
St. Louis Globe-Democrat, March 1924.
St. Louis Post-Dispatch, March 1924; July 31, 1997.
St. Louis Star, March 1924.
Wikipedia, Jasper Newton "Jack" Daniel; Lem Motlow.

PRETTY BOY FLOYD, 1925
Courtaway, *Wetter Than the Mississippi*.
St. Louis Post-Dispatch, September 1925; May 6, 1992.
Wikipedia, Charles Arthur Floyd; Melvin Purvis.
Wallis, Michael. *Pretty Boy: The Life and Times of Charles Arthur Floyd*. New York: St. Martin's Press, 1992.

BERTHA GIFFORD, POISONER, 1928
St. Louis Post-Dispatch, November 28, 1928; December 18, 1928; October 26, 1993.

KIDNAPPED: BUSCH FAMILY HEIR, 1930-31
Hernon, Peter and Ganey, Terry. *Under the Influence*. New York: Avon Books, 1991.
St. Louis Star, January 1931.

HOMER G. PHILLIPS, 1931
Faherty, *St. Louis Portrait*.
Primm, *Lion of the Valley*.
St. Louis Globe-Democrat, June 1931.
St. Louis Post-Dispatch, June 1931; June 17, 1983.

NELLIE TIPTON MUENCH, 1930s
Kirschten, *Catfish and Crystal*.
O'Neil, *Mobs, Mayhem and Murder*.
St. Louis Post-Dispatch, November–December 1936; January 23–24, 1983.
Time, January 7, 1937.
Wilensky, *History of the Post-Dispatch*.

AUGUST LUER KIDNAPPING, ALTON, 1933
Alton Telegraph, July 1983.
The Evening Independent, May 31, 1935.

Time, July 31, 1933.
Wikipedia, Vivian Chase.

KELLAR'S LAST SUPPER, 1933
Dahm and Lewandowski, *Mount Olive to Carondolet*.
St. Louis Post-Dispatch, January 17–21, 1933; January 6, 1989.

THE STRANGE CASE OF MARY CATHERINE REARDON, 1947
Dahm and Lewandowski, *Mount Olive to Carondolet*.
St. Louis Globe-Democrat, February–March 1947.

THE KEFAUVER COMMITTEE, 1951
U.S. Senate Special Committee to Investigate Organized Crime in Interstate Commerce. First Interim Report, August 18, 1950. Second Interim Report, February 28, 1951. Third Interim Report, May 1, 1951. Final Report, August 31, 1951.
Pensoneau, *Brothers Notorious*.
St. Louis Globe-Democrat, February 1951.
St. Louis Post-Dispatch, May 1950; February 1951.

POPULAR POL, CORRUPTION, 1951-52
Grossman, Mark. *Political Corruption in America: An Encyclopedia of Scandals, Power and Greed*. New York: Grey House Publishing Co., 2005
O'Neil, *Mobs, Mayhem and Murder*.
St. Louis Post-Dispatch, March 1952.
Time, August 6, 1951; May 15, 1952; July 12, 1954.

THE AMMONIA BOMB HOLDUP, 1952
St. Louis Post-Dispatch, November 22–23, 1952; July 26, 1997.

THE GREAT ST. LOUIS BANK ROBBERY, 1953
O'Neil, *Mobs, Mayhem and Murder*.
St. Louis Globe-Democrat, April 25–26, 1953.
St. Louis Post-Dispatch, April 24–25, 1953; November 17, 1993.
Wikipedia, Great St. Louis Bank Robbery; Steve McQueen.

GREENLEASE KIDNAPPING, 1953
Deakin, James. *A Grave for Bobby.* New York: William Morrow & Co., 1990.
St. Louis Globe-Democrat, October 1953; October 7, 1982.
St. Louis Post-Dispatch, October 1953; October 7, 1993; September 28, 2003.

STALKING THE STALKER: THE NORTH COUNTY RAPIST, 1957
St. Louis Post-Dispatch, November 13, 1957; January 22, 1960; December 15, 1991.

NOT GUILTY: AN INSANITY PLEA, 1959
St. Louis Post-Dispatch, November 1959; March, June 1960; August 2, 1982.
Interviews of Charles Shaw, William Shaw, Robert G. J. Hoester, George R. "Buzz" Westfall, circa 1982.

PULITZER PRIZE-WINNING REPORTER SHOOTS HANDYMAN, 1960
Lhotka, Michael W. Interview with Jacob H. Wolf, Jr.
Pensoneau, *Brothers Notorious.*
St. Louis Post-Dispatch, July 11, 1960; January 16–21, 1961.

FRANK "BUSTER" WORTMAN, CRIME BOSS, 1960s
Kefauver Committee Reports.
Pensoneau, *Brothers Notorious.*
St. Louis Post-Dispatch, January 2, 1951; August 11, 1968.
Wikipedia, Frank "Buster" Wortman.
Interview of Frank Hudak, circa 1970.

ABOUT THE AUTHOR

Bill Lhotka retired in November 2008 from the *St. Louis Post-Dispatch* after forty-five years in the newspaper business. Lhotka began his career as a sportswriter at the *Alton Telegraph* in October 1962 after graduating with a bachelor's degree in history from Quincy College, now Quincy University. He had also attended the University of San Francisco. After a year as a sportswriter and two years in the U.S. Army, Lhotka returned to the Alton newspaper where he worked until 1973, covering local and state government, police, politics, courts, and corruption.

Lhotka joined the staff of the *Post-Dispatch* and served as bureau chief at the state capital in Jefferson City until 1977. He was the newspaper's labor reporter for five years and then specialized in courts and crime coverage for twenty-five years. He has covered trials and hearings in state and federal courthouses in St. Louis, Clayton, Edwardsville, Alton, Belleville, St. Charles, Union, Jefferson City, Columbia, Hannibal, Fulton, Macon, Cape Girardeau, Kansas City, and Springfield, Illinois.

As an investigative reporter, he either won awards or was nominated for stories that showed the pending decline of organized labor in 1978, even when union membership numbers were at an all-time high; that led to the conviction of a police chief who sold confiscated weapons to criminals; that prompted a federal investigation and conviction of a Missouri House speaker; that led to prison terms for promoters who bribed public officials; that prompted the resignation of a police officer who shot eleven people in his career; and that led to the arrest of a drug-adled stockbroker who swindled his clients, including a teenager who gave him her babysitting money.

The author lives in Olivette with his wife, Susan.

PHOTO CREDITS

FBI, pages 155, 204
Karen Mateyka, page 36
Library of Congress: pages 8, 12, 23, 28, 49, 116